INDIAN LABOUR CONFERENCE
CONCLUSIONS
(1-33 Sessions)

INDIAN LABOUR CONFERENCE
CONCLUSIONS
(1-33 Sessions)

Edited by
C.S.K. Singh

VVG National Labour Institute
Noida

In association with

MANAK
Publications Pvt. Ltd.

First Published in 1998
by **Manak Publications (P) Limited**
G–19, Vijay Chowk, Laxmi Nagar, New Delhi-110 092
Phone : 2453894 Fax : 91-11-2418599

in association with
V.V.G. National Labour Institute
Sector 24, Noida (U.P.)

Branch Office : 3–Na–20, Jawahar Nagar, Jaipur-302004

ISBN 81-86562-16-8

Edited by
Dr. C.S.K. Singh

Style & Layout by
Sudhir Kr. Vatsa

Laser Typeset by
Nidhi Laser Point, Delhi-32
Ph. : 2115424

Printed in India by
Nice Printing Press, Delhi-92

To the
Indian Labour Conference

India is facing difficult problems today and it is very necessary that the organised labour movement should react to them properly. A merely agitational approach is not helpful in the circumstance. We have to consider every problem in its larger context. I would appeal to labour and to employers to ponder over these words and keep the larger interest always in mind while discussing the immediate problems before us.

Jawahar Lal Nehru
last message
to labour
signed three days
before his death.
(Quoted in Chairman's
Speech, 22nd Session)

FOREWORD

Evolution of labour policy is not merely calendering of scores of events and anecdotes; it is a process of objective, dispassionate scanning of such events as they took place, the imagination and vision which contributed to the shaping of such events, their impact on the production system, on the working and living conditions of the working class and in shaping the pattern, ethos and culture of industrial relations in their totality.

Our labour policy derives its origin, inspiration and strength partly from the utterances of important nationalist leaders during the days of freedom struggle in 20s, 30s and 40s, partly from the text of the Resolutions adopted in various sessions of the Indian National Congress, partly from the debates of the Constituent Assembly, partly from the provisions of the Constitution, the Conventions and Recommendations adopted by the International Labour Conference but largely by the decisions taken in the Indian Labour Conferences over a period of 50 years between 1941-97. The ILC has been aptly described as the Labour Parliament of India a confluence of creative forces and energies, the testing ground of tripartite and consensus in decision making. Notable among the decisions and recommendations of ILC which have shaped and influenced the Labour Policy in India are :

- The fifth session of the ILC held in 1943 urged Government to set up a machinery to investigate the question of wages and earnings, employment, housing and social condition of workers.
- The eleventh session of the ILC held in 1951 emphasised the need for training and suggested setting up a Central Training Institute for theoretical vocational skill training to be supplemented by practical training.
- The fourteenth session of the ILC held in 1955 suggested the need for enacting protective laws for child labour.
- The fifteenth session of the ILC held in 1957 recommended the setting up of the Central Board for Workers' Education. It also laid down the norms for fixation of minimum rates of wages.
- The nineteenth session of the ILC held in 1961 recommended

abolition of contract labour where feasible and providing satisfactory conditions for contract labour where abolition of the same was not feasible.

- The twenty-fifth session of the ILC held in 1968 recommended Central Legislation for payment of gratuity.
- The twenty-eighth session of the ILC held in 1985, inter alia, strongly supported the proposal for a comprehensive legislation on child labour.

As subsequent events will go to show these recommendations had considerable bearing on enactment of legislations like Contract Labour (Regulation and Abolition) Act, 1970, Payment of Gratuity Act, 1972 and Child Labour (Prohibition and Regulation) Act, 1986. They paved the emergence and growth of institutional mechanisms like Central Board for Workers' Education and a series of Vocational Skill Training Institutes.

Over the years the recommendations of the Indian Labour Conference have also shaped and influenced labour policy relating to industrial relations, formulation of model grievance procedure, principles of adjudication and voluntary arbitration, functioning of industrial tribunals and labour courts, norms for application of Code of Discipline, workers' participation in management, labour welfare including industrial housing, social security, new economic policy and its impact on labour. While there are sharp differences—both perceptional and ideological on a variety of issues intimately affecting labour amongst the social partners and often irreconciliable, the debates have enriched the literature on a host of issues of interest and relevance to the working class.

While the recommendations reached by way of consensus amongst the social partners have had a salutary impact on labour legislation and industrial relations, it is a sad commentary on the pace of implementation that due to procedural reasons many recommendations like giving a legislative shape to workers' participation in management could not till date be carried to their logical conclusion. This by itself, however, cannot be a reflection on the nature, quality and importance of the recommendation itself which has been made after exhaustive debate and after taking into consideration various implications of a proposal.

Compilation and analysis of these decisions and recommendations arrived at in the ILC from time to time under appropriate heads and in an orderly and scientific manner is a commendable achievement of Dr. CSK Singh, the editor of this publication. The end product which is voluminous and which is the outcome of years of hard dedicated efforts of Dr. Singh will be of immense research and documentation value for numerous social scientists, labour economists, trade union functionaries, grass-root level social activists and so on.

I congratulate the previous Director of the Institute, Shri A.P. Verma, and the present Shrimati Uma Pillai for publishing this work.

Dr. L. Mishra
Union Labour Secretary

CONTENT

	Foreword	*vii*
	Introduction	*xiii*
1.	Indian Labour Conference and Allied Organisations—Genesis, Aims, Objectives, Composition and Fraction	1-16
2.	Rules of Procedure	17-21
3.	Industrial Truce	22-24
4.	Industrial Relations	25-38
5.	Protection against Unemployment	39-51
6.	Trade Unions	52-58
7.	Wage, Dearness Allowance and Bonus	59-69
8.	Consumer Price Index	70-71
9.	Welfare	72-81
10.	Social Security	82-90
11.	Workers' Education and Training	91-96
12.	Workers' Participation in Management	97-103
13.	Contract Labour	104-105
14.	Unorganised Labour	106-109
15.	ILO Conventions and Recommendations	110-112
16.	Code of Discipline, Efficiency and Welfare	113-119
17.	New Economic Policy and Labour	120-126
	Appendices	127-291

INTRODUCTION

The Indian Labour Conference (ILC) stands unrivalled as an epitome of Indian tripartism. It has recently concluded its 33rd Session (October 24-25, 1996). During these years, its contribution to the shaping of the country's labour policy, its role in keeping the wheels of production moving and its response to the economic and political vicissitudes have, indeed, made it, what the Chairman of its 23rd Session remarked, 'the Labour Parliament of India.'

The formative years of the ILC coincided with the period which was a turning point in the political economy of the nation. The freedom struggle wrested provincial autonomy under the Act of 1935. This led to the formation of popular governments in the provinces in 1937. But in protest against entangling the country in the Second World War by the colonial government, the Indian National Congress withdrew from the provincial governments in 1939.

The war also caused economic recession and unemployment. Labour movements were gaining strength day by day. Trade Unions were knitted together more closely under the banner of the national movement. There was a large number of industrial disputes resulting in huge loss of mandays.

The following tables throw light on the labour scenario in the country.

TABLE I

Occupational Distribution of Workers Per 10,000 of Population

Class, Sub-class and Order	Number per 10,000 of total population. Earners (principal occupation) and working dependants	Earners as subsidiary occupation
1	2	3
Non-working dependants-5609		
All occupations	4,391	425
A. **PRODUCTION OF RAW MATERIALS**	2,957	215
I. EXPLOITATION OF ANIMALS AND VEGETATION	2,947	213
Pasture and agriculture	2,923	208
Cultivation	2,766	185
Special crops	47	7
Forestry	9	3
Stock-raising	100	12
Raising of small animals and insects	1	1
Fishing and hunting	24	5
II. EXPLOITATION OF MINERALS	10	2
B. **PREPARATION AND SUPPLY OF MATERIAL SUBSTANCES**	731	115
III. INDUSTRY	438	62
Textiles	117	12
Hides, skins and materials from the animal kingdom	9	1
Wood	47	10
Metals	20	14
Ceramics	29	5
Chemical products property so called and analogous	17	4
Food Industries	42	5
Industry of dress and the toilet	96	15
Building industries	18	2
Construction of means of transport	1	
Production and transmission of Physical force	1	
Miscellaneous and undefined industries	40	4
IV. TRANSPORT	67	12
Transport by air		
Transport by water	10	1
Transport by road	36	10
Transport by rail	18	1
Post Office, telegraph and telephone services	3	

1	2	3
V. TRADE	226	41
Banks, establishments of credit, exchange and insurance	9	4
Brokerage, commission and export	2	
Trade in textiles	13	2
Trade in skin, leather and furs	3	1
Other trades in foodstuffs	110	20
C. PUBLIC ADMINISTRATION AND LIBERAL ARTS	118	19
VI. PUBLIC FORCE	24	3
VII. PUBLIC ADMINISTRATION	28	4
VIII. PROFESSIONS AND LIBERAL ARTS	66	12
IX. PERSONS LIVING ON THEIR INCOME	6	2
X. DOMESTIC SERVICE	311	51
XI. INSUFFICIENTLY DESCRI-BED OCCUPATIONS	222	20
XII. UNPRODUCTIVE	46	3

Compiled from 1931 Census as the 1941 Census, was found defective in many respects.

(*Source* : National Planning Committee)

TABLE II

Registered Trade Unions in British India as on 31st March, 1943

Province	*Number of Registered Trade Unions*	*Number of Unions making returns of Membership*	*Membership of Unions making returns*
1	*2*	*3*	*4*
Ajmer Merwara	3	3	4,794
Assam	5	5	1,948
Bengal	229	147	221,635
Bihar	41	11	18,738
Bombay	77	69	130,688
C.P. & Berar	49	35	29,430
Delhi	30	23	16,895
Madras	143	86	49,451
N.-W. Frontier Province	6	3	418
Orissa	3	3	359
Punjab	24	23	12,493
Sind	28	28	8,934
United Provinces	28	27	20,976
Central Trade Unions (whose objects are not con-fined to one Province)	27	26	168,540
TOTAL	*693*	*489*	*685,299*

(*Source* : National Planning Committee)

TABLE III

Industrial Disputes

Year	Number of Disputes	Number of people involved	Number of working days lost
1	2	3	4
1921	396	600,351	6984,426,
1922	278	435,434	3,972,727
1923	213	301,044	5,051,704
1924	133	312,462	8,730,918
1925	134	270,423	12,578,129
1926	128	186,811	1,097,478
1927	129	131,655	2,019,970
1928	203	506,851	31,647,404
1929	141	531,059	12,165,691
1930	148	196,301	2,261,731
1931	166	203,008	2,408,123
1932	118	128,099	1,922,437
1933	146	164,938	2,168,961
1934	159	220,808	4,775,559
1935	145	114,217	973,457
1936	157	169,029	2,358,062
1937	379	647,801	8,982,257
1938	399	401,075	9,198,708
1939	406	409,189	4,992,795
1940	322	452,539	7,577,281
1941	359	291,054	3,330,503
1942	964	772,653	5,799,965
1943	716	525,088	2,342,287

(*Source* : National Planning Committee)

Under these circumstances, the first conference of the labour ministers was held on January 22-23, 1941. It discussed the recommendations of the Royal Commission on Labour, 1926 (Whitley Commission), which had inter alia recommended constitution of a tripartite industrial council for regulating the labour condition all over the country. The Chairman of the conference however indicated that the time was not yet conducive to the formation of an industrial council. He informed that he held discussions separately with all-India labour representatives and the employers' representatives.

The second labour ministers' conference took place on January 30-31, 1942. This was followed by a tripartite labour conference on August 7, 1942. It was for the first time that representatives of workers, employers and government (both from the provinces and the Indian states) sat across a table which resulted in a tripartite body at the national level.

It is noteworthy that the tripartite labour conference on 7th

August 1942, was going to witness the very next morning a political volcano, the Quit India Resolution, which was adopted by the Indian National Congress on 8th August 1942.

To appreciate the gensis of the ILC one has to go still go further to back and familiarise himself with the undercurrents of the national movement. Labour was a potential force in the political struggle of the country. The Indian National Congress, in its Karachi Session in 1931, passed the famous Resolution on Fundamental Rights :

- The organisation of economic life must conform to the principle of justice, to the end that it may secure a decent standard of living.
- The state shall safeguard the interests of industrial workers and shall secure for them, by suitable legislation and in other ways, a living wage, healthy conditions of work, limited hours of labour, suitable machinery for the settlement of disputes between employers and workmen, and protection against the economic consequences of old age, sickness and unemployment.
- Labour to be freed from serfdom and conditions bordering on serfdom.
- Protection of women workers and specially adequate provision for leave during maternity period.
- Children of school-going age shall not be employed in mines and factories.
- Peasants and workers shall have the right to form unions to protect their interest.
- The state shall protect indigenous cloth; and for this purpose pursue the policy of exclusion of foreign cloth and foreign yarn from the country and adopt such other measures as may be found necessary. The state shall also protect other indigenous industries when necessary against foreign competition.
- Intoxicating drinks and drugs shall be totally prohibited except for medicinal purposes.
- Currency and exchange shall be regulated in the national interest.
- The state shall own or control key industries and services, mineral resources, railways, waterways, shipping and other means of public transport.
- Relief of agricultural indebtedness and control of usury, direct or indirect.
- The state shall provide for military training of citizens so

as to organise a means of national defence apart from the regular military force.

The election manifesto of the Congress in 1936 also spelt out the policy of the party in regard to labour such as standard of living, hours of work and conditions of labour, as well as machinery for settlement of disputes, protection against the economic conditions of old age, sickness and unemployment, and the right of the workers to strike for the protection of their interests.

The manifesto emphasised to remove hindrances in the way of the growth of trade unionism and to promote collective bargaining.

The Congress policy on labour was further summarised in the declaration of the first Congress ministry in Bombay in 1938 during the provincial autonomy. It declared its programmes for providing minimum human needs, security of services, protection against unemployment, minimum wage fixing machinery, housing, social insurance, sickness benefits, weekly holidays, rest, hours of work, settlement of trade disputes etc.

The Congress, under the presidentship of Subhash Chandra Bose, appointed a National Planning Committee in 1938, which commenced its work in 1939, under the chairmanship of Jawahar Lal Nehru. The committee was tripartite in composition in so far as it consisted of, besides Nehru as chairman, great leaders of the national movement, eminent trade uninonists and captains of industries as well as scholars of high repute. To mention a few, Gulzari Lal Nanda, Vijayalakshmi Pandit, among political luminaries, N.M. Joshi, eminent trade unionist, Purushottamdas Thakurdas and Walchand, captains of industries, Megh Nad Saha and Radha Kamal Mukerjee, the reputed scientist and ecomomist respectively.

The National Planning Committee appointed eight Sub-committees. The Sub-committee on Labour consisted of the workers' representative, namely, N.M. Joshi as chairman and eminent personalities like B. Shiva Rao, V.V. Giri, N.V. Phadke, Godavari Gokhale (Now Godavari Parulekar), Dewan Chaman Lal, Padampat Singhania as members of the Sub-committee.

The Sub-committee was required to deal with the following terms of reference :

(a) Labour, other than agriculture labour, including the problem of unemployment.

(b) The general policy relating to labour, with special reference to the terms and conditions of employment, nationalisation of output and efficiency, rates of wages, methods of wage determination, laws and conditions of work in factories, mines, workshops, plantations, railways and transport services, docks etc., insurance against sickness, industrial accidents, old age, maternity, unemployment, and other contingencies of industrial life.

(c) The problem of employment of women and children.
(d) Measures and legislation for the safety of workers in mines, factories, workshops, plantations etc.
(e) Adequate provision for their housing, health and sanitation.
(f) Organisaion of labour.
(g) Provision of apprenticeship for industrial workers.
(h) Other incidents of Industrial life, e.g., strikes, lockouts, and labour disputes in general and the ways and means (including legislation) of settling them by conciliation or arbitration.

The report of the Sub-committee covered practically all aspects of labour, such as, hours of work, child labour, health and safety, creches, wages, some special problems like unregulated industrial undertakings, plantations, seasonal works on inland vessels, dock workers, building workers, problems of domestic servants, shop assistants and workers employed in commercial establishments, problem of housing, holidays with pay, social insurance, education, trade unions, trade disputes, statistics, organisation of labour inspection, labour legislation and workers' voice or control.

The last recommendation of the Sub-committee, workers' 'voice or control,' is worth mentioning here. The Sub-committee said that it would not be enough to provide social insurance and machinery to fix the workers' wages. The workers will require to be given a 'voice or control' in the conduct of the industrial system "As in politics, 'good government is not a substitute for self-government,' so is in industrial system...." The Sub-committee said: "It is too early to decide what will be the nature, form and extent of that voice or control which will depend upon the nature and form of the machinery that will be devised to settle and to carry out the plan and also upon the political constitution under which it will be carried out."

These were the undercurrents which set the stage for the tripartite labour conference of August 1942 which made the following recommendation :

> This tripartite labour conference recommends that with a view to provide adequate material on which to plan a policy of social security for labour, the central government in cooperation with the governments of provinces of British India, Indian states and chamber of princess should immediately set up machinery to investigate

> question of wages and earnings, employment and housing and social conditions generally, and that as soon as possible after receipt of required statistics and other data the central government should appoint a mixed committee to formulate plans of social security.

The discussions in the session revolved around dearness allowance, bonus, wage, employment, housing, social conditions, dispute settlements etc.

It was during the sixth session that the tripartite conference deliberated over its own structure, composition and constitution. The other specific subjects of discussions were, mainly, amendment of Trade Disputes Act, organisation of employment exchange, statutory provision of minimum wage, sickness insurance scheme, special ration, ESI, provident fund, industrial housing and the Industrial Disputes Act. But the most important was the resolution proposed by the All India Trade Union Congress (AITUC) on the amendment of the Defence of India Rules affecting labour rights. The resolution read :

> Resolved that the government of India should consult the tripartite organisation before issuing rules under the Defence of India Act affecting labour interest. Where such possible consultation is not possible on account of urgency of action, the rules issued and the action taken should be placed before the tripartite organisation at its next meeting for consideration.

But there was a volte-face on the part of the government on such an important subject. The central government observed :

> The Resolution was beyond the scope of the Conference. If any member desired a discussion on any matter concerning the working of the Defence of India Rules, it would be carefully considered by the government, but there was no reason why the time of the Conference, which usually had a larger agenda, should be taken up in advance discussion of every rule affecting labour, particularly as the Conference might not be a suitable place for such discussion in all cases. The government would be prepared to consider any proposal by any member of the Conference regarding the Defence of India rules. The government already undertook a good deal of consultations, with the result that the labour side often complained of slow progress.

In the 7th session, the tripartite conference further considered the recommendation of the committee regarding its composition and nomenclature. The committee suggested that the tripartite conference be called Labour Conference. The tripartite conference instead decided to call it Indian Labour Conference.

The 8th session was preceded by a series of strikes in coal mines. The Wage Enquiry Committee for the collieries was already set up, but its terms of reference could not be finalised because of the strikes. The government informed the Conference that it had constituted a Board of Conciliation. Labour was also represented on the Board. The government also informed that it was constituting tripartite industrial committees and was also examining if similar committee could be constituted for the Railways. The Chairman expressed concern on the widespread 'industrial unrest' accentuated by continued scarcities of essential goods, an acute shortage of housing and a fear of unemployment resulting from contraction of war-time activities. "This is not an isolated Indian phenomenon, but a part of the general industrial unrest that follows the end of every war."

The discussions of the ILC during the subsequent few years, therefore, were on the subjects like industrial employment (Standing Orders), Central Rules, 1946, Bill for Dock Labour, Housing for Coal-mines, Provident Fund and War Injury Scheme.

The ILO conventions and recommendations were perhaps for the first time discussed in the 9th session. The 10th session was the special session which was called to discuss the Labour Relations Bill, Compulsory Arbitration, Negotiations, Conciliation, Collective Bargaining and Trade Unions Bill. The Trade Unions Bill sought to reduce the proportion of outsiders in the executives of trade unions. This, according to the Chairman, would build up "... a strong, self-reliant and responsible trade union movement which will cease to be a pawn on the political chess board..."

The Second Five Year Plan was approaching when the 14th session of the ILC took place. The Chairman said that the country strove for national development and socialistic pattern of society, and implementation of the Second Five Year Plan. He said the First Plan had definite purpose and it had limitations. For the first time the equity found a vent in the discussion of the Conference. The Chairman said that the wealth had to be distributed to the advantage of common man and the gap between 'haves' and 'have nots' had to be narrowed down "But wealth can be shared only if it is created, and production of more wealth required greater production."

In the 16th session, the Chairman further stressed the 'socialistic pattern of society' which, he said, was not the slogan of a party but the nation's programme to ensure justice, equity and conquest of poverty. While right to strike was considered to be the legitimate right, the exercise of that right had to be viewed in relation to the consequences of stoppage of work disrupting the national economy which was detrimental to workers' own interest, he said.

Against this background the Conference in its next session deliberated on the Code of Conduct, Voluntary Arbitration, Adjudication, Trade Union Registration and other such matters.

Social peace and economic progress became the watch words during the 18th session[1] which was preceded by the general strike of the central government employees disrupting the process of national development. In the context of social justice, the Chairman remarked that concentration of urban wealth and income was increasing and disparities were widening. This, he said, was in sharp contrast to the professed national policy of egalitarian land policy through fixation of the ceiling of landholdings.

The prevailing industrial relations in the public sector was viewed with all seriousness. The Chairman emphasised that the public sector should function as small community which should not only be conscious of their rights but also of their obligations. For the first time, during the 20th session, the management of public sector was invited to attend the session.

The Chinese aggression put the national economy in shambles. The country faced the double burden of defence and development with visible impact on its economy. During this period the ILC discussed industrial relations situation, particularly dispute settlement, adjudication, rights and privileges of non-recognised unions, arbitration, price stability, cooperative societies, fair price shops, pay roll saving scheme, review of the code of discipline; and it adopted the Industrial Truce Resolution.

The adoption of Industrial Truce Resolution showed signs of improvement in the industrial relations. The number of mandays loss declined. The business community solemnly pledged to maintain the price list and to abstain from taking advantage of any scarcity situation.

Again, there was aggression by Pakistan across the eastern border which resulted in a chaotic economic situation. There was also further threat from the Chinese aggressive postures and constant provocations. The Chairman, therefore, appealed to the ILC in its 23rd session to devote itself to support the defence efforts to guard the freedom and integrity of the country and development of the national economy.

The Conference reviewed the whole situation. It expressed whole-hearted support to the Prime Minister's call for self-reliance in

1. See Appendix IV for proposals on Labour Policy for inclusion in the Third Five Year Plan as approved by the Standing Labour Committee at its 18th session, also see Appendix V for Five Year Labour Programme.

every sphere of economc activities, congratulated the defence forces and expressed full support of all sections of the Conference. It welcomed the significant declaration by labour to avoid work stoppage and greeted the employers for maintaining uninterrupted production.

It also recommended that compact standing tripartite bodies be constituted at the central and state levels, with labour ministers as chairmen, to review and resolve major labour and management problems and, when necessary, forward them for action to an inter-ministerial committee to be set up by the central government.

In due course of time, the country witnessed the militant form of workers' protest. There were a number of 'gheraos' in different parts of the country.

The central government had also appointed the National Commission on Rural Labour to undertake a comprehensive review of the development of labour policy and legislation and to formulate policy guidelines to take a fresh and comprehensive view of the labour situation.

The ILC deliberated over the recommendations of the commission in the 25th session and in the subsequent sessions, such as Industrial Relations Commission, Preventive and Post-closure Measures, Wage Policy, Inter-Union Rivalry, Bonus and Gratuity.

The burden of maitaining millions of victims of the military tyranny who came as refugees from Bangladesh added fuel to fire. The mounting expenditure caused high inflation situation. As a result, there was erosion of real income of the workers. This disturbed the industrial relations situation further. There was increase in closures and work stoppage. Hence the 27th session of the Conference felt the need for bipartite committee for labour management in public sector beside giving a fresh look on other matters including the Consumer Price Index.

After the 27th session of the ILC, there was a gap of nearly 14 years when it held the next session. Again, a gap of nearly 5 years when it held its 29th session in 1990. The Conference placed added emphasis on workers' participation in management; the problems of unorganised labour, and child labour figured more prominently in the deliberations.

The 30th, 31st, 32nd and 33rd sessions took up the cause of workers in the changing industrial relations scenario owing to the new economic policy of liberalisation and structural adjustment. The Conference discussed the Ramanujan committee report on industrial relations, as well as Trade Union Bills, Exit Policy, Retraining and

Redeployment, productivity, industrial competitiveness, social clause etc.

The present volume is the subject-wise compilation of the conclusions arrived at by the ILC. My information is based on the reports of the proceedings of the conference available with the Ministry of Labour, Government of India, I have at times also drawn on the extracts of the Chairman's speeches to put the matter in right perspective.

I have appended the summary of the proceedings of 31st, 32nd and 33rd sessions because of their relevance in the context of the New Economic Policy. For similar reason, I have appended the text of the speech delivered by the Chairman of the 31st session, Shri P.A. Sangma and his concluding statement as well as the text of the speech delivered by the Chairman of the 33rd session Shri M. Arunachalam. In addition, the appendices contain the reports of the various important committees and the list of the chairmen of different sessions.

I hope this volume will be a useful source material for researchers, policy-makers and practitioners.

I acknowledge with gratitude the Foreword given by Dr. L Mishra, Union Labour Secretary, and his usual encouragement and support.

I express my deep sense of gratitude to the then Union Minister for Labour, Shri P.A. Sangma (now Speaker, Lok Sabha) who indeed suggested the need for undertaking such work and evinced keen interest in its progress.

I am extremely grateful to Shri A.P. Varma, Director of the Institute whose constant supervision and valuable suggestions and support have enabled this work to see the light of day.

Shri D.K. Trehan, Labour and Employment Advisor, Ministry of Labour and officiating Director of the Institute made valuable suggestions for improvement of the draft. Ms Uma Pillai, Director of the Institute evinced keen interest in the publication of the volume. I am grateful to them indeed.

I am thankful to Shri Hari K. Mathur of the Ministry of Labour for his sustained and personalised support in carrying out this work.

But for the secretarial assistance enthusiastically extended by Shri Rajesh Karan, Shri Tarun Kumar and Shrimati Sudha Ganeshan, the completion of work would not have been possible. I am indeed grateful to them.

Last but not the least, I am grateful to Manak Publications in general and Shri M.P. Yadav in particular, for designing and publishing the book in an appreciable manner.

1

INDIAN LABOUR CONFERENCE AND ALLIED ORGANISATIONS—GENESIS, AIMS, OBJECTIVES, COMPOSITION AND FUNCTION

The Indian Labour Conference (ILC), as it is known today, had its predecessor in the first Labour Ministers' Conference held in January, 1941. It was that Conference of the Labour Ministers which considered the recommendation of the Royal Commission on Labour for setting up a tripartite Industrial Council. The Chairman of the session was of the opinion that setting up of an Industrial Council would be a bit premature. But the proposal did materialise in the very next session.

The ILC also underwent changes in its nomenclature such as, Tripartite Conference, Plenary Conference, Labour Conference and finally, Indian Labour Conference. The determination of aims, objectives, composition and functions constituted the main agenda of the Conference up to the 6th Session, though improvements continued to take place thereafter as well.

THE GENESIS

It was at the first session of the Labour Ministers' Conference held in January, 1941 that the recommendation of the Royal Commission on Labour to set up an Industrial Council, consisting of representatives of government, employees and employers, to coordinate labour conditions all over India, was considered. The Chairman of the Conference declared in his address that the Government of India was not opposed to the establishment of an Industrial Council and that it welcomed the recommendations of the Royal Commission. However, he said that it was the considered opinion of the Government of India that setting up of an Industrial Council would be somewhat premature at that stage. He expressed the view that the Labour Ministers' Conference, which represented not only the Provincial Administration but also the Indian States, was the beginning of tripartism in the country which would make possible the creation of Industrial Council foreshadowed by the Royal Commission.[1]

Later, in the second session of the Labour Ministers' Conference,[2] the Chairman informed that he had, prior to the Conference, held meetings with the representatives of employers and employees separately, and it was a step forward towards the formation of an Industrial Council which, he hoped, would materialise soon.

He also proposed to depart from the existing practice of holding separate meetings with representatives of employees and employers and to develop a practice of joint meetings of employers, workers and government representatives. He said that there were many advantages in bringing all the concerned parties face to face at a tripartite conference on the pattern of the League of Nations. "It is only by sitting around one table that persons defending different ideologies and economic interests can resolve their differences in a most pleasant and convincing manner..." He appealed to the Conference to consider the proposal for convening a joint conference of government, employees and employers in the following year.[3]

First Tripartite Meeting

On 7 August, 1942, the first tripartite meeting was held. It was represented by the Government of India, Provincial governments, Indian States and Chamber of Princes, as well as workers and employers in British India.

The purpose for calling such a conference was as stated by the Chairman, a growing realisation that the industrial problems could not be solved unless the three parties—government, employees and employers—developed a sense of responsibility towards one another, exhibited more respect for the views of one another and agreed to work in mutual interests. A plan to bring them together, and to let them talk to each other, across the table was necessary for the realisation of this purpose.

1. 1st Session of Labour Ministers, 22-23 Jan., 1940.
2. Extracts from Chairman's Speech, Conference of Labour Ministers, 22-23 Jan., 1940.
3. Extracts from the Chairman's Speech at the Conference of Labour Ministers, 3rd Session, 30-31 Jan., 1942, See Appendix VI for Report of the Sub-committee on the constitution of tripartite organisation, also see Appendix VII for note on the constitution of the Indian Labour Conference and the Standing Labour Committee.

Although the idea of such tripartite organisation was there, it was, the Chairman observed, doubtful if it would have taken a concrete shape so quickly had the War not made the maintenance of labour morale an urgent and immediate necessity. "The Conference had its genesis in the exigencies of the War but it was foreseen to last beyond the War. It was intended to be an institution which would have a permanent place in the economic structure of the country."[1]

Change in Nomenclature

The Chairman said that the Conference was meeting under different names, such as Labour Ministers' Conference, Tripartite Conference and Plenary Conference. The Committee constituted by it had decided to call it the 'Labour Conference.' "Notwithstanding what Shakespeare has said, there is much in a name. The name 'Labour Conference' may not have a sweet smell. But it certainly has the merit of being simple and less loud than the name 'Tripartite' or 'Plenary'." He commented that the name as proposed by the Committee 'lacked colouring,' a defect which could be easily removed "if instead of calling it 'Labour Conference,' we decide to call it the 'Indian' Labour Conference.' I take it that you are in agreement with me on this point."

AIMS, OBJECTIVES AND COMPOSITION OF THE TRIPARTITE ORGANISATION[2]

The aims and objectives of the tripartite organisation were declared to be mainly the following three :

(i) Promotion of uniformity in labour legislation;
(ii) Laying down of a procedure for the settlement of industrial disputes; and
(iii) Discussion on all matters of all-India importance as between employers and employees.

It was clarified at the Conference that the last item included in the aims and objectives was deliberately kept wide and flexible in its scope so as not to exclude from the purview of the Conference anything that was of importance to labour and capital.

1. Extracts from Chairman's Speech, Tripartite Labour Conference, 5th Session.
2. *Ibid.*, 4th Session, 1942.

Plenary Conference and Standing Advisory Committee[1]

The Tripartite Conference considered the proposal to constitute two bodies, namely, (1) Plenary Conference and (2) Standing Advisory Committee. It adopted the following resolution was :[2]

> This conference of the representatives of the central and provincial governments of British India and of the Indian states and the Chamber of Princes, and of the representatives of workers and employers in British India, being convinced that a collaborative body of governments, employers and workers in India should be established forthwith for the consideration of all questions relating to the conditions of labour, resolves that a plenary conference shall be constituted as follows :
>
> (i) Labour Member of the Government of India, Chairman;
> (ii) Three representatives of the Government of India, including one representative to represent Minor Administration;
> (iii) Eleven representatives of provinces;
> (iv) Six representatives of the industrially important states;
> (v) Two representatives of the Chamber of Princes to represent other states;
> (vi) Eleven representatives of employees of whom four will be nominated by the government in agreement with the All-India Trade Union Congress, four will be nominated by the government in agreement with the Indian Federation of Labour, and three will be nominated by the government as representatives of other employees' interest; and
> (vii) Eleven representatives of employers of whom four will be nominated by the government in agreement with the Employees' Federation of India, four will be nominated by the government in agreement with the All-India Organisation of Industrial Employers and three will be nominated by the government to represent other classes of employers.

1. Extracts from Chairman's Speech, Tripartite Labour Conference 4th Session, 7 August, 1942.
2. Tripartite Conference, 4th Session, 7 August, 1942.

Composition of Standing Advisory Committee[1]

The composition of the Standing Advisory Committee was proposed to be as follows :

(i) One representative of the Government of India,
(ii) Six representatives of the provinces,
(iii) Three representatives of the employers, and
(iv) Five representatives of the employees, with the labour member of the central government as chairman.

The Chairman made the following statement :

In suggesting the composition of the Standing Advisory Committee the Government had closely followed the principles underlying the League of Nations : First, equality of representation between government and non-government representatives. We have given effect to this principle by giving 10 seats to government and 10 seats to industry. Second, equality of representation as between employers and employees. This is provided by the Article whereby the 16 non-government seats are divided equally between the employers and the employees. We recognise this by distribution of the 10 seats allotted to Industry equally between the employers and the employees. Third, an assurance of representation to certain interests by reservation. We propose to adopt this principle by allowing one representative from the quota of both employers and employees, to be nominated by the Labour Member of the Central Government. This will ensure some representation of interests other than those represented by the main employers' and employees' organisations.

Composition of Standing Labour Committee

On the composition of Standing Labour Committee the following resolution was moved and adopted :

This Conference further resolves that a Standing Labour Committee would be constituted with the following composition :

(i) Labour Member of the Government of India, Chairman;
(ii) One representative of the Government of India;
(iii) One representative each of the Governments of Bengal, Bombay and the United Provinces;

1. Extracts from Chairman's Speech, Tripartite Labour Conference, 4th Session, 7 August 1942.

(iv) (a) One representative to represent the Provinces of Assam, Bihar and Orissa;
(b) One representative to represent the Provinces of the Punjab, Sind and NWFP;

(v) Three representatives of Indian States, including one representing the Chamber of Princes;

(vi) Five Representatives of employers; and

(vii) Five representatives of employees.

The Conference decided that the Standing Labour Committee should be revived and it should meet once in six months. The Committee should be compact and its composition should be left to be decided by the Union Labour Minister.[1]

Principles of Election of Standing Labour Committee[2]

The Conference decided the principles of election of the Standing Labour Committee as under :

(i) Representative of single provinces will be selected by the governments of those provinces;

(ii) Representatives of two or more governments will be selected by agreement between those governments. A system of selection by rotation might be adopted.

(iii) Representatives of states to be selected by the governments of the states; and,

(iv) Representative of the Chamber of Princes to be selected in the usual manner.

Representatives of Employers

The following provisions were made for employers representation on the Standing Labour Committee :

(i) Four representatives to be nominated by the Labour Member in agreement with the two leading all-India associations of employers.

(ii) One to be nominated by the Labour Member.

Representatives of Employees

As regards representation of employees, the following provisions were made :

1. 28th Session, 28.5.
2. 4th Session, 4.3.

Four to be nominated by the Labour Member in agreement with the two main associations of employees.

(i) One to be nominated by the Labour Member.

It was decided that the Standing Labour Committee would not be a deliberative body. It would perform the specific duties assigned to it by the Conference from time to time.

The Chairman expressed his opinion on the points raised during the discussion:[1] There were :

(i) The Constitution was in no sense final and it was open to the delegates to make suggestions. But the Constitution should be allowed to work for some time before trying to alter it.

(ii) As regards advisers to delegates and whether the proceedings of the Conference should be open to Press, the matters might be decided by the Conference and the Committee.

(iii) As regards employers, outside the two all-India bodies, it was necessary that the number should remain at three as proposed, so as to balance the number of three corresponding workers' delegates.

(iv) that delegates should be drawn only from the most representative organisation. It was very difficult in the present circumstances to agree to a provision. As regards nomination, if it was for giving representation to an organisation would be done in agreement with that organisation.

(v) As regards the suggestion for 'alternate' or 'substitute' delegates, there would be no difficulty about it provided that the names of the substitute delegates were communicated prior to the Conference, as it was essential to have finality in the composition of the Conference.

(vi) Regarding voting, it should left it to the Conference to decide.

(vii) As regards the term of appointment of delegates, the delegates they should be appointed afresh each meeting of the Conference.

(viii) In respect of the suggestion that the Conference and the Committee should have some link, it should be decided by the and as far as possible, the members of Standing Committee should also be members of the Corference.[2]

---

1. 4th Session, 4.4.
2. 6th Session.

Labour Welfare Committee

The Conference decided to create a new body namely, Labour Welfare Committee.

Its composition was proposed to be as follows :

(i) Members elected by the Standing Labour Committee;
(ii) One representative of the employers and one representative of the employees drawn from organised industries and municipal and other bodies employing labour;
(iii) Persons nominated by government from non-official cadre;
(iv) Persons representing Indian States; and,
(v) Representatives of Provincial Governments.

The Conference suggested that the matter relating to criteria for workers' representation on the Indian Labour Conference should be left to be discussed and decided by the Central Trade Union Organisations and in case of any differences among them, the government might take a decision in the matters.

It also suggested that the practice of holding tripartite discussions at the state level should be revived.[1]

> The principle of tripartism having been the very essence of industrial relations in the country all along, the meetings of the ILC should invariably be preceded by SLC meetings, in order that the ILC decisions were followed up with action in an orderly manner. There should also be regular meetings of the tripartite review committee. There should be two such review committee meetings, apart from the meeting of the SLC, before every ILC meeting. Thus there should be four tripartite meetings—two of the review committee, one each of the SLC and the ILC. The meetings of the SLC and ILC should be scheduled well in advance.[2]

It was suggested that the conclusions reached at the ILC meeting should be construed as matters of continuing importance until they were disposed of by appropriate follow-up action. Those conclusions of the 31st Session of the ILC which had not been implemented so far should be pursued including those of the Review Committee meetings.[3]

---

1. 31st Session, 31.2
2. 32nd Session, 32.1.
3. 32nd Session, 32.2.

REVIEW, MONITORING AND FOLLOW-UP OF THE WORKING OF PLENARY CONFERENCE AND STANDING LABOUR COMMITTEE

The two-year working of the plenary conference and the Standing Labour Committee was reviewed in the Sixth Tripartite Labour Conference.[1] Based on the review the following conclusions were drawn :

(i) There is no clear-cut division of functions between the Conference and the Standing Labour Committee. It is not that one is a deliberative body and other is an executive body. Both appears to be deliberative bodies.

(ii) There is an overlapping in the work they do. The subjects discussed by both are of the same nature.

(iii) There being no clear-cut distinction between general questions and concrete problems, the discussions in the Conference as well as in the Committee become too general to be of much use. Even concrete problems are treated like general problems.

(iv) There is no machinery to undertake the task of examining special problems and reporting upon them. It is an important function and there must be some machinery charged with such a function.

(v) There is no machinery to study and advise on problems of industry specific labour welfare.

Representation of Different Parties[2]

There were also complaints regarding the representation of the different parties on the Conference and on the Standing Labour Committee. The employers stated that it was not proper on the part of the government to reserve three seats for employers to be nominated by the government. They said that the Employers' Federation of India and the All-India Organisation of Industrial Employers were the ackonowledged representatives of employers. Hence, the provision for appointing more employers' representatives by nomination was unnecessary. The method of representation of labour was also considered faulty as those who represented labour did not actually belong to the labouring classes.

---

1. Extracts from Chairman's Speech, Tripartite Labour Conference, 6th Session, 27-29 Oct., 1944.
2. Ibid.

The Chairman during the Seventh Session of the Conference admitted that there was much force in the suggestions made with regard to the composition. If the two employers' organisations were fully representative, as they claimed to be, there was no justification for nominating employers. It was also necessary to see that the working classes should have not only their problems of employment and welfare considered but that they should be trained to represent themselves. They should, therefore, ensure their participation in all Labour Conferences.[1]

The clarified that the government was not averse to making appropriate changes in the composition of the Conference. At the same time, the government felt that the matters relating to changes in the composition of the Conference were not very urgent. "We could well afford to postpone their consideration for a while. As I said in the course of the first Tripartite Conference, we must not keep on pulling out the plant every now and then to see whether it has taken any roots. This is a way to kill the plant."

Delegates, Advisors and Substitutes

The Procedure Sub-committee, appointed by the Standing Labour Committee, submitted its report to the Conference. On the recommendations of the Sub-committee, the Conference adopted the following Rules of Procedure :[2]

(i) Each delegate representing more than one province or state may be accompanied by one adviser each for such province or state other than his own.
(ii) A delegate representing the Government of India may be accompanied by not more than three advisers.
(iii) Each delegation representing employers or workers may be accompanied by advisers not exceeding the number of delegates constituting the delegation.
(iv) The Chairman can permit any adviser to speak in the meeting if the delegate himself does not wish to speak. But if the delegate himself speaks, the Chairman will ordinarily need special reasons before permitting an adviser to speak.
(v) Advisers are not entitled to vote.

Substitute : A delegate may, by notice in writing addressed to the

1. Extracts from Chariman's Speech, Tripartite Labour Conference, 7th Session, 27-28 Nov. 1945.
2. 1st Session, 30 Nov.-1 Dec., 1942.

Chairman before the sitting of a meeting, appoint a substitute. The notice shall specify the sitting or sittings in which the substitute will participate.
A substitute may take part in debates and vote like a delegate.

Representation on the Tripartite Bodies[1]

It was suggested and that some convention should be laid down for representation of delegates and regarding invitation to and participation by observers and advisers. The Committee met at New Delhi on 5 September, 1959 and adopted the following conclusions :

(a) The existing procedure in respect of representation and participation in discussion, as detailed below, was generally approved :

  (i) *Delegate* : In giving representation to the workers and employers' sides on tripartite bodies, parity is maintained between the two sides. Seats within the groups are allocated among the central organisations of workers and employers on the basis of their relative strength. All the state governments are invited to send their representatives to the sessions of the Indian Labour Conference and the Standing Labour Committee. In the case of the meetings of Industrial Committee, representatives of the Central Ministry and the State Government concerned are also invited.

  (ii) *Advisers* : Each delegate is permitted to bring one official adviser. Requests are, however, received from time to time from the organisation to increase the number of advisers. Sometimes permission is given to bring non-official adviser.

  (iii) *Invitation to Members of Parliament* : In the meeting of the Standing Labour Committee, held at Bombay in October 1958, it was decided that some of the Members of Parliament on the Consultative Committee of the Labour Ministry might be invited. In the seventeenth session of the Indian Labour Conference all the 64 members of the Consultative Committee were accordingly invited.

  (iv) *Invitees* : The Director, ILO, India Office, is usually invited. Invitations have also been extended at times, to individuals or representatives of the organisations having

1. 17th Session, 17.7.

a special interest in the particular subject to be discussed.

(v) *Observers and visitors* : Requests to invite observers or visitors are considered on merit. Permission is given, wherever possible, subject to the availability of space and other facilities at the place of the meeting.

(vi) *Participation in discussions* : Both delegates and advisers participate in the discussions. As a matter of convention all decisions are taken by agreement and not by voting.

(vii) Invitees and observers usually do not participate in discussions, but can be permitted to do so by the Chairman. Non-official advisers are not permitted to participate.

(b) Organisations claiming representation on the Indian Labour Conference should have an all-India character with a minimum membership of one lakh spread over a number of states, and a sizeable membership at least in the majority of industries. The entitlement to representation on the Standing Labour Committee should be more restricted. The allocation of seats to each organisation should be determined in accordance with the latest available data regarding its membership. It was also agreed that observers, etc., should not participate in the discussions of the Conference. They might, however, speak on particular issues only with the specific permission of the Chairman if there are special reasons for the same.

(c) In addition to the present practice of permitting one adviser for every delegate, non-official advisers might also be allowed to attend the Conference depending on the number of important items on the agenda and taking into consideration the number of delegates and advisers already allowed to the various organisations. It was, however, agreed that an organisation having only one delegate might be allowed to bring one non-official adviser also.

(d) The various suggestions made at the meetings should be taken into account by the Minister of Labour and Employment in deciding these matters from time to time.

Representation of the Public Sector on Indian Labour Conference and other Tripartite Committees[1]

(i) The principle of participation by the representatives of the

1. 20th Session, 20.5.

public sector undertakings in tripartite conference and committees was agreed to. Those representatives would, however, form part of the government delegation for the present.

(ii) The conclusions of Conference and Committees would apply equally to the public sector including the employing ministries.

Allocation of Subjects to Plenary Conference and Labour Welfare Committee

On the allocation of subjects the Chairman suggested the following changes :

(i) The Conference would have two lists of subjects : List-I will contain all general subjects such as:

A. terms and conditions of employment;
B. labour legislation; and
C. questions relating to social security.

(ii) List-II will include all concrete questions

A. relating to labour welfare; and
B. relating to the administration of labour laws.

(iii) Subjects in list-I will be assigned to the Plenary Conference.

POWER AND FUNCTIONS

Power and Function of 'Plenary Conference'[1]

The 'Plenary Conference' shall advise the Government of India on any matter referred to it for advice taking into account the suggestions made by provincial governments, states and the Chamber of Princes and the representative organisations of employers and workers recognised for the purpose of the Conference.

The Conference shall exercise the power

1. To make recommendations to government on matters relating to terms and conditions of employment and all questions of social security which are placed on the agenda.
2. To refer any such matter or any part of it to the Standing Labour Committee with a direction (a) to report back to the Conference, or (b) to make a recommendation to the government.

---

1. 4th Session.

3. To appoint an ad hoc committee to consider any matter on the agenda with a direction to report (a) to the Conference, and (b) to the Standing Labour Committee, with a view to making recommendations to the government, and making a further report to the Conference.

Power and Functions of the Standing Labour Committee[1]

The powers and functions of the Standing Labour Committee were specified as under :

The Standing Labour Committee shall meet as often as it may be convened by the central government for the consideration of the issues which may come before it. The Committee shall consider and examine such questions as may be referred to it by the central government taking also into account the suggestions made by provincial governments, States, the Chamber of Princes and representative organisations of workers and employers. It is an agency of the Conference from which it derives its authority. The Standing Labour Committee, with the exception mentioned below will conduct no business other than that which has been delegated to it by the Conference. It is, however, open to the government to refer a matter directly to the Standing Labour Committee on which it wants an early opinion. The Committee in that case will report to the Conference or the recommendations shall be made available to the government which would be placed before the Conference. The Committee is competent :

(i) to advise the government on any matter referred to it by the government. Copies of any such advice shall be forwarded to all members of the Plenary Conference.
(ii) to report to the Plenary Conference upon any matter referred to it by that Conference.

The Standing Labour Committee will be empowered :

(i) to make recommendations or reports to the Conference on matters referred to it by the Conference;
(ii) to make recommendations to the government in a case in which the Conference has directed the Standing Labour Committee to report to the government; and
(iii) to appoint ad hoc committees to consider any matters on the agenda with directions to report to the Standing Labour Committee.

1. 26th Session, 4.2.

It was felt that the Indian Labour Conference should be strengthened further, keeping in view the level of importance and sanctity attached to the institution, and its decisions/ recommendations by senior captains of the industry and stalwarts of the trade union movement.[1]

> It was therefore, suggested for holding regular meetings of the Indian Labour Conference and the Standing Labour Committee annually.

Proposal for Separate Secretariat for Labour Conference[2]

Some members felt the necessity of a separate secretariat of the Conference. They suggested that a Secretariat should be set up to discharge the following functions :

(a) Preparation for meeting (i.e., circulation of papers, informing members of the dates, fix agenda, etc.)
(b) Preparation of records of the proceedings.
(c) Propaganda through of leaflets.
(d) Financial administration, such as payment to staff and travelling allowance bills of non-government members attending the Conference.
(e) Research and collection of information to serve as a basis of discussion and recommendations.
(f) Taking stock of the action taken by the government.

The demand for a separate secretariat, according to the Chairman, was based on the analogy of the ILO and that the government saw a fundamental difference between the ILO and Tripartite Organisation. The ILO was an independent organisation created by the Peace Treaty of Versailles. Its Conventions and Recommendations placed definite obligations on all State members and failure to fulfil those obligations involved certain definite international liabilities. It was regulated by its own constitution and it was not subject to any outside authority.

The Conference, on the other hand, was not independent in the same sense as the ILO was. It had no independent finances. It was only an advisory body which was constituted to advise the Government of India on such matters as were referred to it and was not a decision-making body. To allow it to do so would be to permit it to usurp the functions of the legislature. Having regard to those differences it was obvious that an independent secretariat for the

1. 31st Session, 31.1
2. 6th Session.

'Labour Conference' would create friction between the Government and the Conference.

The Government of India felt that all the functions of the Secretariat, with the exception of the "research and information," were such as could be discharged efficiently by the Labour Ministry of the Government of India. As regards "research and information," the Labour Department had certain proposals under consideration for re-organizing its activities which would inter alia include the setting up of necessary machinery for research and collection of information on labour and allied questions.

Hence, the Government of India did not favour the idea of a separate secretariat for the 'Tripartite Organisation.'

2

RULES OF PROCEDURE

The Rules of Procedure of the Indian Labour Conference are the outcome of its continuous deliberations. Initially, those were laid down in 1942 itself. What would be the position of the ILC vis-a-vis legislature was significant decision which was taken in the 9th Session. Continuous efforts have been made to strengthen its functioning which is evident from the fact that in its recent session held in November, 1995 as well, it took a number of decisions to strengthen its Committees particularly the Standing Labour Committee.

Committees : The Standing Committee and the Conference may appoint committees to consider and report on any matter and may appoint technical experts to any committee. They shall be advisers without right to vote.

At public sittings, if so decided, arrangements shall be made to accommodate the Press.

One secretary for each member and for each adviser representing a province or state not represented by a delegate, may be allowed admission to the meeting hall.

Closure : The president (chairman) may, on the move of a member or otherwise, put a motion for closure of the discussion. The decision on such a motion shall be by a simple majority vote.

Agenda : The agenda for a meeting shall be settled by the Government of India which shall consider any suggestion for inclusion in the agenda that may be made by any state government, any all-India organisation of employers or workers or by any member.

The agenda shall be sent to the members, as far as possible, at least one month before the date of the meeting, excepting during a war when Government of India may send the agenda with less than one month's notice.

Resolutions : Any delegate may move a resolution on any matter specially placed before the meeting, which on being seconded and discussed shall be put to vote.

Voting : Every delegate shall be entitled to vote individually on all matters which are put to vote. The decision shall be by a majority of two-thirds of votes cast by the delegates present except when otherwise provided for.

Interpretation : The chairman of the meeting shall have powers to decide on any question of interpretation of the rules.

Sittings : There shall be at least three sittings of either the Conference or the Standing Committee during the year, at least one of which shall be a meeting of the Conference.

The sittings of the meeting shall not be public, and the Press shall not be admitted to them except when the meeting expressly decides by a simple majority vote.

Regarding periodicity of the meetings, it was decided at the 15th session that the Conference[1] shall meet at least once a year at such places as may be decided upon from time to time.

Circulation of Agenda Papers[2]

Agenda papers for such meetings would be circulated at least fifteen days in advance of the meeting so that the organisations had sufficient time to consult their constituents.

Right to Fix Agenda[3]

The matters relating to preparation of agenda gave some grounds for complaint. The existing procedure regarding the agenda was said to be defective in two respects. The members of the Conference and the Committee were not entitled to place on the agenda any matter, in which they were interested. And the memoranda which accompanied the agenda reached members so late that they had hardly any time to study and hence they were not able to effectively participate in the discussion.

The contention of the government was that it cannot surrender its right to fix the agenda of the Conference. The Conference was not legislature. It was an advisory body and the government decided the matters on which it needed advice from the Conference. Besides, it was not possible for the government to accept an obligation to place a

1. 15th Session, 15.8.
2. 17th Session, 17.7.
3. 17th Session, 17.7.

subject on the agenda unless the government was in a position to furnish the Conference factual statements which could guide members in their deliberations and had time to examine the matter sufficiently enough to express its own view. It was not possible for the government to be ready with such statements without sufficient notice.

The government was willing to frame the agenda to revise the procedure without surrendering the right.

According to the existing procedure, the Labour Department invited suggestions from state governments, and employers' and workers' associations after the conclusion of a meeting from which items were selected for the agenda of the next meeting. There was no consultation between the government and the Conference or Committee before a decision was taken. But by a revised procedure, the government would receive suggestions for the agenda if the concerned parties desired to send them. Otherwise the government would also invite suggestions from delegates at each meeting.

The other change which the government was prepared to make in this regard was that while the final decision would be that of the government, all suggestions received for the framing of the agenda would provide the government with opportunity to consult the members and the members would have the opportunity to express their views.

Preparation of Record of Proceedings for ILC[1]

As regards the preparation of the records of proceedings of the Conference, it was felt that only the statement of the decisions and conclusions should be recorded. It was felt that preparation of the summary of the entire proceedings was not necessary. As far as practicable the statement of conclusions of the Conference should be finalised by a small Drafting Committee and placed for adoption during the Conference itself. It will be circulated to the organisations participating in the Conference.

Recording of Conclusions of Tripartite Conference & Committees[2]

The preparation of the records of proceedings was again discussed. It was decided that the existing practice of recording only the conclusions and recommendations would continue. It was also reiterated that the conclusions of such meetings would continue to be finalised by the Drafting Committee.

1. 20th Session, 20.6.
2. 20th Session, 20.7.

Permission to Admit Observers[1]

It was agreed that requests for permission to attend as observers or visitors should be considered on merit, and permission granted wherever possible, subject to availability of space and other facilities.

Strengthening the Working of the Tripartite Committee

It was generally agreed that the working of the Tripartite Committee could be made more effective. For the purpose, the following suggestions found general acceptance :

(i) A session of the Tripartite Committee should be preceded by an examination in depth of subjects on the agenda by small committees, bipartite or tripartite.

(ii) Public sector employers including those under the centre and the states should be given separate representation.

(iii) The decisions arrived at in the Tripartite Committee should be fully honoured and implemented.

The question of representation of national trade union organisations on the National Tripartite Committee, including minimum qualifying membership, was, however, deferred after some discussion.

Complaints[2]

Sufficient notice should be given to the parties concerned before any allegations or complaints were made against them in the Conference so that they might be in a position to collect the relevant facts and given an adequate reply to the charges.

Implementation of Recommendations[3]

It was felt that the implementation of the recommendations should be effected as voluntary obligations on the part of all the concerned parties instead of levelling charges of violation against each other.

Tripartite Bodies and Legislature

Referring to the contention that it was not right for the Legislature to make radical changes when a matter was considered in the Tripartite Conference or the Standing Labour Committee, the Labour Secretary pointed out that the Tripartite Conference was an advisory

1. 24th Session, 24.1.
2. 17th Session, 17.7.
3. 9th Session, 9.1.

body whose advice was communicated to the government but that the Legislature was a sovereign body and as such it would be difficult to prevent it from making the changes. He, however, agreed to bring prominently to the notice of the Legislature in future all points of agreement reached at Tripartite Conference.[1]

While admitting that there was lack of uniformity and co-ordination between the centre, the provinces and the states, he pointed out that it was not due to any lack of desire on the part of either the centre or the provinces to co-ordinate and cooperate but that it was due to the physical defects and to the delays in postal communication.

The Conference in its thirty-third session further emphasised the need for revival of the practice of holding tripartite consultations at the state level. It lamented that through some of the state governments had set up such bodies, quite a few of them were neither truly tripartite in nature nor did they hold meetings regularly.

It was therefore felt that the Labour Minister should again impress upon the state governments the need for reviving the practice of tripartite consultations by constituting truly and appropriately representative tripartite bodies and by holding its meetings atleast twice a year.[2]

1. 9th Session, 9.1.
2. 33rd Session.

3

INDUSTRIAL TRUCE

The different partners of ILC exhibited exemplary solidarity during the threat to the national sovereignty on account of the Chinese aggression. It adopted the industrial Truce Resolution on 3 November, 1962 and affirmed to prepare itself for the defence of the country and repeal the invasion of its territory. Following the Truce Resolution, the industrial relations situation showed a perceptible improvement. But after the national crisis was over, the improvements did not sustain.

The Chairman was happy to note that all the parties had accepted the Resolution on Industrial Truce.[1] He made it clear that the government did not propose to limit profits or dividends. So long as the government was not going to do away with the private sector economy there must be some incentive for the private enterprises to invest their capital in the industry. Although the government was for nationalisation of certain industries, due to certain limitations the employers had been given a period of ten years. He however pointed out that a very vast field for private enterprises was left open and there was no reason why the employers should complain that by giving a life of ten years, the government would make the industries capital shy. He pointed out that by profit sharing, the government did not mean limiting dividends or profits, but if the employers were inefficient they should be satisfied with whatever percentage of profits might be fixed. He assured the conference that all points raised by the various parties would be examined by the government, but expressed the view that the suggestion that the determination of their returns on capital should be examined by the three departments

1. See Appendix VIII and Appendix IX for Industrial Truce Resolution, 1967, and Industrial Truce Resolution, 1962 respectively.

concerned of the Government of India was not valid. All policy questions were first discussed by all the concerned departments and then a decision was reached. Therefore, vital aspects of this question would certainly be discussed by all departments concerned.

He promised immediate action in regard to setting up the necessary machinery and the collection of data as regards housing. He pointed out that one of the main difficulties was that the cost was to be shared by many parties, e.g., the central and provincial governments, employers, local bodies and labourers. He said the matter would be discussed at the Labour Ministers' Conference. Thereafter, it would be possible for the government to announce what the government was going to do during the next twelve months.

He appealed to both sides to observe industrial truce in letter and spirit.[1]

Review of the Working of the Industrial Truce Resolution[2]

There was a general discussion on this subject. Summing up the discussion, the Chairman observed that the Industrial Truce Resolution had generally worked well. There had been instances of its violation by certain parties but it should not be a ground for similar lapses by others. Effective steps were needed to ensure a more satisfactory working of the Truce Resolution. A high-level Tripartite Standing Committee could also be constituted to supervise the implementation of Industrial Truce Resolution. The proposed committee would consist of the Union Labour Minister as its Chairman and a representative for each of the four central organisations of workers and of the three employers' organisations represented on the Indian Labour Conference. The Committee should meet at frequent intervals and would be free to go into any connected matter for the successful implementation of the Resolution.

To quote the Chairman :

> We are meeting for the first time after the conference held on 3 November, 1962, at which a resolution on Industrial Truce was adopted unanimously by all the participants. There was a realisation that a grave emergency had overtaken the nation on account of the Chinese aggression. The Resolution expressed satisfaction over the immediate and spontaneous response of the employers and workers to the call of the nation and their determination to take urgent steps in every direction in order to

1. 9th Session, 9.9.
2. 21st Session, 21.2.

prepare adequately for the defence of the country and to repeal the invasion of its territory.

The Industrial Truce Resolution spread a wave of enthusiasm throughout the country. A profound change had occurred in the climate of industrial relations. Disputes almost vanished and the spirit of cooperation prevailed in all sections of the industry. The number of mandays loss declined abruptly in the month of November 1962. In December, January and February, the monthly rate of mandays loss was about a sixth of the monthly average of the corresponding period of the previous year. This stretch of four months constituted the most peaceful period in the industrial history of India.

There was, naturally, a marked accent on price stability in the text of Industrial Truce Resolution. The business community pledged itself solemnly to maintain the price-line and abstain from taking advantage of any scarcity that might develop.

A programme for setting up consumers' cooperative was accepted by the government. The Labour Ministry took upon itself the task of establishing cooperative stores in the mining areas.

I am sure you will share with me the keen regret that this happy state has not lasted in its fullness. The spirit generated by the emergency has waned, the number of cases of dismissals and discharges has gone up and the degree of redressal through arbitration, promised by the Resolution has not been obtained. The answer which immediately comes to the mind is that we should restore that sense of urgency and recapture the shining spirit of the earlier days.

4

INDUSTRIAL RELATIONS

It was towards the end of the 1950s that the ILC started deliberating over specific problems relating to industrial relations, like grievance redressal, settlement of disputes, wage negotiations, tripartite negotiation machinery etc. Matters like labour productivity, environment and labour protection received priority after the new economic policy was launched. It was in this context that the working conditions in export processing zones became an important matter of concern. Hence, it was felt necessary to consider the Sanat Mehta Committee recommendations on Industrial Relations Commission. What is more important it that the workers' representatives pressed for a comprehensive industrial relations laws in the context of the economic reforms.

GRIEVANCE REDRESSAL PROCEDURE AND INDUSTRIAL TRIBUNALS

Draft Grievance Redressal Procedure[1]

The ILC discussed the draft Grievance Redressal Procedure. It decided that only the guiding principles should be drawn up and referred to the employers' and employees' organizations for comments. The drafts would be modified in the light of the comments received and thereafter it would be placed before the next meeting of the sub-committee.

Approval of the Model Grievance Redressal Procedure[2]

The Model Grievance Procedure placed before the Committee was approved subject to certain amendments.

---

1. 3rd Session, 3.2., see Appendix X and Annexure thereto for model grievance procedure and guiding principles for a grievance procedure respectively.
2. 4th Session, 4.1.

Inclusion of Grievance Procedure in Model Standing Order[1]

The proposal for inclusion of Grievance Procedure in the Model Standing Orders was withdrawn.

Adjudication and Voluntary Arbitration[2]

(i) There should be more and more recourse to mediation and voluntary arbitration in place of adjudication. Matters of local interest not having any wider repercussions should, as a general rule, be settled through arbitration.[3]

(ii) The consensus was that it was not the suitable time for suspension of adjudication for settlement of industrial disputes. The government side made it clear that there would be no element of compulsion in the matter. The employers agreed to extend their full cooperation in evolving the mechanism for settlement of industrial disputes through mediation and arbitration.

(iii) A panel of arbitrators should be maintained by the central and state governments in order to assist the parties in the matter of choosing suitable arbitrators. The parties, however, will be at liberty to choose arbitrators outside the panel.

(iv) The question of making the provisions of the Indian Arbitration Act applicable to the arbitration procedures under the Industrial Disputes Act, 1947, should be examined afresh by the Central Government.

(v) The principles and norms so far evolved through awards and judicial decisions on important issues should be compiled and made available for guidance of the parties and arbitrators.

(vi) Every case of refusal to have recourse to arbitration should be recorded and referred to the evaluation and implementation machinery in the states or at the centre, as the case might be.

Emphasis on Bipartite Mechanism

The Conference noted the general improvement in the industrial relations situation. It felt that as far as possible, disputes should be resolved through bipartite mechanism. Where this was not possible, tripartite mechanism could be resorted to in the case of the dispute referred to voluntary arbitration.

---

1. 27th Session, 27.11.
2. 17th Session, 17.2, see Appendix XI for functions of the National Arbitration Promotion Board. Also see Appendix XII for Model Principles for reference of Disputes to voluntary arbitration under the Code of Discipline.
3. 17th Session,17.2.

Clarification of the Model Principles for Reference of Disputes to Adjudication[1]

While referring disputes to adjudication under Clause (iii) of the Model Principles, the government should not determine the date from which the award of the tribunal should be operative.

Complaints Regarding Adherence to Voluntary Arbitration[2]

While discussing the action taken on the decision of the previous meeting, the workers' representatives, pointed out there was reluctance on the part of some of the employers to go for arbitrations. The employers' representatives said that they had been doing their best to persuade their affiliates to accept voluntary arbitration as a means to settle the industrial disputes. It was explained that difficulties, if any, coming in the way of employers in this regard would be dealt with in detail at the next meeting of the Central Implementation and Evaluation Committee.

Appointment of District Judges as Presiding Officers[3]

(a) The proposed amendment to Section 7(a) (3) of the Industrial Disputes Act, 1947, to enable the appointment of serving or retired district judges as presiding officers of the Industrial Tribunals was agreed.

(b) It was also desired that an assurance should be obtained from the district judges appointed to the Tribunals that they would not practise before the same Tribunal after their retirement from the Tribunals.

(c) It was also decided that while amending the Act for this purpose, the provisions in the U.P. Industrial Relations Act in this regard would be taken in to consideration.

Appointment of Practising Advocates

The proposal for amendment to Section 7 and 7A of the Industrial Disputes Act for relaxing the qualification of presiding officers to enable appointment of practising advocates was withdrawn.

Proposal to Exempt Hospital Staff[4]

Regarding the suggestion of the West Bengal Government that the

1. 20th Session, 20.3.
2. 22nd Session, 22.2.
3. 16th Session, 16.3.
4. 16th Session, 16.3.

hospitals staff should be excluded from the purview of the Industrial Disputes Act, the consensus was that a convention should be established whereby the staff would not go on strike provided that an effective machinery for the speedy redressal of their grievances was set up by the employers.

Individual Dismissals[1]

The Conference Committee discussed the proposed amendment to the Industrial Disputes Act to empower Tribunals to go into the merits of individual dismissals. The different views in this regard were as follows :

(i) Employers' representatives felt that this provision would result in Tribunals interfering with the quantum of punishment and upsetting the consistency of the particular punishment practices followed by an undertaking. As a result there would be avoidable grievances.

(ii) Employers' representatives also pointed out that the proposed amendment would provide no remedy against perverse judgement of Tribunals etc.

(iii) Workers' representatives said that this could be brought to the notice of the Tribunal while considering individual cases.

Job Security

Employers' representatives raised the question of job security and pointed out that the government's decision to go ahead with the proposed amendment to the Industrial Disputes Act to empower the Tribunals to go into the merits of individual dismissals, seemed to be contrary to previous tripartite decisions. And in any case, since the stand of the employers had not been fully understood, they should be given another chance to put forward their views before the government went ahead with the proposal.

The Chairman explained the various stages leading to the government's decision to go ahead with the proposed amendment, and pointed out that the government's action was in accordance with the decisions taken at the Indian Labour Conference and the Standing Labour Committee. It would not be possible to reopen the issue unless there was an agreement to this effect between the two sides.

After some discussion the Conference constituted a small

1. 20th Session, 20.4.

committee comprising representatives of the workers, employers state governments and the Union Labour Secretary, to look into the matter. It was agreed that the government might take further decisions and action in the matter taking into consideration the views expressed by the two sides.

Time Limit for Raising Disputes[1]

The proposed amendment to the Industrial Disputes Act, 1947 seeking to prescribe a time limit within which an industrial dispute could be raised by the workmen was not agreed to.

Employers' representatives, however, said that they would be free to raise this issue after the disposal of the pending case in Calcutta in which an industrial dispute regarding dismissal had been referred for adjudication after a period of 20 years.

Delay in Settlement of Disputes

The Conference was concerned about long delays in settlement of disputes by labour courts. The Conference also suggesting the government to take decisions on the recommendations of the Sanat Mehta Committee for setting up an Industrial Relations Commission.[2]

Industrial Relations

It was suggested that in view of the economic implications of major industry-wide strikes in sectors such as banking, coal, textiles including jute etc., the Labour Ministry should facilitate prompt and effective settlement of disputes in such sectors.[3]

It was felt that industrial adjudication was being seriously handicapped on account of delays in filling up of the vacancies of presiding officers and for want of adequate secretarial staff to support them. The procedure should be simplified so that the vacancies were filled up promptly.[4]

Introduction of Standing Orders in Large Industries[5]

On the above subject, the central government representative summed up the discussion as follows :

The general opinion seemed to be that standing orders should be

1. 24th Session, 24.9.
2. 28th Session, 28.9.
3. 32nd Session, 32.3.
4. 32nd Session, 32.5.
5. 5th Session, 5.6.

introduced in industrial concerns employing 500 or more persons as soon as possible. It was also felt that the standing orders should have statutory force. But how the standing order could have statutory force had not been decided. The Employers' representatives had asked for a statutory authority to decide cases of disagreement with the Labour Commissioner. The workers' representatives suggested that there should be a statutory authority to deal with the disputes arising out of the standing orders. It was suggested that in both cases, an industrial court should settle the disputes. The Workers' representatives also suggested that the standing orders should inter alia include security of service.

Model Standing Order

The Chairman added that it was considered necessary that the model orders might be drawn up by the Government of India and circulated.

Retrenchment[1]

It was proposed that Section 2(00) of the Industrial Disputes Act should be amended to change the definition of 'retrenchment.'

Full Compensation for Closure[2]

An amendment to Section 25-FFF of the Industrial Disputes Act was proposed to provide for payment of full compensation in the case of closure of an undertaking on account of expiry of lease, licence, or exhaustion of reserves.

The Chairman informed that the deficiencies in the Industrial Disputes Act were being examined and the revision of the Act would be taken up.

Security of Employment[3]

During the course of the general discussions, the Conference considered the question of security of employment in the context of certain judicial decisions, according to which Industrial Tribunals, while adjudicating cases of dismissal of individual workers, could only go into the questions: (1) whether the principles of natural justice had been applied, (2) whether there was victimisation, or (3) whether there was mala fide intention on the part of the employer.

1. 20th Session, 20.4.
2. 20th Session, 20.4.
3. 20th Session, 20.1.

The state governments and workers' representatives were of the view that this was not adequate and that in such cases Tribunals should be empowered to consider fully the merits of the case and the propriety of the punishment awarded. The Tribunals should give their award in the light of their findings. The employers' representatives, however, felt that the provisions of the law were quite adequate and there was no need of change in the existing legislation.

The Chairman agreed to the views of the state governments and workers' representatives, and paid that the matter would be further examined and it would be accordingly decided if there was a need for amending the legislation.

Model Principles for Reference of Disputes to Adjudication

The following model principles were approved :

A. Collective Disputes

(i) All disputes may not be referred for adjudication unless efforts at conciliation had failed and there was no further scope for conciliation and the parties were not agreeable to arbitration;

(ii) If there was a strike or lockout which was declared illegal by a court, or a strike or lockout which was resorted to without seeking settlement by means provided by law and without proper notice or in breach of the Code of Discipline as determined by the machinery set up for the purpose unless such a strike (or direct action) or lockout was called off;

(iii) If the issues involved were such as to contribute the subject matter of recent judicial decisions or in respect of which undue delay had taken place; and

(iv) If in respect of demands other legal remedies were available, i.e., matters covered by the Factories Act, Workmen's Compensation Act, Minimum Wages Act, etc.

B. Individual Disputes

Industrial disputes raised in regard to individual cases, i.e., cases of dismissal, discharge or any action of management on disciplinary grounds, might be referred for adjudication when the legality or propriety of such action was questioned and, in particular under the following circumstances :

(i) if there was a case of victimisation or unfair labour practice;

(ii) if the standing orders in force or the principles of natural justice had not been followed; and

(iii) if the conciliation report was that injustice had been done to the workman.

It was also agreed that the question of evolving a 'clearer' definition of the term 'illegal strike' would be further considered.

Additional Measures for Protection Against Victimisation[1]

The subject was partly covered during the general discussion. It was agreed that it should be further considered at the next meeting of the Standing Labour Committee.

Machinery for Dealing with Disputes Relating to Individual Dismissals, etc.

(i) Disputes relating to individual cases, including dismissals should, as far as possible, be sponsored by a union.

(ii) In the absence of a union to sponsor such cases, or the union concerned declining to sponsor them, the aggrieved individuals might approach the government conciliation machinery for redressal.

(iii) The government official authorised for the purpose should be empowered to refer such cases to the labour court for adjudication.[2]

There was a consensus that a 30-day period of direct action before the I.R.C., undertakes adjudication in cases of disputes in non-essential industries, was unnecessary and uncalled for and should be dispensed with.[2]

The representatives of the state governments emphasised that several disputes involved question of law and order and, therefore, it would not be appropriate for the state government to approach the I.R.C. as petitioner for the reference of such disputes for adjudication. They suggested that the over-riding power of reference to adjudication should be retained by the state governments. There was, however, a consensus that the representative union and the employers should also be able to approach the I.R.C. for reference of disputes for adjudication.

1. 20th Session, 20.3.
2. 24th Session, 26.4.

Industrial Relations Commission[1]

The Chairman referred to the situation that prevailed at the time of the appointment of the National Commission on Labour, particularly the rising expectation of workers for higher wages, better standards of living and improved amenities. The Commission had been called upon to make a comprehensive survey of the labour scene in the country and suggest measures for the reorientation of the labour policy and programme so as to further the interest of the workers and help establish a stable relationship between the workers and their employers. He also drew attention to the salient features of the recommendations made by the Commission and invited members to give their considered views on the recommendations so as to help the government to come to appropriate decisions thereon.[2]

The representatives of all the state governments and union territories were opposed to the setting up of the proposed Industrial Relations Commission (IRC) in the form recommended by the National Commission on Labour (NCL). They said that conciliation and adjudication functions should not be performed by any Industrial Relations Commission, and that the functions of conciliation should continue to remain with the State Labour Departments. In their opinion, the state conciliation machinery had functioned well. It was, therefore, necessary that the experience gained by the officers of the state governments in this regard should be utilized.

The representatives of the INTUC and employers' organisations were, however, of the opinion that Industrial Relations Commission should combine all functions, including conciliation as recommended by the NCL. In their opinion the IRCs should be competent to handle the functions of conciliation with the help of the existing experienced officers of the state conciliation machinery. The conciliation wing of the IRCs should be separate from the adjudication wing.

The representatives of the AITUC expressed opposition to the setting up of the proposed IRCs on the line suggested.[3]

Summing up the deliberations of the Conference, the Chairman observed that conflicting views were expressed on the scope and functions of the proposed Industrial Relations Commissions as conceived by the National Commission. While the representative unions and the employers might be given the right to approach the

1. 26th Session, Extracts from Chairman's Speech.
2. 26th Session, 26.2.
3. 26th Session, 26.17.

Commission for adjudication, the state government should also continue to have such powers.[1]

There was also a consensus that the period of 30 days of direct action before intervention by the Industrial Relations Commissions should be done away with. As regards conciliation the state governments were in favour of the retention of the functions of conciliation with the State Labour Department.

INDUSTRIAL RELATIONS IN PUBLIC SECTOR UNDERTAKINGS

Strikes[2]

There was a discussion on strikes in the public sector undertakings. The discussion was mainly in the context of the strike by the government employees that took place in July, 1960. There was a unanimity of opinion that effective measures should be taken to create suitable measures to ward off the possibility of such strikes.

In this regard the following suggestions were made :

1. Creation of a negotiating machinery at departmental level.
2. Compulsory arbitration.
3. Making strike illegal in certain situations.

It was clarified by the government that the proposal to declare strike illegal in certain situations was not at variance with the existing law. The Industrial Disputes Act already imposed some restrictions on strike. The government also clarified that it would favour compulsory arbitration rather than exercise the freedom to refuse arbitration.

Mobilisation of Internal Resources

The Conference welcomed the suggestion of the Union Finance Minister that a small group should be set up by the Ministry of Labour to assist the government in seeing that the internal resources from the public sector undertakings to the tune of Rs. 35,000 crores in the Seventh Five Year Plan could be mobilised. The Conference felt that a tripartite group should be set up in consultation with the Minister of Finance.

1. 26th Session, 26.4.
2. 18th Session.

Implementation of Labour Laws[1]

(i) In respect to implementation of labour laws in public sector the Conference noted the position stated in the Memorandum and urged that Public Sector Undertakings should ensure full compliance with the requirements of labour laws.

(ii) The proposal concerning constitution of a special committee to review the status of implementation of labour laws in the public sector was however not approved.

(iii) The proposal concerning the review of industrial relations in each public sector undertaking, at least once in three years, was approved.

Management Relations[2]

The Conference recommended that a high powered bipartite committee consisting of the representatives of all the central organisations of workers and representatives of public sector undertakings should go into the question of industrial relations in public sector. The Chairman said that he would take up the matter with the Bureau of Public Enterprises.

Application of the Code of Discipline[3]

The workers' organisation desired that the Code of Discipline and other decisions taken in respect of recognition of unions, mediation and arbitration should also apply to public sector with such adjustments as might be considered necessary. Facts regarding non-observance of these decisions in public sectors should be forwarded to the Ministry of Labour and Employment so that those could be taken up with the respective ministries.

Negotiation on Charter of Demands

The Workers representatives advocated for permission to the managements of the public sector units to commence negotiations with the unions on their charter of demands immediately.

Wage Negotiation and Wage Settlement

The Workers' representatives expressed concern that though the government had permitted wage negotiations in the central public sector enterprises, wage settlements was not being concluded, which

1. 24th Session, 24.2.
2. 27th Session, 27.16.
3. 17th Session, 17.7.

was a matter of serious concern. They suggested that the government should review the situation and facilitate speedy conclusion of wage negotiations and settlements. They also suggested that PSUs should enjoy autonomy for negotiating wage settlements.

Workers' representatives reiterated that the managements of public sector enterprises should be given full functional autonomy, including on issues relating to wage settlement.

Working Conditions of Workers in Export Processing Zone

The conference was concerned about the long delays in the settlement of disputes by labour courts. The Conference also urged on the government to finalise its view on the recommendations of the Sanat Mehta Committee regarding setting up of an Industrial Relations Commission.[1]

Labour and Productivity

The Conference expressed its serious concern at the low productivity of Indian industry and expressed its determination to improve, wherever necessary, productivity, enhance quality and reduce the price of goods to make them internationally competitive. The Conference decided to strive for improvement in discipline and attitude to work at all levels. It also decided that bipartite efforts to improve productivity and quality should be institutionalised.[2]

While fully recognising that productivity of economic enterprises as a whole was of paramount importance, a need was felt to provide it through :

(a) Broadbasing and diversification of production, including by better capacity utilisation.

(b) Well thought-out measures and practices for achieving higher levels of output and to produce goods and services of high quality to enhance the competitive edge of the country's enterprises.

Environment and Labour Protection[3]

The measures for environment protection, the Conference felt, had wide ranging implications for labour. Hence, workers' organizations should be in charge of establishing and regulating environment standards.

1. 32nd Session, 32.4.
2. 31st Session, 31.3, 31.4, 31.5.
3. 32nd Session, 32.23.

National Commission on Labour

Workers' representatives indicated that the first National Commission on Labour was appointed about 25 years ago and a time had come to set up another National Commission on Labour to examine the issues that labour was facing as a result of many developments that had taken place.[1]

Amendment of Industrial Disputes Act

The Chairman said that the defects in the Industrial Disputes Act were being examined and the question of revision of the Act would be taken up in due course. He explained that the memorandum of the Ministry of Labour was placed before the Standing Labour Committee and the Conference and that all points raised would be kept in mind while drafting the Bill. He assured the house that all views expressed by the All India Trade Union Congress, or by any other organisations would be placed before the Select Committee.[2]

Review of Industrial Relations (Covering proposed amendments to ID Act and Trade Unions Act)[3]

The employees' representatives generally felt that in the light of the new approach in regard to workers' participation in management, changes to be brought in the industrial relations also required a fresh thinking. The employers' representatives also broadly agreed with this but emphasised that any further exercise should attempt to provide a package which taking into account all such areas.

Following further discussion on the subject, the Conference agreed to make the following recommendations :

(i) The Trade Union and the Industrial Disputes (Amendment) Bill, introduced in the Rajya Sabha in 1988, be withdrawn.

(ii) To formulate specific proposals for further legislation, a bipartite committee be constituted with Shri G. Ramanujam as Chairman. The Workers' representatives also suggested the names for the Committee. The employers' organisations undertook to forward the names of their nine representatives to the Ministry of Labour. It was decided that secretarial assistance for the Committee would be provided by the

1. 30th Session, 30.10.
2. 9th Session, 9.1.
3. 29th Session, 29.3.

Ministry of Labour and the Committee would give its report by 31st July, 1990.

It was observed that the Government of India had before it the considered views of the Central Trade Union Organisations, the Central Employers' Organisations and the state governments on the recommendations of the Ramanujam Committee. In this context, it was felt that it would be more useful to discuss the matter after the views of the Government of India were known.

The Chairman assured that the drafts of the proposed Industrial Relations and Trade Unions Bill would be prepared, keeping in view the ideas and suggestions expressed by all the parties and the changes that had since been taken place both inside and outside the country. The Chairman offered to have a discussion on the matter with the select group of representatives of the parties present at the Conference.[1]

Comprehensive Industrial Relations Laws

The workers representatives said that it was a matter of concern that despite discussions in the various tripartite fora, including the Indian Labour Conference, over the years and despite efforts on the part of successive governments, a comprehensive industrial relations law had not become a reality. They said that in the present scenario of vast changes in the socio-economic front, the central and state governments and the social partners should come together in making this comprehensive Industrial Relations Law a reality.[2]

1. 30th Session, 30.4.
2. 31st Session, 31.3.

5

PROTECTION AGAINST UNEMPLOYMENT

Rising unemployment in the post-war situation were the important and the immediate issues that engaged the attention of the ILC in its initial sessions. Several measures were discussed to tide over the situation. It was for this reason that the establishment of Directorate General of Resettlement and Employment, and Employment Exchange became necessary. Closure of industrial units was viewed with all seriousness, and it is significant that as early as 1958, the 16th Session of ILC emphasised the need for modernisation of textile industries.

The issue of rationalisation assumed importance following the Second Five Year Plan which stressed the need for promoting increased productivity and laid down the Labour Policy and Programmes.

Problem of industrial sickness became an important issue particularly after the new economic policy. An important suggestion made in the context of structural adjustment was the revival of labour cell in the Planning Commission to facilitate consultations with trade unions in the formulation of labour policy.

INVOLUNTARY UNEMPLOYMENT, UNEMPLOYMENT IN TRANSITION PERIOD AND EMPLOYMENT EXCHANGE

Involuntary Unemployment Due to Shortage of Coal, Raw Materials, etc.[1]

The question before the Conference was whether the involuntary unemployment caused by the war situation needed special provision to tide over the problem. The central government's tentative view was that relief to the unemployed labour was necessary which should however, be of a purely temporary nature. The Government made it

1. 5th Session, 5.1.

clear that a permanent unemployment scheme was not under its consideration. It suggested that the entire cost of the proposed temporary benefits should be borne by the employers who should compensate it by price addition to their products.

Involuntary Unemployment Resulting from Controls[1]

The central government representative stated that there was no immediate proposal for an Act on this subject. Legislation would take considerable time to come into existence whereas the problem had to be tackled immediately.

It was the general opinion that immediate action was required to mitigate the hardship caused to the workers on account of involuntary suspension of work. The .employers felt that the responsibility for action devolved on the authority responsible for such hardship. It was felt necessary to consider whether the Conference should accept any obligation on the part of the employers? If the circumstances leading to a stoppage were likely to be very rare, there should be no reluctance to undertake the obligation. So far as the moral obligation was concerned, the provision regarding a waiting period of seven days for six months should be accepted in order to eliminate the chances of advantage of periodical stoppages by employers.

Unemployment in Transition Period[2]

The ILC considered the Establishment of Directorate General of Resettlement and Employment and setting up of Employment Exchange. A memorandum in this regard outlining was placed before the Conference. What the government proposed to do and seeking suggestions either by modification or addition to the scheme. Both the employers' and the workers' organizations were requested to extend their cooperation in running the Employment Exchanges as efficiently as possible.

The central government representatives expressed gratitude for the acceptance of the proposal by the Conference.[3]

> The question of Employment Exchanges has now come to the fore and would demand the active and urgent attention of all

1. 7th Session, 7.1.
2. 7th Session, 7.2.
3. 6th Session, 6.3.

the parties. This was a very big problem and it was impossible to conceive of any satisfactory solution unless it was jointly tackled by the Government of India, Provinces, employers and workers. Experience in other countries has shown that these exchanges have failed for want of co-operation and co-ordination. India should learn from that experience. It should be clearly understood that these exchanges do not solve unemployment problems but do regulate employment and can make a big contribution towards the smooth working of labour and capital. The exchanges should go a long way to abolish haphazard employment and supplant the unsatisfactory system and contract labour.

Through an oversight, labour was not represented on the Advisory Committee for Technical Training and the error would quickly be rectified. Labour would nominate persons who were aware of technical aspects of training and would help to arrive at sound decisions. Employment Exchanges in provinces should have committees attached to them on which labour should be equally represented with employers. There should be greater interest and enthusiasm on the part of all concerned. The centre should give lead to the provinces. The suggestion for an ad hoc committee was accepted.

Another important issue was the displacement of workers by retrenched servicemen. It was felt this could also be watched through a system of Employment Exchanges.

The Conference came to an agreement that the Employment Exchanges should not give their services in the following cases :

(i) for placement of the workers on strike if strike was declared 'illegal' after refusal to submit the dispute to a public authority or to a conciliation committee appointed or proposed or to accept the settlement of the dispute proposed by a public authority or conciliation committee thus appointed; and

(ii) for placement of the workers who had refused to submit a dispute for enquiry or had refused to accept the decisions with respect to the dispute by a public authority or a conciliation committee or had declared a lockout without previously having recourse to the authority or board or after refusal to comply with their decision.

Representation of Agricultural Labour on Central Employment Advisory Scheme[1]

The suggestion for representation of workers' representatives agricultural workers on the Central Employment Advisory Committee had been taken note of.

Employment Organisation for Discharges and Placements[2]

The government informed that the employment organisation was trying to collect all statistics to have a clear idea of the manpower position in the country, as the data supplied by private industrial concerns were incomplete. The government would however, try to publish the detailed figures which would give some idea of discharges and placements.

Closure of Industrial Units and Unemployment[3]

The Chairman expressed his deep concern on the incidence of closures of Industrial Undertakings. He said :

> A large number of closures of industrial understakings in the country posed several problems and some kind of emergency legislations had to be put into effect in West Bengal. That is why, when we think in terms of any law on closure, we have to think in a comprehensive manner.
>
> I do not propose to go into the remaining subjects included in the agenda. I would only say that government's policies have been framed by a keen desire to secure a fair deal for labour as well as for employers. To my mind, it is one of the compulsions of the current economic situation that full encouragement is needed to all productive enterprises. Curbs should also be placed on all speculative activities. It is equally necessary that the leadership of trade unions show full awareness of the imperatives of development while raising the demands of the workers.

Take-over of Closed Units[4]

The Conference in this regard discussed the following :

1. Adoption of suitable measures by the government to meet the situation arising from closures due to shortage of raw materials or threats of strikes;

---

1. 8th Session, 8.1.
2. 8th Session, 8.1.
3. 27th Session, extract from Chairman's speech.
4. 24th session, 24.1.

2. Take-over of units which had closed down on account of mismanagement; and
3. Suitable arrangement to provide financial assistance to ensure satisfactory running of such units.

Plantations[1]

It was felt that suitable steps should be taken by the central and the state governments after examining the recommendations of the Plantation Inquiry Commission, the Industrial Committee on Plantations in consultation with the Tea Board.

Cotton Textile[2]

(a) There were more than a dozen units which had been closed for a number of years. These were beyond the economic viability and could not be reopened the government was convinced, on expert advice, that these old units could not be run. However, licenses for new units of equivalent capacity should be considered in the same locations if parties were willing to seek such licenses;

(b) For the other closed mills, or for units which had given closure notice, an expert committee should be appointed to examine each individual unit and make recommendation for suitable remedial action to restore normal working;

(c) The present difficulties were confined to coarse and medium count mills. Steps might be taken to make available, if possible, long staple cotton to the mills as a special relief measure to enable them to produce finer cloth;

(d) When adequate additional securities were available, scheduled banks, including the State Bank of India, should be requested to reduce the margin required by them for advance of working capital. This recommendation should be of a temporary character and should continue only till heavy stocks with the unit were disposed of;

(e) Rehabilitation and modernisation, through the National Industrial Development Corporation, might be expedited. In all cases of modernisation, however, the recommendations of the fifteenth session of the Indian Labour Conference on Rationalisation should be kept in mind;

(f) For such units, which were found uneconomic, the grant of

1. 16th Session, 16.6.
2. 16th Session, 16.6.

licence for necessary balancing equipment, either in spindles or in looms or in preparatory equipment, might be favourably considered by the government after examination of the unit concerned;

(g) In Kanpur and Indore, where the situation was more difficult, expert committees might be appointed to enquire into the existing conditions of units located there and to suggest remedial action;

(h) Any steps that might be taken to remedy the situation in cotton textile industry, should also take into account the position of the hand-loom industry and of exclusive spinning units; and

(i) Liberal exports of the year, particularly on the basis of Open General Licence, might be considered to help the spinning units in the country.

Jute[1]

(a) In the case of jute textiles outside West Bengal, the transfer of looms from one unit to the other should be effected only after the permission was accorded for such transfer by the government concerned;

(b) The Conference took note of the diversification of jute products which was already taking place and recommended that efforts in this direction should be further intensified; and

(c) Possibilities of further action should be explored at a meeting of the Industrial Committee on Jute to be convened in Calcutta at an early date.

Engineering[2]

The Conference drew the attention of the government to the acute shortage of steel and imported raw material for all industries—big, small and medium—and urged that unless immediate steps were taken by the government in this regard, a large number of full or partial closure would take place in this important sector of national economy.

General Recommendation Regarding Closure[3]

(a) The standing orders might be so amended that no shift working

1. 16th Session, 16.6.
2. 16th Session, 16.6.
3. 16th Session, 16.6.

should be closed without two months' notice and that no total closure should take place without three months' notice to the workers as well as to the government. However, in the case of units of engineering industry, the period could be reduced in individual cases, if the state government concerned was satisfied that because of the circumstances of any particular unit, a shorter period (one month) was adequate.

(b) Lacunae in the present provision for the lay-off compensation whereby labour could be denied compensation by working nominally for some days in a week after 45 days lay-off to avoid payment of compensation should be immediately remedied. In the meantime, such practices should not be resorted to.

(c) Liquidation proceedings took an unreasonably long time. Where government was convinced that a mill, company or a unit could not be worked unless ownership was changed, some measures—legal, if necessary—might be devised for an early completion of the liquidation proceedings or the sale by transfer or open auction of such property even before liquidation. It would enable the new party to restart working of such units. As an interim measure, the government should, as far as possible, ensure the working of the mill as a measure of unemployment relief with such conditions as agreed to between the government as employer and the workers concerned. In such cases, steps should be taken to overcome the difficulties caused by the normal financial procedures of the government.

(d) The Government of India should consider favourably any request of the state governments for enquiries, and in conducting such enquiries, should associate the concerned state governments if it so desired.

Preventive and post closure measures :[1] It was generally agreed that the problem of closures had two aspects—one preventive and the other relating to taking over and reopening of units already closed. While the workers' representatives and many state governments suggested that the period of notice should be increased to three months, the employers felt that it was not feasible to give notice in all cases.

It was also agreed that notice alone would not help to prevent closures. A Standing Tripartite Cell for each major industry should be

1. 25th Session, 25.4.

set up to keep a watch over the working condition of all the units in the industry, particularly the marginal ones. Legislative provisions and governmental machinery for takeover should ensure continuity of employment and production. Consequent upon the takeover, there should not be any reduction in employment or emoluments nor should there be any adverse effect on service conditions and benefits.

The workers' representatives favoured an immediate ordinance empowering the government to take over units already closed or likely to be closed and to carry out any amendments in the law to ensure that any action for taking over is not rendered justifiable. The unit taken over should not be handed back.

The state governments suggested that the central government should streamline procedures for takeover and provide sufficient funds to run the taken over units.

Ensuring Effective Functioning of the Textile Corporation[1]

The Conference noted with concern the deteriorating situation in the textile industry resulting in the closure of a number of mills and recommended that the Commerce Ministry might be requested to organise a Conference at an early date to discuss the problems of this industry and to suggest effective solutions.

The workers' representatives suggested that the question of providing unemployment relief to the affected workmen in the textile and other industries should also be considered.

RATIONALISATION AND LOSS OF EMPLOYMENT

Model Agreement to Guide Employers[2]

The Second Five Year Plan stressed the need for promoting increased productivity for the general benefit of the community, the enterprise and the workers. In this context, rationalisation, that is, better utilisation of men, machines and management in industrial undertakings, had assumed greater importance. The task of drafting a model agreement on this issue was entrusted to the Conference Committee.

In pursuance of the above task, the Committee discussed measures for rationalisation and the procedure to be adopted by the establishments which were willing to introduce schemes involving

1. 27th Session, 27.14.
2. 24th Session, 24.1.

higher productivity. It was decided that government make arrangements to ensure that measures of rationalisation which did not serve real economic interest in the existing conditions of the country might be avoided. This would be applicable even in the case of those units which had already taken initial steps to introduce rationalisation and had not completed the process. The recommendations of the Committee were mainly based on the principles laid down in paragraphs 28 and 29 of the chapter on Labour Policy and Programmes in the Second Five Year Plan document. Those recommendations were :

(i) There should be no retrenchment or loss of earnings of the existing employees except in the cases of natural separation or wastage. Workers could, however, be provided with suitable alternative jobs in the same establishment or under the same employer, subject to agreement between the employers and the workers;

(ii) There should be an equitable sharing of benefits of rationalisation between the community, the employer and the worker; and

(iii) There should be a proper assessment of work-load by experts which should be mutually agreed upon. Suitable improvement in the working conditions should accordingly be made.

Keeping in view the above conditions, some broad procedure was suggested to smoothen the progress of rationalisation. The union, or unions, in an undertaking and the employer could agree to a working arrangement on the following lines :

(i) The company may seek to make such changes in machinery, layout and organisation as it deems necessary for efficient operation of machinery and rational use of labour and material without prejudice to the provisions of any law for the time being in force;

(ii) Before any such change is effected, the company should give reasonable notice, to the unions of its intention to effect the change. The notice shall be in the form as mutually agreed upon, and shall contain full information regarding the nature of the proposed change, approximate date of such change, proposed duties for workers concerned and their job assignment and the expected earnings. However, where an appropriate procedure for notice of such changes exists under the current legislation, the same should be observed in preference to the above;

(iii) The employer shall also give information regarding the change and the reduction in the number of jobs and also the effect of the change on the number of jobs in other departments;

(iv) The employer and employees shall meet and discuss the proposal as soon as possible after the notice has been given under para (ii) above. The employer shall furnish all information necessary for a complete understanding of the proposed change and shall explain the contemplated change to the union(s);

(v) The union(s) shall, within a week after the discussion with the employer, present its views or proposals to the employer. If there is agreement between the parties, the employer may introduce the change on the due date in accordance with the agreement;

(vi) The union(s) shall be given adequate opportunity to study the new change so as to enable it to gauge the work load and the earnings of the employees engaged in the new operation; and

(vii) If there are differences between the parties on any matter covered by this working arrangement, the matters in dispute shall be referred for arbitration or adjudication.

Automation[1]

The employers' representatives adopted the recommendations and said that any resistance or delay in automation would impede country's progress. It was generally felt that there was a need for regulation of the pace of technological change to facilitate a smooth and orderly transition, with the minimum social costs. It was felt that the requirements of the Model Agreement on Rationalisation should be fully complied with in the case of automation as well. The Chairman expressed the view that installation of Computers in the Life Insurance Corporation, Oil Companies, etc., should also be subject to the above requirements. He agreed that the Government's policy in regard to automation should be selective and while introducing the scheme, Mould Agreement would be taken into consideration.[2]

1. 24th Session, 24.1.
2. 27th Session, 27.12.

Regarding problems in the LIC and other establishments the Chairman agreed to convene a special session of the Indian Labour Conference in June or July, 1968, for discussion on the subject. Meanwhile, he made an appeal to the employers to maintain the status quo and to the workers not to precipitate matters.

Industrial Sickness in the Context of New Industrial Policy

The growing sickness of industrial units was viewed with concern. It was felt that immediate preventive steps should be taken to go into the cause of sickness and effective remedial action initiated to combat it. Emphasis should be laid on quick programmes for rehabilitation and revival of sick units. A Standing Committee should be set up to monitor the problem of sickness in industries and also to undertake indepth study of individual cases of closed sick units as well as units identified as potentially sick.

The Conference generally welcomed the Sick Industrial Companies (Special Provisions) Bill, 1905, which was introduced in Parliament. It, however, suggested that the government might consider amending it to bring within its purview sick industrial units as also the potentially sick units to prevent the latter from closing down. The Conference also felt that the interests of labour should be fully represented on the Board and the state government should also find representation thereon.

It was of the opinion that there was a crying need for speedy and orderly investigation into the rehabilitation of sick industrial enterprises registered with the BIFR, minimising distress for the workers and disabilities for the employers. Important measures required were :

(a) Review of the working of the BIFR so far and suggestion for changes, if necessary.

(b) Creation of adequate number of benches of the BIFR on a zonal basis.

(c) Hearing by BIFR benches to be so organised as to have its sittings in different places to suit, to the extent possible, the convenience of the parties called for hearing.

(d) Appointment of members of the BIFR with adequate professional expertise in handling matters relating to structuring and restructuring of industries, management and industrial relations with trade union experience.

(e) The BIFR procedure should be simplified and statutory

provision should be made to make it time bound.

(f) Registration of an enterprise with the BIFR under the Sick Industrial Companies Act should not result in cessation of fund flows from the financing institutions until a decision was taken on rehabilitation.

(g) Wherever rehabilitation proposals had been approved, the government should ensure flow of funds for such rehabilitation. Wherever joint revival packages were submitted, those packages should be given full support by the government and financial institutes.

Restructuring of National Textile Corporation

The scheme for NTC restructuring should be implemented.

Restructuring of Jute Mills

Financial support for jute mills restructured on cooperative basis should be extended without delay.

Restructuring of BIFR

The BIFR should be restructured with experts from the areas of management and labour. The BIFR procedures should be significantly simplified to cut down delays in the restructuring of sick enterprises; inordinate delays that occur now in the disposal of winding up and liquidation proceedings should be cut down by necessary simplification of laws.

Study of Industrial Sickness

Detailed and comprehensive studies of sickness in industrial enterprises should be undertaken for evolving appropriate remedial and preventive measure.

Structural Adjustment and Employment

On the impact of the new industrial policy, the Chairman referred to the assurance given by the Prime Minister that it would not lead to any human distress and the legitimate interests of labour would be protected.

For absorption of surplus labour, if any, and for maximising capacity utilisation, the Conference suggested diversification and broad-basing by working the units round the clock and on all days of the week.

Priority in the use of resources of the fund should be given for training, retraining, vocational counselling and guidance for redeployment of workers affected by rationalisation. Side by side, investments should also be made by drawing on appropriate sources of finance for the rehabilitation of the rationalised enterprises.

The present employment scenario in which organised sector employment had become stagnant and the agrarian sector was not absorbing more job seekers, meaningful action should be taken in pursuance of the report of the NDC Committee on employment to create more job opportunities in the economy as a whole and to protect existing levels of employment to the maximum possible extent.

The Economic Reforms Process should be geared to expansion of employment opportunities by evolving an employment policy which would arrest the loss of job opportunities and provide suitable rehabilitation package for sick industries.

The conference suggested that detailed studies should be undertaken in various sectors in respect of employment generation; the progress in promoting employment in agro-based industrial sector should also be studied. Special measures including employment reviewing the existing laws and amending them where appropriate, should be taken to augment employment appropriate for women.

It was suggested that the Labour Cell in the Planning Commission should be revived to facilitate consultation with Trade Unions in policy formulation. The views expressed in the Conference with regard to employment policy might be conveyed to the Planning Commission for its consideration and for the consideration of the two sub-committees of the Planning Commission/NDC which were working out the strategies for implementation of the employment policy.

6

TRADE UNIONS

The Trade Unions Act, 1926 figured prominently in the various sessions of the ILC. It discussed at length the registration, verification and recognition issues as well as applicability of the Code of Disciplines to unrecognised unions. Though it did not favour the proposal to amend the Act to limit the number of outsiders as office-bearers, it emphasised that as far as possible, workers at the enterprise level should be the office-bearers. It also suggested that technicians and supervisory staff could have either their separate unions or represent themselves through the general unions.

Proposed Amendment of the Trade Unions Act, 1926

The Conference considered a draft bill to amend the Trade Unions Act, 1926. It was decided to have a small committee comprising two members from the employers' side and two from workers' side, besides representatives of the government. The government would call the meeting of the committee at short notice and place before it the final proposal with regard to the Trade Unions Bill.

Labour Relation Bill, 1950, and Trade Unions Bill, 1950

(a) After a general discussion on the underlying principles of the proposed Labour Relations Bill and the Trade Unions Bill the various provisions of the Bills were discussed and the views expressed were noted.[1]

(b) It was suggested that the delay in the registration of trade unions should be avoided.[2]

(c) If out of the seven signatories to an aplication for registration,

1. 10th Session.
2. 16th Session, 16.1.

one or two got discharged during the pendency of the application and if the signatories were entitled to apply for registration at the time of application, registration should not be refused on the ground that they had since ceased to be workers.[1]

Recognition and Verification

It was felt necessary that certain conventions should be evolved for the voluntary recognition of trade unions by employers. The criteria agreed to for such recognition were as follows :[2]

(a) Where there were more than one unions, the union claiming recognition should have been functional for at least one year after registration. Where there was only one union, this condition would not apply.

(b) The membership of the union should cover at least 15 per cent of the workers in the establishment concerned. For this purpose, membership would be counted only of those who had paid their subscriptions for at least three months during the period of six months immediately preceding the reckoning.

(c) A union might claim to be recognised as a representative union for an industry in a local area if it had a membership of at least 25 per cent of the workers of that industry in that area.

(d) When a union has been recognised, there should be no change in its position for a period of two years.

(e) Where there were several unions in an industry or establishment, the one with the largest membership should be recognised.

(f) A representative union for an industry in an area should have the right to represent the workers in all the establishments in the industry, but if a union in a particular establishment had a membership of 50 per cent of workers or more, it should have the right to deal with the matters of purely local interest, like handling of grievances pertaining to its own members. All other workers who were not members of that union might either operate through the representative union for the

1. 16th Session, 16.1.
2. 16th Session, 16.1, see Appendix XIII for criteria for recognition and verification of unions. Also see Appendix XIV for Procedure for Verification of membership of unions evolved in the 16th Session, and Appendix XV for verification of membership for the purpose of recognition under the code of discipline.

industry or seek redressal directly.

(g) As regards the procedure for verification of the strength of unions, the Conference approved the following suggestions :

(i) Copies of the claims of membership submitted to the Chief Labour Commissioner by each of the Trade Union Federations should be made available also to the other Federations so that the claim of membership by the different Federations were known to each other and in the case of any wrong claim, rectification measures were taken.

(ii) After the Chief Labour Commissioner has completed verification, and before finalising it, he should furnish particulars of the verification to the Federations concerned. If any of the unions claimed by the Federations have not been accepted for inclusion, the reasons should be indicated. A specified period should be given to the Federations to bring to the notice of the Chief Labour Commissioner any errors or omissions which they might wish to point out.

It was further agreed that the verification procedure for the determination of the representative character of a union should be made more adequate. Where the result of verification by the departmental machinery was not accepted by the parties, a committee composed of the representatives of all central trade union organisations should go into the question and resolve the dispute. For this purpose, the central trade union organisations, which could act as a standing machinery, would provide panels of suitable persons for different localities. If this machinery failed, the question should be left to the decision of an agreed independent agency or a tribunal. The state governments should also evolve similar procedures concerning industries within their sphere.

(h) In the case of trade union federations which were not affiliated to any of the four central organisations of labour, the question of recognition should be dealt with separately.

(i) Only those unions which observed the Code of Discipline would be entitled to recognition and the procedure for recognition should form a part of the Code of Discipline.

(i) Union-shop and Check-off : The proposals for the introduction of union-shop and check-off were rejected. It was, however, agreed that a recognised union should be entitled to collect membership fees every month within the premises of the undertaking.

(ii) Suspension of Adjudication : The consensus was that the time was not appropriate for the suspension of adjudication for settlement of industrial disputes though adjudicaton would be the last resort in the process.

(iii) Works Committees : The present position should be fully examined.

(iv) Grievance procedure : The sub-committee of the 15th session of the Indian Labour Conference should draft a simple and flexible grievance procedure in accordance with the principles evolved by it.

(v) Steps to be taken to mitigate the Trade Union rivalry : This was discussed separately in a meeting of representatives of the different central organisations of workers held on 21 May, 1953, and an Inter-union Code of Conduct was adopted at this meeting.

(vi) Membership Fee and Registration of Trade Unions :

(a) A trade union should prescribe a minimum membership fee of Rs. 4 per month and the Registrar of Trade Unions should be empowered to inspect the books of the union.

(b) Delay in the registration of trade unions should be avoided.

Time Limit for Registration of Trade Unions[1]

(i) Application for registration should be decided expeditiously. It should not take more than three months to complete the procedure. In those cases in which the registration procedure exceeded three months the reasons for the delay should be recorded and reported to the State Implementation Committees. For this purpose, the time taken by the applicant in carrying out any correction in the application forms should be excluded. The authority should indicate all the defects and mistakes in the application immediately.

(ii) Though no further restraint should be placed in the law regarding the minimum number of persons who must be shown as members for the purpose of registration, care should revertheless be taken by unions that the membership

1. 17th Session, 17.2.

should not fall short of 5 per cent of the full strength of workers eligible to become members of the union.

Decentralisation of Registration[1]

The proposal, concerning decentralisation of the work of the Registrars and delegation of the powers of the Registrars to other authorities, viz., Additional and Deputy Registrars, with a view to avoid delays in the registration of unions, was approved.

Powers of Registrars[2]

It was decided that Registrars should have powers to inspect the account books, membership registers and minutes books of the trade unions to verify the correctness of the annual returns. The inspection should, as far as possible, be done at a place within a reasonable distance (within city limits or within a distance of 10 miles, whichever may be more) from the office of the union concerned or at the union office itself.

Number of Unions in an Industry or Undertaking to be Registered[3]

There was a consensus that there should not be any restriction on the number of unions that might be registered in a particular industry or undertaking.

Number of Outsiders as Office Bearers[4]

(i) There should be no change in the existing legal provision in respect of statutory restrictions on the number of outsiders on the executive of trade unions.

(ii) Conduct of affairs of trade union should be placed more and more in the hands of persons drawn from the ranks of the workers engaged in industry; or who had actual work experience in the industry. To facilitate the process, the following steps should be taken :

(a) educational activity for the benefit of the workers and their children should be greatly extended. For this pupose, besides the state, the union and the employers should participate and assist as much as possible. A sufficient number of scholarships should be provided to

1. 17th Session, 17.2.
2. 17th Session, 17.2., see Appendix XVI for Inter-union Code of Conduct.
3. 17th Session, 17.2.
4. 17th Session, 17.2.

the workers and their children. Evening classes and extension courses should be developed on a large scale;

(b) the work of trade unions and the labour departments of the government and the undertakings should, as far as practicable, be carried on in regional languages.

Rules and Constitution of Unions[1]

It was suggested that central organisations of workers should ensure that the unions affiliated to them carried out the provisions and requirements of the rules and constitution, especially with regard to the holding of meetings, election of office bearers and adoption of annual reports and statements.

Representation of Technicians, Supervisory Staff etc. by a Representative Union[2]

It was agreed that technicians, supervisory staff, etc. should be free to form their own unions to represent their interests. If, however, a majority of technicians, etc. were members of a general union and the union was a representative one, such a union would be entitled to represent the interests of technicians, supervisory staff etc. also.

Rights of a Recognised Union Under the Code of Discipline vis-a-vis an Un-recognised Union

1. It was agreed that unions granted recognition under the Code of Discipline should, for the present, enjoy the following rights :

   (i) to raise issues and enter into collective agreements with employers on general questions concerning the terms of employment and conditions of service of workers in an establishment or, in the case of a representative union, in an industry in a local area;

   (ii) to collect membership fees/subscriptions payable by members to the union within the premises of the undertaking;

   (iii) to put up or cause to be put up a notice board on the premises of the undertaking in which its members were employed and affix or cause to be affixed thereon notices relating to meetings, statement of accounts of its income and expenditure;

1. 17th Session, 17.2.
2. 19th Session, 19.4.

(iv) to protest against use of abusive, indecent or inflammatory language or expressions which are subversive of discipline or otherwise contrary to the Code. In pursuance of the prevention of industrial disputes or settlement of industrial disputes the unions will have the right to :

(a) to hold discussions with the employees who were members of the union at a suitable place or premises of office/factory/establishment as mutually agreed upon;

(b) to meet and discuss with an employer, or any person appointed by him for the purpose, the grievances of its members employed in the undertaking;

(c) to inspect, by prior arrangement, any place in an undertaking, where any member of the union was employed.

(v) to nominate its representatives on the Grievance Committee constituted under the Grievance Procedure in an establishment;

(vi) to nominate its representatives on Joint Management Councils; and

(vii) to nominate its representatives on non-statutory bipartite committees, e.g., production committees, welfare committees, canteen committees, house allotment committees, etc. set up by managements.

2. The rights referred to above would be without prejudice to the privileges being enjoyed by the recognised unions at present, either by agreement or by usage.

The question of grant of special casual leave to office bearers and permission to employees to work as full-time union functionaries was briefly discussed. It was, however, decided to defer those questions for detailed discussion at a future tripartite meeting. The organisations agreed to send full information regarding the existing practices on the subject of rights and privileges of recognised unions.

The question of rights and privileges of non-recognised unions was deferred for future consideration because of difference of opinion.

7

WAGE, DEARNESS ALLOWANCE AND BONUS

Wage, Dearness Allowance and Bonus became the subject matters of extensive discussions mainly from 13th Session onwards. The importance of the discussions lay in the fact that efforts were made to determine rational principles for fixation of minimum wage, dearness allowance and bonus. Thus, in determination of minimum wage, the recommendation of Dr. Akroyd on calorie norm was taken into consideration. The representatives of the AITUC and the West Bengal Government in the 26th Session of the ILC rejected the inclusion of capacity to pay, as one of the criteria for minimum wage fixation. The findings of the first All Indian Agricultural Labour Enquiry were also considered for fixing minimum wage for agriculture workers, though in a very general way.

MINIMUM WAGE

The Conference considered the various suggestions made by the different interests groups regarding all aspects of wage and recommended the following steps :[1]

(i) The time for implementation of the Minimum Wages Act in respect of Part I of the Schedule be extended till 31 December, 1954;

(ii) The Central Advisory Board should lay down principles and criteria for the fixation of minimum wages.

(iii) The manner in which the Act was so far being implemented should be immediately examined by the Central Advisory Board. It should formulate a code of directions to be issued by the central government to state governments; and

1. 13th Session, 13.5.

(iv) The government should issue notifications for covering additional employments on the advice of the Central Advisory Board.

General Considerations regarding Minimum Wage[1]

The Conference considered the following issues pertaining to minimum wages :

(i) The implementation of the Minimum Wages Act with regard to various employments;
(ii) The principles involved for fixing the minimum wages under the Act;
(iii) Lack of uniformity in the actual fixation of wages under the Act;
(iv) The lacunae in the various provisions of the Act; and
(v) The need for widening the scope of the Act to cover additional sweated employments and also to secure improvements in the existing provisions.

Principles of Fixation

The recommendations of the conference committee, were as follows :[2]

The minimum wage should be 'need based' and should ensure the minimum human needs of the industrial workers irrespective of any other consideration.

(i) In calculating the minimum wage, the standard working class family should be taken to consist of consumption units for one earner; the earnings of women and children excluding the adolescents.
(ii) Minimum food requirements should be calculated on the basis of a net intake of 2,700 calories, for an average Indian adult of moderate activity as recommended by Dr. Akroyd.
(iii) Clothing requirements should be estimated at a per capita consumption of 18 yards per annum for a family of four persons, i.e., 72 yards per worker's family.
(iv) In respect of housing, the norm should be the minimum rent charged by the government in any area for houses provided under the Subsidised Industrial Housing Scheme for low income groups; and

1. 13th Session, 13.5.
2. 15th Session, 15.6.

(v) Lighting and other 'miscellaneous' items of expenditure should constitute 20 per cent of the total minimum wage.

The committee suggested that Government Study Group might usefully collect available material on the following subjects for information of all concerned :

(i) Work-load and job evaluation;
(ii) Rationalisation of management in industries including those in the public sector;
(iii) Working conditions; and
(iv) Relative share of workers, capital, management and the public exchequer in the factory product.

While suggesting this, the Committee recognised the difficulties in the collection of such material and its interpretation for the purposes of wage fixation, but felt that a beginning might be made in that direction.

Capacity to Pay[1]

While the representatives of the AITUC and the West Bengal Government rejected the inclusion of 'capacity to pay' among the criteria for determining need-based minimum wage, employers' representatives were emphatic that 'capacity to pay' should be a determinant factor.

Fair Wage Committee[2]

As regards fair wages, it was agreed that the Wage Boards should go in detail in respect of each industry on the basis of the recommendations of the Fair Wage Committee. The recommendations of the Committee should also be made applicable to the employees in public sectors.

Collective Bargaining for Wage[3]

There was a consensus on the need to encourage collective bargaining between employers and workers' representatives to negotiate wage rates and conditions of employment. However, with the exception of the representatives of West Bengal Government and AITUC, it was generally felt that the existing system of Wage Boards should continue subject to the removal of the defects and deficiencies in their functioning.

---

1. 26th Session, 26.10.
2. 15th Session, 15.6.
3. 26th Session, 26.8.

Implementation of Recommendations[1]

While agreeing to the guidelines for fixation of the minimum wage for industrial workers throughout the country, the Committee recognised that difficulties might be experienced in implementing those recommendations. Wherever the minimum wages fixed were below the recommended level, it would be incumbent on the authorities concerned to justify the circumstances which prevented them from adherence to the norms laid down.

The Committee took note of the steps taken by the government for conducting (a) a wage census and (b) family budget enquiries in various industrial centres.

Minimum Wages Fixation Machinery[2]

The discussion regarding the need for Statutory Machinery for fixation of Minimum Wages revolved round a choice between Wage Boards and Industrial Courts. The central government representative observed that there was a distinction between Wage Boards and Industrial Courts. While the High Court judges might be available for the industrial courts, it might not be so for Wage Boards which, like Trade Boards, would be usually required to sit for long period.

The Boards will have to go further than merely fixing subsistence wage or minimum wage rates. As such the rate must be related to normal working week and over-time and to piece rate and time rate. It was made clear that it was not the intention of the Conference that the Boards should fix hours of work.

The suggestion that the Boards should not consider the general conditions of employment was also accepted by the central government representatives.

Tripartite Wage Boards[3]

There was an agreement that the appropriate machinery for wage fixation would be Tripartite Wage Boards similar to that already appointed for the cotton textile industry. It was suggested by the workers' representatives that the government might set up Wage Boards for the following sectors : (a) Jute, (b) Plantations, (c) Mines (other than coal), (d) Engineering, (e) Iron and Steel, (f) Chemicals, (g) Sugar, (h) Cement, (i) Railways, (j) Posts and Telegraphs, (k) Civilian Employees in Defence Establishments covered under the Industrial Disputes Act, 1947, and (l) Ports and Docks.

1. 15th Session, 15.6.
2. 6th Session, 6.5.
3. 15th Session, 15.6.

Employers' representatives were of the view that it might be left to the discretion of government.

It was acknowledged that the Tripartite Wage Boards had generally done a good job. There were complaints about delay and the abnormally long time the Wage Boards took to complete their deliberations. The question of setting up a committee to go into the matter and make recommendations to improve the functioning of such Boards was said to be under consideration.

Recommendations of Wage Boards[1]

There was a consensus that unanimous recommendations of Wage Boards should have statutory force. As regards the recommendations which were not unanimous, the general opinion was that the recommendations of the Chairman, provided such a Chairman was appointed with the consent of all the parties, should be considered as an Award which should be statutorily binding. The representatives of Tamil Nadu Government, however, stated that it was essential to have independent members on the Boards and that the decisions which were not unanimous could be left to the appropriate government.

Wage Freeze[2]

The proposal for freezing of the existing wage structure in industry, where a Wage Board was functioning was withdrawn. The Chairman remarked :

> Wage-freeze was not a solution to our problems nor was it practicable. Any proposal for wage-freeze can be considered only along with a proposal for price-freeze and profit-freeze. The existing policy of effecting selective wage revision and granting relief were called for and, to the extent practicable, would seem to meet the requirment adequately.

Minimum Wage for Agricultural Workers[3]

The Conference considered the findings of the first All India Agricultural Labour Enquiry and made suggestions for improving the economic conditions of agricultural workers specially with reference to the fixation of minimum wages under the Minimum Wages Act.

1. 26th Session, 26.9.
2. 24th Session, Extract from Chairman's Speech.
3. 14th Session, 11.4.

Appointment of Wage Commission[1]

There was a discussion on the subject but no conclusion was arrived at.

Common Secretariat for Wage Boards and Wage Committees

It was agreed that there should be a common secretariat for all wage boards as well as for wage committees under the Minimum Wages Act.

The Conference discussed the need for a national minimum wage. Till such time as this was not feasible, it was felt desirable to have regional minimum wage for which the central government should lay down the guidelines.

The minimum wages should be revised at regular periodicity and should be linked with rise in the cost of living.

Uniform Minimum Wages

It was felt necessary that the scope for introduction of uniform minimum wages in the country should be investigated further so that drastic wage disparities did not contribute to flight of industries and sudden unemployment in those pockets.

DEARNESS ALLOWANCES AND BONUS

General Uniform Principles for DA

It was felt that a general uniform principles for fixing dearness allowances or bonus should be decided. The central government representatives raised the following issues :[2]

(a) What should be the general principles? Should there be different rates for different industries and for different regions? If so, what should be the governing factors and the demarcation of regions?

(b) Should it be laid down so that the degree of assistance given towards the increased cost of living should diminish as wages increase above subsistence level? If so, how?

(c) If and when such principles are laid down should they be so worked out that not only the tendency to give higher allowances is checked but also such allowances, if they fall below the prescribed standard, are raised?

1. 14th Session, 14.7.
2. 5th Session, 5.5., see Appendix XVII for the Gregory Committee's Report on the General Principles of fixing dearness allowance to employees and Industrial Concerns, 1944.

(d) Should the allowance automatically increase or decrease according to the cost of living index? And should the scale of neutralisation diminish as prices rise above a certain level?

(e) Should the allowances be fixed on a percentage of wages or income or at flat rates varying according to various wage levels?

(f) If the allowances are at flat rates should there be only one flat rate or two flat rates or more?

(g) Should there be a limitation that no allowances or/and bonuses place the person in a better position than he enjoyed in 1939 before the war?

(h) In view of the need to fight inflationary tendencies, should the cash element of allowances be fixed at a minimum and the bulk of the allowances be made available in kind, through supplies of essential articles at concessional rates?

(i) How should the general principles be implemented? Should there be legal compulsion or can voluntary experiment achieve the desired results? Should the authorities be set up in different regions or for different industries to decide finally on all questions relating to dearness allowance and bonus apart from the already provided adjudication procedure?

(j) How should the principles agreed to be extended to the states?

(k) (i) Are profit-sharing bonuses desirable, and to what extent?

(ii) Should the grant of such bonuses affect the quantum of dearness allowance or be related to dearness allowances? If so, how?

(iii) To check inflation, was it desirable that the payment of some proportion of profit-sharing bonus should be deferred. Are there objections to this proposal? If so, what are they? If not, what proportion of bonus should be deferred?

(iv) Whether a sub-committee should be appointed to formulate precise recommendations in the light of the discussions at the Conference?

The central government representative summed up the discussion as follows with reference to the above points :

(i) The consensus of opinion was clearly in favour of general uniform principles for fixation of dearness allowance.

(ii) (a) The weight of opinion seemed to be (i) allowances should be fixed with reference to the cost of living on a regional basis and (ii) separate rate should not be applied to separate industries.

(b) The general opinion seemed to be that the degree of assistance should decrease in proportion to increase in wage rate.

(c) There was some difference of opinion. Workers' representatives felt that there should be no reduction in the existing rates. But others answered this question in the affirmative. They maintained that the tendency to give higher allowances should be checked and allowances which fell below the prescribed standards should be raised.

(d) Here, again two opinions had been expressed. First, allowances should not be automatically related to increase or decrease in the cost of living, but there should be periodical revision, and secondly, the allowances should fluctuate with the cost of living index.

(e & f) There was unanimity of opinion that allowances should be fixed on the basis of flat rates in slabs, and there should not be more than two flat rates.

(g) There was a division of opinion on this point. One section felt that no consideration should be taken of the pay and wages drawn by labour before the war in 1939, while the other considered that labour should not be allowed to draw anything in excess of what was drawn in 1939 allowing for certain exceptions.

(h) Opinion here seemed to be that a large proportion, as far as possible of the allowances should be made available in kind provided the necessary supplies were available.

(i) The general opinion on this point was that some form of compulsion would be necessary. But before compulsion was applied, it should be endeavoured to pursuade the parties to agree. Otherwise, the government should rely on Defence of India Rules, or other rules, instead of introducing a fresh legislation.

(j) The question of having authorities in the regions to decide dearness allowance, was raised by one or two sections but no general opinion was expressed on that point. The representatives of the states assured full cooperation in the matter.

Merging Portion of D.A. with Normal Wage Rates[1]

There was some discussion on the question of merging portion of Dearness Allowance with normal wages, but no specific recommendation was adopted on the subject.

Linking of D.A. with Consumer Price Index[2]

The Conference reiterated the decision reached at the Standing Committee on Industrial Truce Resolution that dearness allowance should be suitably linked with the cost of living index.

The workers' representatives argued that any proposal to impose a wage-freeze was not justifiable or practicable and would not be acceptable to the working class in the existing conditions. They said that there should be linkage of dearness allowance with the consumer price index. Some of the workers' representatives were in favour of an ordinance to ensure such linkage. They said that it would maintain the real wage.

Neutralisation for Rise in the Cost of Living[3]

About the extent of neutralisation for rise in the cost of living, the representative of the AITUC stressed that calculation of 95 per cent of neutralisation should not be fixed at the minimum level as recommended by the NCL but should be applied at all levels.

The representatives of employers, however, emphasised that neutralisation should only be at the minimum level and that 95 per cent neutralisation should be adopted without protecting the higher rate followed by some industries and future increases should be on the basis of a common consumer price index series for all centres. The 1960 series should be taken as the basis for merger of D.A.

Grant of Bonus

It was unanimously felt that bonus should be treated separately from dearness allowance and that primarily it was to be settled by employers in consultation with their employees. The grant of bonus had been mentioned as being desirable, subject to the extent to which the Finance would grant concessions in the matter of tax, and employers were able to pay.

The workers' representatives emphasised that bonus should not be deferred.[4]

1. 11th Session, 11.4.
2. 24th Session, 24.1.
3. 26th Session, 26.12.
4. 5th Session, 5.5.

Review of Payment of Bonus Act

The issue of bonus was discussed at length. The workers' representatives unanimously demanded promulgation of an ordinance providing for a minimum bonus of 8.33 per cent. The state government generally agreed with this demand. The employers' representatives opposed the proposal.

Committee to Review Scheme

It was generally felt that the entire scheme of bonus should be reviewed by a committee which could be bipartite or tripartite. The employers' representatives on the Committee should also include representatives of the public sector. The committee should submit its report within a period of six months.[1]

Suggested Amendment

Amendments to the payment of Bonus Act, 1965 to give effect to the provisions struck down as ultra virus by the Supreme Court and to clarify provisions regarding rebate on taxes for computing the surplus.

The workers' representatives said that the payment of Bonus Act should be amended to take care of the situation arising from the striking down of Section 34 (2) by the Supreme Court and also to evolve a simpler formula for the determination of bonus. On the other hand, the employer's representatives urged that the Act should not be amended at all.

The Chairman said that he would wait for the decision of the Supreme Court on the Indian Oxygen case before undertaking any amendment to the Act.[2]

Report of Bonus Commission

The Conference recommended that government should take a quick decision of the report of the Bonus Commission.[3]

RECENT CONCLUSIONS ON DEARNESS ALLOWANCE AND BONUS

Public Sector Enterprises

It was felt that the revised DA formula under implementation for the

1. 25th Session, 25.5.
2. 24th Session, 27.6.
3. 22nd Session, 22.1.

employees of public sector enterprises should be further discussed.

The workers' representatives suggested immediate implementation of the DA rate of Rs. 2 per point of the Consumer Price Index (1960 series).

Bonus

The workers' representatives asked for the removal of ceiling on bonus both for eligibility and for computation through an ordinance. But the employers' representatives wanted postponement of the decision on removal of ceiling on bonus both for eligibility and computation of bonus by one year so that a well-thought out scheme could be evolved. They also wanted productivity-linked bonus as prescribed under the law.[1]

The workers' representatives expressed serious concern on the delay in taking action pursuant to earlier deliberations on amendment of the Payment of Bonus Act and introduction of DA slabs for employees of the Public Sector Enterprises. The statutory bonus formula, as implemented was, ·according to them, discouraging to skilled workers. They, therefore, suggested that the provisions relating to eligibility and calculation of ceiling should be immediately scrapped. They wanted a quick decision on introduction of DA slabs, keeping in view the fluctuations in the cost of living indices. The Employers had reservations on the matter.[2]

Again, in the 32rd session the workers' representatives suggested that the eligibility and calculation of ceilings for bonus under the Payment of Bonus Act should be scrapped. They argued that the ceiling on bonus militated against skilled workers who were in comparatively higher wage segment.[3]

1. 30th Session, 30.9.
2. 30th Session, 30.8.
3. 32nd Session, 32.7.

8

CONSUMER PRICE INDEX

The important decisions with respect to the Cosumer Price Index (CPI) were, change of nomenclature from 'Working Class Cost of Living Index Numbers' to 'Consumer Price Index Numbers for Working Class,' the principles thereof, association of employees' and employers' representatives as well as of the state governments in conducting the Family Budget Enquiry and Neutralisation for Rise in the Cost of Living.

Change of Nomenclature[1]

The Conference accepted the proposal to substitude the nomenclature the name of "Working Class Cost of Living Index Numbers' by "Consumer Price Index Numbers for Working Class.'

Consumer Price Index Numbers[2]

The following decisions were taken :

(a) The index for individual centres in the new series of Consumer Price Index for Industrial Workers should be published replacing the old series.

(b) The All India Index, 1960, as basis, should also be published forthwith replacing the old series taking 1949 as basis since 26 out of 27 constituent series had already been corrected.

(c) The linking factor (multiplier) for deriving the old All India Index from the new All India Index would be derived on the basis of the ratio between the two series taking an average of 12 months ending with the month with effect from which the old series was discontinued.

---

1. 14th Session, 14.8.
2. 27th Session, 27.3.

(d) The linking factor should be carefully determined so that the need for revision might be minimal.

(e) The effect of using the uncorrected index for Madras in the matter of the All India Average Index would be negligible. However, in order to enable the publication of the new series for Madras, replacing the old one at an early date, their decision on the recommendation of the expert committee which had already examined the old Madras Series should be taken into account.

New Family Budget Enquiry[1]

The Conference also endorsed the proposal conducting the next Family Budget Enquiry during 1969-70. It was agreed that the state government should be associated with this enquiry at all stages. It was also agreed that the employers' and workers' organisations should be associated with the planning of the enquiry.

Neutralisation for Rise in the Cost of Living[2]

About the extent of neutralisation for rise in the cost of living, the representative of AITUC stressed that 95 per cent of the neutralisation should not be only at the minimum level, as recommended by the NCL, but at all levels. The representatives of the employers emphasised that neutralisation should only be at the minimum level and that 95 per cent neutralisation should be adopted without protecting the higher rate followed at present by some industries and future increases should be on a common consumer price series for all centres and that the 1960 series should be taken as the basis for merger of D.A.

1. 27th Session, 27.3.
2. 26th Session, 26.12.

9

WELFARE

The Indian Labour Conference took a number of important decisions relating to welfare measures for workers. Important among them were reduction of working hours under the Factories Act, and in Seasonal Factories, Railways, Hazardous occupations etc., Health and Safety Scheme, Voluntary Agreement between employers and employees for Pay Roll Saving Scheme, Industrial Housing, Canteens, Fair Price Shops etc.

FACTORIES ACT

Reduction of Working Hours Under the Factories Act[1]

The central government representative noted with satisfaction that the Conference had reached a very 'fine measure of agreement' as the employers' representatives agreed in principle to the reduction of working hours in factory to 48 hours a week and workers' representatives agreed to the principle of 'good work and no loitering' during the prescribed working hours.

However, the employers' representatives wanted an exemption in the case of textile industry. They felt that reduction of working hours in textile industries would result in loss of production which would be detrimental to the interest of the country as clothes were already in short supply. Workers' representatives did not subscribe to the above view.

The central government said that the amendment process would take some time as the proposed Bill had to be first passed by the Legislature and even after the passage of the Bill, its enforcement would be notified by the central government. Besides, the provincial

1. 7th Session, 7.3, Nov. 27-28, 1945.

governments would have powers to grant exemption. Hence, it was advisable on the part of the government to initiate the process of amendment as the situation, in the meantime, would improve.

Hours of Work in Seasonal Factories[1]

The central government informed that the existing discrepancy with regard to hours of work in seasonal factories would be removed when the Factories Act was amended.

Amendment of Sections 79 and 80 of the Factories Act[2]

The Amendment was proposed to provide for the rate of payment for the period of leave according to the wages of the normal post held and for the grant of leave according to exigencies of work in a factory.

Health and Safety

The Conference felt that the existing measures for the safety and health of the workers should be strengthened and they should be effectively implemented and monitored. It acknowledged that those measures could be implemented only with the active cooperation of both the employers and the workers. It suggested suitable training of workers in safety measures.[3]

The Conference noted that the Ministry of Labour was considering proposals for amendment of the Factories Act and desired that the proposed amendments should be expedited. It also felt that punishment for repeated violations of provisions of the the Factories Act pertaining to health and safety should be made more deterrent.

REDUCTION OF WORKING HOURS

Reduction of Working Hours in Railways[4]

The conference discussed the question of reduction of working hours in the railways which was under adjudication and decided that the Labour Ministry should ensure implementation of the adjudicators' recommendations.

1. 8th Session, 8.2, April 21-22, 1947.
2. 20th Session, 20.4, August 7-9, 1962.
3. 28th Session, 28.7.
4. 8th Session, 8.1.

Reduction of Working Hours in Hazardous Occupations[1]

It was agreed that all the safety measures recommended in the reports on hazardous occupations should be tried out expeditiously and if the minimum standards of safety were assured through these measures, it might not be necessary to reduce the hours of work. If in spite of all the precautionary measures recommended in the reports it was found that the minimum standards of safety were not ensured, then hours of work would have to be reduced.

Pay Roll Savings Scheme

The Pay Roll Savings Scheme was approved. To implement this scheme, following modalities were worked out :[2]

(i) The collection charge at the rate of one per cent, paid by the government on amounts collected in respect of the National Plan Savings Certificates, should be utilised for distribution among the staff engaged in actual collection and the balance left after such distribution should be utilised for welfare of the employees.

(ii) The pass-books might be kept with the employer but should be made available for inspection to the employees concerned during working hours. An employee could also keep the pass-book with him if he wanted to do so.

It was suggested that the collection should be made by a government agency only. The money so collected should not be left with the employers.

Investment of Saving

This scheme was based on a voluntary agreement between employers and the employees for the regular investment of savings in small saving securities. The main features of the schemes were : (i) display of notices and distribution of pamphlets, posters etc. by the employers and exhibition of films produced by the National Savings Organisation, (ii) formation of bipartite saving committees to obtain letters of consent from the employees for deduction of specific amounts from the wages for investment in saving securities, (iii) arrangements by the employers to collect and remit the moneys so collected to the concerned authorities and to arrange for distribution

1. 19th Session, 19.3.
2. 17th Session, 17.4.

of workers' pass-books, certificates etc. and (iv) collection charges of employers for the services rendered.

Employees and trade unions were requested to give wider publicity to the scheme and extend their full cooperation to ensure satisfactory working of the scheme.[1]

Welfare Trust and Welfare Fund[2]

After discussing the modality of the Welfare Trust and Welfare Fund it was decided that out of the cash of the Welfare Fund of eight annas, four annas would be utilised for general welfare work, eight pies for starting dispensaries and three annas, four pies for housing. The expenditure would be regulated on the advice of a tripartite committee and a report giving details of the expenditure would be published in the Gazette.

Supply of Foodgrains[3]

It was considered essential that adequate supply of foodgrains and other essential commodities at reasonable prices should be ensured to the workers. Since the main difficulties was the problem of transport the central government was requested to remove or ease the situation by granting a very high priority for the transport of foodstuffs. The workers' representatives suggested for the opening of grain shops in larger numbers. Suggestions were also made for greater collaboration with workers' representatives.

SUBSIDISED INDUSTRIAL HOUSING SCHEME[4]

(i) The Committee noted with regret that the funds allocated for construction of houses to the various agencies, viz., the government, employers' and workers' cooperatives, had not been fully utilised. It urged that steps be taken to remedy the unsatisfactory situation.

(ii) The Committee examined the reasons for the poor response from employers and workers to the Subsidised Industrial Housing Scheme and concluded that workers were not interested for such houses in many cases because those were located far from their work place.

1. 22nd Session, 22.4.
2. 8th Session, 8.2.
3. 4th Session, 4.4.
4. See Appendix XVIII and Annexure thereto for Report of the Industrial Housing Sub-Committee of the Standing Labour Committee (Extracts) and Minimum Standards recommended respectively for workers' houses.

It was felt that there was a need for coordination of the Industrial Housing Scheme with that of the slum clearance. The Employers complained of administrative delays in getting financial sanctions, non-availability of building materials and the soaring land prices. The state governments also pleaded for (a) modifications in the procedure for the allocation of funds, (b) distribution of interest of the allotted funds between the different agencies, (c) the procedure for acquisition of land for construction of houses, and also, (d) the types of accommodation on the basis of local conditions.

(iii) Rising costs and non-availability of land were considered major impediments to industrial housing. In order to overcome those difficulties, it was necessary that steps should be taken by the government to freeze land prices at suitable levels and to make land available for construction of houses under the industrial housing schemes.

(iv) The workers' representatives sought information whether the government contemplated integration of following schemes :

(a) Industrial Housing
(b) Housing for Low-Income Group and
(c) Other Subsidised Housing

It was explained by the government that it had received some suggestions on this subject but before taking any decision, the matter would be placed before the Indian Labour Conference.

(v) There was a general feeling that the ceiling on cost for tenements should be raised and that the matter examined immediately. The Committee also requested the central government that alongwith the central subsidy which the centre gave to the states, the employers and the co-operatives of workers, there should be a guarantee that the necessary supplies of building materials would be made available if the distribution of such material was controlled by the central government.

(vi) (a) It should be incumbent on employers to provide at least a reasonable number of houses for their workers.

(b) The housing department of the state government should assist employers and co-operatives in the procurement of essential building materials. Steps should be taken by the central government to enact a National Housing Act.

(c) Housing Co-operatives have to handle long-term finance and management of real estate. Unlike co-operatives formed for other purposes, the housing department of the state government should, organise housing co-operative movement, and for this purpose a special unit should be established in the office of the Registrar of Co-operative Societies which should function under the administrative control of the State Housing Department.

(d) For effective implementation of the housing schemes for workers and other low-income groups, a greater coordination among various departments at the state-level was necessary. At present most of the departments faced difficulties, particularly in taking full advantage of the Subsidised Industrial Housing Scheme. Hence, each state government should have a housing department dealing with all matters relating to housing in an integrated manner.

(e) The quantum of financial assistance to employers should be raised from 62.5 to 75 per cent—50 per cent loan plus 25 per cent subsidy—and guarantees from scheduled banks and co-operative banks might be accepted as alternative security.

(f) The central government had been advancing short-term loans, under the Low-Income Group Housing Scheme, at low rates of interest to the state governments for acquisition of land and its development with essential services such as water-supply, drainage, electricity, roads, etc. The state governments should be permitted by the central government to sell part of such developed land to employers and co-operatives on a no-profit no-loss basis for the construction of houses under the Subsidised Industrial Housing Scheme. Where the housing colonies were located far away from the factory area, transport should be provided to workers on a no-profit no-loss basis.

(g) Taking into account the inability of many workers to share their own contributions, viz., 25 per cent of the cost, the central government might permit the state governments to build houses under the Scheme and allot them to workers on a hire-purchase basis. However, if some of the workers preferred to own the houses straight way, they might be permitted to withdraw their contribution of 25 per cent from their accumulations under the Employees' Provident Fund Account.

(h) The present arrangement of providing 50 per cent of the cost of housing as loan and 25 per cent as subsidy should be changed to 60 per cent loan and 30 per cent subsidy in the case of workers' co-operatives.

(i) The various agencies should take full advantage of the funds allotted to them for the construction of houses.

The employers' representatives agreed to undertake construction of houses on a voluntary basis. With a view to encourage the employers to discharge their responsibility towards their workers in respect of housing, the following measures were recommended :[1]

(a) The present quantum of loan to employers under the scheme be raised from 37.5 per cent to 50 per cent. The quantum of the subsidy, viz., 25 per cent should remain unchanged;

(b) The rules for the allotment of tenements should be left to the employer to be finalised in consultation with the workers of the establishments, subject to certain broad principles being laid down by the government; and

(c) The matter of giving some income tax relief to employers who built houses for the workers should be examined by the government in greater detail.

If the state governments found that industrial housing was not making progress for want of suitably developed plots, they should spend as much of their allocation under the Subsidised Industrial Housing Scheme as was needed for the acquisition and development of land. Such land should be utilised or sold at a no-profit no-loss basis to employers for building the houses.

The central government clarified that it had not withdrawn its offer of subsidy of 12.5 per cent on housing. The state governments, however, felt that this subsidy was inadequate, in view of the increased costs of construction. It was also informed that the Labour Department was making an experiment with the construction of 50,000 houses in the coalfields. This would enable them to work out the actual cost of construction. The government was also looking into the question of allocation of supplies for industrial housing.

---

1. 16th Session, 16.4.

Housing for Coal Mines[1]

The Chairman pointed out the difficulties in speeding up the housing of coal-miners. Apart from the difficulty in getting coal-free land, there was also difficulty in land acquisition in Dhanbad area and in Asansol. There was considerable resistance from the rural population who did not want to part with their land. He explained that steps were being taken to overcome those difficulties and, hoped the situation would improve.

FAIR PRICE SHOPS

Setting up of Fair Price Shops[2]

The Conference reviewed the position concerning the setting up of fair price shops and consumer stores.[3] It was felt that the progress had not been quite satisfactory. Establishments which had not yet set up stores/fair price shops should do so without further delay. The Chairman concluded that the legislation would soon be enacted as already agreed to at the meeting of the Standing Labour Committee in December, 1963.

Legislation on Fair Price Shops[4]

Workers' representatives suggested that for the provision of fair price shops, the government should pass the proposed legislation for which there had been agreement. The employers' representatives raised the question of supplies which was crucial for satisfactory working of such shops. The setting up of a committee to go into all these matters and for drawing up of the proposed legislation was also suggested. It was noted that the legislative measures were kept pending so as try persuasive measures. Eventually it was decided that the Chairman should look into the matter and take necessary action.

Payment in Cash and Kind Through Fair Price Shops[5]

The Conference discussed in detail the current price situation. It came to the conclusion that in view of the hardship caused by the high

1. 9th Session, 9.1.
2. 22nd Session, 22.1.
3. See Appendix XIX and Annexure thereto for memorandum on organisation of consumer co-operative in the Industrial Sector and Scheme for a Consumer's co-operative store respectively.
4. 24th Session, 24.2.
5. 22nd Session, 22.1.

prices of essential commodities, and the imperatives needed for ensuring the supply of those commodities to the industrial workers at reasonable prices, part of their wages should be paid in kind. If necessary, a legislative provision for this would be made. The payment in kind should consist of the supply of rice, wheat or wheat substitutes, sugar, pulses, one or two popular varieties of cloth and cooking medium. The government should supply to the employers the commodities excepting textile, pulses and cooking medium at controlled prices for distribution to the industrial workers through fair price shops. The employers should distribute the textiles, pulses and cooking medium at prices equivalent to the wholesale prices. The cost of distribution should be borne by the employers. The Standing Committee on Industrial Truce Resolution should work out the details of the Scheme.

There was a concern on the inflationary trends and increase in the price of essential commodities eroding the living standards of workers. It was, therefore, suggested that the government should pay special attention to streamlining and expanding the public distribution system, particularly where there was concentration of workers.

Further the delivery of essential commodities through the public distribution system should be streamlined with special emphasis on ensuring adequacy of supplies.

INDUSTRIAL CANTEENS

Supply of Ration[1]

The central government representatives informed about the decision of the Government of India to supply ration to industrial canteens. The workers doing manual work were also entitled to supplementary ration. They said that there were difficulties in getting right type of rice. However, the Department of Food would extend all possible support to run the industrial canteens. In appreciation of the difficulties being faced it was not feasible to make the provision of canteen compulsory unlike the system in the UK. Such provision could be made after the initial experiments proved to be successful. It was felt that properly run canteens would attract more workers than the ordinary shops in the market.

1. 6th Session, 6.7.

Statutory Provision[1]

Workers' representatives agreed to the government's proposal for statutory provision of industrial canteens. But they wanted the following two conditions to be kept in mind while laying down the provision. First, canteens should be established if the workers in the establishment were likely to take advantage of the provision. Secondly, the establishments which lacked space for canteen should be exempted from the statutory obligation. The government assured that it would not impose the obligation on such establishments which had genuine problems.

1. 7th Session, 7.6.

10

SOCIAL SECURITY

Regarding Social Security, the measures that were decided included extension of Compulsory Provident Fund Scheme to industrial workers which were initially introduced in the coalfields of Bihar, Bengal and Central Provinces, extending the coverage of Employees' Provident Fund Act of 1952, Insurance Scheme, need for a separate central law on Payment of Gratuity and expansion of its coverage as well as that of Workmen's Compensation Act.

PROVIDENT FUND

Model Provident Fund Rules[1]

It was decided that the subject be taken up by the Standing Labour Committee at its next meeting. In the meantime, suggestions, if any, on the draft rules might be sent to the Government of India.

Compulsory Provident Fund Scheme for Industrial Workers[2]

The Chairman said that the Compulsory Provident Fund Scheme had been introduced in the coalfields of Bihar, Bengal and Central Provinces where there were mostly casual workers and that if the scheme was successful it would be possible to extend it to other industries which might take about six months. In the meantime, the Ministry of Labour would prepare a comprehensive scheme for other industrial workers and the employers should persuade their other colleagues to agree to the idea.

---

1. 5th Session, 5.8.
2. 9th Session, 9.8.

Coverage of Employees' Provident Fund Act, 1952[1]

(i) All industries with an employment strength of 10,000 workers throughout India in the factories employing 50 or more persons should be covered.

(ii) The representatives of the state governments suggested that they should be consulted before new industries were added to Schedule I of Employees' Provident Fund Act. Employers' representatives raised the question of capacity of the industry to pay and they too suggested that employers should also be consulted before any industry was included in the schedule. It was, therefore, decided that the Government of India should give due consideration to the suggestion while extending the scope of the Employees' Provident Fund Act.

(iii) It was felt that there was no bar to the inclusion of seasonal industries in Schedule I of Employees' Provident Fund Act. For this purpose, however, the eligibility qualification should be suitably reduced. It was agreed that an employee who had worked for two-thirds the number of working days in the preceding season would be eligible for provident fund benefits. The number of working days for a seasonal industry and other details would be determined by the central government and incorporated in the scheme.

Compulsory Deductions[2]

It was felt that in view of the proposed increase in the rates of provident fund contributions and other deductions, there was no justification for any further compulsory deductions from the workers' wages in the public as well as private sectors for investment in government securities under the Non-contributory Provident Fund Scheme.

PROVIDENT FUND SCHEME

It was generally felt that the contribution should be raised from 8 per cent to 10 per cent. However, a majority of the employers' group had reservations about.[3]

The workers' representatives suggested enhancement of the rate of interest on Employees' Provident Fund to at least 13 per cent.[4]

1. 14th Session, 14.3.
2. 19th Session, 19.8.
3. 28th Session, 28.13.
4. 30th Session, 30.8.

It was felt that since social security was particularly important in the present situation, the government should introduce the Pension Scheme for provident fund subscribers on a priority basis. There should be tripartite consultations on the details of the Scheme before its introduction. Management of Social Security Funds should be professionally handled so that returns on investments of the resources of the funds were maximised. Agreements/settlements on pension matters should be implemented on a priority basis.[1]

Vigilance machinery in the Employees' Provident Fund Organisation should be tightened up particularly at the cutting edge level so that the subscribers avail of the services without let and hindrance.[2]

Insurance Scheme

The present employment limit of fifty persons or more, prescribed under Sub-section (3) of Section 1 of Employees' Provident Fund Act, 1952, should be reduced to twenty persons or more. Employees in commercial establishments should also be covered.

Provident Fund Contribution for Paid Holidays

The proposal for provident fund contribution for paid national and festival holidays was agreed.

Rate of Contribution

The employers' representatives were opposed to raising the rate of provident fund contribution from existing 8 per cent to 10 per cent.

Conversion of Provident Fund Scheme into Old Age/Survivorship Pension[3]

The proposal for conversion of the Provident Fund Scheme into an old age and/or survivorship pension (for widows and children) scheme should be further examined provided that it worked within the limit of 16-2/3 per cent of wages recovered by way of contributions from employers and workers covered by the Employees' Provident Fund Act.

1. 31st Session, 31.9.
2. 32nd Session, 32.17.
3. 16th Session, 16.2.

Difficulties in Insurance Schemes[1]

The central government representative summed up the discussion held on insurance scheme. There was no common measure of agreement. A good number of difficulties had been pointed out. Apart from these, there was really a bad risk as no private insurer might accept it. The question of controlling the premium might also be a difficult one. The matter required thorough investigation and the Government of India should be asked to undertake it in consultation with provinces, associations of employers and employees and the insurance companies. Whether, state insurance would cover every worker should also be considered by any further inquiry.

Sickness Insurance for Industrial Labour[2]

The central government noted the general appreciation of Prof. Adakar's report and felt that the report gave credit not only to the author but also to India as a whole. Prof. Adakar had dealt with the matter thoroughly and threw new light on several points. The government would, it said, carefully consider the recommendations. The Government of India and provincial governments would take up the question of sickness insurance and other labour legislations along with the general industrial policy of the country in totality and not in isolation. The medical matter was dealt with under two headings—medical assistance and medical insurance. There was a thinking that organisation for medical assistance for agricultural population might have to be dealt with by medical assistance method through rural dispensaries and not by insurance as the collection from agricultural labour of any portion of the premium would cause great difficulty. There was, however, it was clarifed no intention to divide industrial and agricultural labour. The Philadelphia recommendation was being followed in covering industrial workers in the first instance, the others would be covered as far as practicable.

Unemployment Insurance Scheme[3]

The Conference discussed briefly the Unemployment Insurance Scheme and the workers' representatives generally welcomed the idea in principle. The employers' representative however desired more time to study the scheme. It was decided to place the item before the next session of the Standing Labour Committee.

1. 6th Session, 6.1.
2. 6th Session, 6.4.
3. 23rd Session, 23.2.

Special Casual Leave[1]

The proposal for grant of casual leave was agreed subject to adjustment against the Employees' State Insurance benefits where those were available. The special cash incentive, paid by the Employees' State Insurance Corporation, should, however, continue.

As for those workers, not covered by the Employees State Insurance Act, such special casual leave would be granted only on submission of medical certificate.

Employees' State Insurance Scheme (ESIS)

(i) *Share of State Government Towards Cost of Medical Care* : The state government's share on extension of medical care of the families of workers insured under the scheme should be 1/8th of the total expenditure during the Second Five Year Plan period and thereafter revision should be made only on the terms, which were mutually agreed upon.

(ii) *System of Medical Care* : The state government concerned might adopt any system of medical care (service panel or mixed) which they considered feasible.

(iii) *Capitation Fee for Panel Doctors* : It would be desirable for the Employees' State Insurance Corporation to approach the medical profession through the state government concerned.

(iv) *Arrangements for Maternity Cases* : A sum of Rs. 30 per case should be paid to the wives of insured persons on extension of medical care to the families.

(v) *Improvement in Cash Benefits* : Further improvements in the quantum of cash benefits might be made till such time the scheme has been extended to the entire coverable population in the country.

Coverage of the Employees' Provident Fund Act, 1952

(i) Some improvement in the rate of maternity cash benefit was, however, necessary under the Employees' State Insurance Act as some State Acts on this give more benefits than the Central Acts. Persons suffering from T.B. might also be given special consideration.

(ii) The question relating to revision of the waiting period should

1. 27th Session, 27.13.

be examined.

(iii) The families of insured persons should be covered for medical care and treatment. Hospitalisation should also be provided for them as soon as possible.

In this regard the employers' representatives were of the view that medical care and treatment should be extended to the families of insured persons only after the Employees' State Insurance Scheme has been extended to insurable persons in all coverable areas.

(vi) The employers' contribution should be raised to 4 per cent as already provided for in the law.

(iv) The administration of the Employees' State Insurance Scheme and of the Employees' Provident Fund Scheme should be integrated.

The employers' representatives reserved their opinion on items (vii) to (xii) above as they felt the need for consulting their constituents before making any commitment in this regard. It was agreed that, if possible, the employers' representatives would be consulted before further action was taken.

It was suggested that the labour ministry should present a status paper on the existing social security schemes under implementation in the country, particularly reflecting the experiences of the various states and bring the matter for consideration in the SLC. And the scope for extension of the existing social security laws and systems to the unorganised sector, should also be considered.

GRATUITY

Central Enactment for Payment of Gratuity[1]

It was the general opinion of the conference that there was a need for a separate central law on gratuity. In this regard the views of the different groups were as under :

Workers' View

The workers' representatives suggested the law should preferably be brought into force through an ordinance covering the following points :

(i) It should apply to all establishments irrespective of the size of the workers.

1. 25th Session, 25.3.

(ii) It should cover all wage earners including those in hospitals, educational institutions, etc. without any limit of salary.
(iii) There should be no ceiling on the quantum of gratuity.
(iv) There should be no requirement of any qualifying period of service for entitlement of gratuity.
(v) Gratuity should be payable at the ratio of one month's total wages for every year of service.
(vi) In the case of death or disability while in service, the rate of gratuity should be higher.
(vii) Dismissal from service should not be a disqualification for entitlement to gratuity.

Employers' View

The employers agreed on the need for central legislation which should also cover employees in educational institutions. They did not want it by way of an Ordinance. They were opposed to the concept of gratuity which would render it different from a reward for continued and satisfactory service. They also wanted that the Draft Bill on the subject should be circulated for comments. They also suggested that a comprehensive study of all social security and fringe benefits should be undertaken to assess the total benefits as well as the total incidence.

State Government's View

The state governments endorsed the need for an immediate Ordinance and supported the extension of the scheme to all wage earners.

There was consensus on the Gratuity Insurance Scheme as proposed by the Ministry of Labour.

The Conference suggested to ensure that the workers were not adversely affected in the payment of gratuity in the event of non-payment of insurance premium by the management.[1]

The Conference expressed concern on the default of gratuity payments. It suggested that measures should be taken to ensure payment of such defaults apart from settlement of the defaulted dues.[2]

Pension

The workers' representatives suggested enforcement of the agreement regarding Pension Scheme at the earliest.[3]

1. 28th Session, 28.8.
2. 32nd Session, 32.16.
3. 30th Session, 30.8.

Social Security

The workers' representatives said that while the pension scheme for subscribers to the provident fund under the Employees' Provident Fund Act was welcome, it should be further modified, taking into consideration the various constructive suggestions that had emerged in the series of consultations held by the Labour Minister with various interest groups. They also suggested that the details of the pension scheme should be widely publicised and steps for efficient management of the pension fund and for prompt and accurate disbursal of pension dues should be taken. However, some workers' organisations such as CITU, UTCC and UTCC (LS) expressed their reservations about the scheme.[1]

WORKMEN'S COMPENSATION ACT

Amendment of the Act[2]

The Conference endorsed a Draft Bill to amend the Workmen's Compensation Act, 1923, to widen its scope by raising the prescribed maximum monthly wages level from Rs. 3,000 to Rs. 4,000 for workers covered under the Act and for providing consequential changes in the rates of compensation.

Revision of Rate of Compensation[3]

The Conference set up a committee to consider this item. The committee subsequently met at New Delhi on September 5, 1959 and recommended the following proposals :

(i) The system of payment of compensation in a lump sum should be replaced by a system of periodical payments as far as practicable.

(ii) The rates of compensation payable under the Workmen's Compensation Act, 1923, should be raised in accordance with the recommendations of the study group on social security.

(iii) The implementation of the Employees' State Insurance Scheme should be expedited to cover the coverable population as early as possible.

(iv) The Employee's State Insurance Corporation would be the

1. 32nd Session, 32.15.
2. 7th Session, 7.7.
3. 17th Session, 17.5.

appropriate agency for the disbursement of the periodic payments of compensation, and

(v) The scope of the Workmen's Compensation Act, 1923, might be extended to cover persons drawing wages upto Rs. 500 per month.

Introduction of compulsory insurance to cover the risk of accidents was briefly discussed. The employers' organisation agreed to collect and provide full information regarding the prevailing practice amongst their affiliates in the matter of taking up such insurance policies on a voluntary basis.

11

WORKERS' EDUCATION AND TRAINING

Extension of Workers' Education besides workers' training has been one of the earliest areas of concern of the ILC. In the 10th Session it was emphasised that Workers' Education Programme should also cover the workers' children and that there should be evening classes and extension courses with the involvement of workers' representatives, employers' representatives and government's representatives. In this regard the ILC endorsed the recommendations of the Study Team on Workers' Education. In the field of training it suggested multi-training programmes such as training within the industries, full time training course, vocational training and apprenticeship. It also suggested for vocational training schemes for agriculturists, (rather than the agriculture labour). Speedy implementation of the Schemes for retraining and redeployment as proposed under the Structural Adjustment Programmes was an important decision taken in the recent sessions.

EDUCATION[1]

It was emphasised by the Conference that there was a great need for extending worker's education programmes. It felt that the workers' children should also be brought under the purview of the programme. For the success of the programme, it was necessary that governments, unions and employers should participate and assist with all sincerity.

An increasing number of scholarships should be provided for workers and their children.

Evening classes and extension courses should be developed on a large scale.

1. 10th Session, 10.7.

Recommendation of Study Team on Workers' Education[1]

The Conference endorsed the following recommendations of the Study Team on Workers' Education which suggested for establishment of central board, state and regional boards and local boards and prescribed their functions on the following lines :

Recommendation No. 1

A central board, having semi-autonomous authority, should be established comprising representatives from the trade unions, employers, the government (including Ministers of Labour and Education) and educational institutions with the following tasks :

(a) to formulate the policy for the purpose of giving education and training to the workers;
(b) to administer the programme, allocate funds, inspect, coordinate, audit, account etc.;
(c) to arrange the provision of educational materials;
(d) to establish standards for teachers and programmes;
(e) to encourage the establishment of active educational departments within the national unions and federations; and
(f) to stimulate and promote the development of workers education.

Recommendation No. 2

At the instance of the Central Board or when a local demand is made, State and/or Regional Boards, on the pattern of the Central Board should be set up.

Within their respective areas, the function of these boards should be similar to that of the Central Board.

Recommendation No. 3

Local Workers' Education Boards should be created in industrial centres by the existing boards.

The local boards should encourage the workers of their areas in the educational activities and administer the approved programmes.

Recommendation No. 4

Any industrial worker, whether, literate or illiterate, trade union member or non-member and full-time union officials and staff should be eligible for the services provided by the boards.

1. 15th Session, 15.2.

Selection of candidates for the Workers' Education Programme should be made by the local boards.

Recommendation No. 5

Applications for workers' education may be channelled through such trade unions. In the absence of trade unions, workers may apply directly to their respective boards.

Recommendation No. 6

A series of programmes should be organised in the educational institutions, at local union level, community centres, place of employment or at local colleges and schools to provide instructions in :

(a) trade union consciousness;
(b) the purposes, functions and administration of trade unions;
(c) the conduct of union-management relations and knowledge of the industry; and
(d) the development of a mature individual and his role as a citizen.

Recommendation No. 7

Instructions should also be given for :

(a) Single-session conference;
(b) Part-time classes;
(c) Full-time course from one week to three months or of a longer duration when required;
(d) Such other methods for pursuance of the principles laid down.

Full attention should be paid to the techniques of instruction and a beginning should be made for informal discussions, role-playing, field work, seminars, lectures, films, correspondence courses, etc.

Recommendation No. 8

Provision should be made for training the teachers and programme administrators for full and part-time assignments.

Existing facilities should be used to their maximum, and initial project of teacher-administrator instruction should be inaugurated forthwith.

Recommendation No. 9

Suitable materials in the regional languages should be prepared in the shape of (a) Pamphlets, books and charts; (b) Teaching manuals and guides; and (c) Audio-visual aids.

Recommendation No. 10

Institutions and individuals interested in workers' education should be encouraged to form a 'Non-official Workers' Education Association acting in cooperation with the Adult Education Programme.

Recommendation No. 11

The sources of financing the Workers' Education Programme should be :

(a) Central and state government grants;
(b) Contributions from the trade unions;
(c) Assistance, in kind, from educational institutions, e.g., class rooms, libraries, teaching etc.;
(d) Support by employers through payment of release time wages for the duration of the training period; and
(e) Grants from funds consisting of unpaid wages, fines, canteen profits, etc.

In allocating the resources, priority should be given to the programmes, contents, and services. Any ambitious programme involving capital expenditure on buildings, etc. should be taken care of only latter.

There was also some discussion for fixing a limit of the number of workers who might be given release-time wages, but it was ultimately decided to leave that matter to the local boards.

Recommendation No. 12

Priority should be given to those matters which might provide a more favourable climate to accomplish the goals of workers' education by :

(a) instituting measures calculated to bring about a strong trade union movement;
(b) providing courses in labour-management relations in educational institutions;
(c) meeting the requirement of setting up an example of an ideal employer.
(d) encouraging a wage policy that provides for wage and/or incentive bonus adjustments as productivity rises; and
(e) undertaking a study of legislation at the central and state

government levels with the objective of strengthening and coordinating all legislation affecting the trade union movement.

TRAINING[1]

Report on the Activities of the Director-General of Resettlement and Employment[2]

The Director-General of Resettlement and Employment, in his report, expressed his gratitude to the members for their valuable suggestions and for the general feeling of the Conference that the organisation had done valuable work and had potentialities of doing further such work and that it should be made permanent. He pointed out that although the apprenticeship of craftsmen for industry was a provincial subject, the Government of India felt, as had been stressed by the Advisory Committee on Technical Training, that there should be some degree of central coordination, guidance and inspection.

The provincial governments and the industries should realise the necessity for having a Central Technical Institute for the training of instructors.

He informed that the training of Factory Inspectors was being organised in three ways—the first being a regular course for beginners, the second, refresher course and lastly, the memoranda on various points were being circulated to the inspectors for their information. He, however, agreed that the number of inspectors being trained was small.

Training Course for Workers[3]

(i) The proposal that it would be desirable to relieve the workers in large numbers for three weeks full-time training course, rather than for the normal three-month part-time course with daily time-off facilities was by and large accepted.

(ii) There should be an independent assessment of the working of the Workers' Education Scheme, to evaluate its functioning. It should also be assessed if the benefits of the Scheme had been commensurate with the expectations and what further improvements were possible.

---

1. For training also see Chapter 17, New Economic Policy and Labour.
2. 9th Session, 9.3.
3. 24th Session, 24.8.

Training within Industry[1]

While acknowledging that the scheme deserved greater support from the employers and others concerned, the following suggestions of the Conference Committee were accepted :

(i) Training within the industry should be intensified by having definite programmes drawn up for (a) Groups of typical industries; and (b) Groups of industries on a regional or state basis, dealing, in order of priority, with areas where larger industries were located.

(ii) Special programmes should be arranged for industries in the nationalised sectors, and potential supervisors required for the new industries to be developed during the Second Five Year Plan.

(iii) Persons trained under the scheme should, as far as possible, be continued on the job for which they had received training so that their training might be of greater utility.

(iv) The scheme should be implemented in consultation with the workers' organizations.[2]

Vocational Training and Apprenticeship

The Conference agreed, in principle, that suitable arrangements should be made for the training of retrenched workers with a view to finding alternate employment for them.

Central Institute for Training[3]

The Acting Chairman, in winding up the discussion on the subject, concluded that all the sections agreed to the felt need for a Central Training Institute for Factory Inspectors and Labour Officers to impart theoretical training supplemented by practical training.

He hoped that the government would prepare a draft scheme taking into account the suggestions made in the meeting, particularly the one regarding the training of trade union workers.

Vocational Training in Agriculture

It was agreed that such varied training as was practicable within the resources of the country, should be made available for 'agriculturists'

1. 15th Session, 15.3.
2. 11th Session, 11.2.
3. 11th Session, 11.5.

12

WORKERS' PARTICIPATION IN MANAGEMENT

Workers' participation in Management has been an important subject of discussion by the ILC. It set up Sub-Committee and Tripartite Committee to suggest the details of the Scheme. Besides the Works Committee, setting up of a Joint Management Council was also decided. In one of the sessions, the Employers' representatives expressed their reservation on statutory provisions for participation. They suggested for a bipartite mechanism instead.

Proposal for Works Committee[1]

Towards introducing the system of workers' participation in management, a decision was taken to set up a small tripartite committee consisting of four representatives each from among the employers and workers and a few representatives from the government side. The tripartite committee would examine the matter on the subject and draw up "guiding principles" relating to the composition and functioning of works committees. It would also consider further action in respect of workers' participation in management.

Proposal for Joint Management Council[2]

It was felt that in addition to works committee, a Joint Management Council should be set up. Its function should be different from those of the works committees. Agreeing to this view the representatives of

1. See Appendix XX and Annexure thereto for conclusions of the tripartite committee on works committees and Illustrative list of items to be dealt with by the works committee.
2. See Appendix XXI for model agreement regarding establishment of Joint Councils of Management.

the Assam Government suggested that a Joint Management Council should be set up in public sector undertakings as well.[1]

The questionnaire prepared for the use of the Sub-committee was discussed and the following conclusions were arrived at :

(i) The question of the Joint Council having separate sub-committees or technical committees, to deal with different subjects should be left to the option of the parties at the undertaking's level.

(ii) During the period of the experiment, the employee's representatives on the Joint Council should be nominated by the trade union concerned. At a later stage, the intermediate method of submission of a panel of names by the trade unions might be considered.

(iii) The bulk of employees' representatives should be the workers themselves. But, if the local trade unions wanted to induct outsiders it should be limited to 25 per cent of the employees' representatives on the Joint Councils. The question of how many outsiders were to be entertained within this upper limit and in what capacity was left to local option.

(iv) If the decision was taken to constitute technical committees, or sub-committees, their constitution should be decided according to specific needs and situations.

(v) Outsiders might be taken on technical committees, or sub-committees.

(vi) The size of the Joint Councils should be restricted to twelve persons.

(vii) Any member of the Joint Council could bring forward items for discussion.

(viii) The Joint Councils should meet during working hours.

(ix) The worker-members of the Joint Councils should be compensated for loss of earnings, but nothing more should be given by way of remuneration.

(x) There should be a provision for recall of members of the Joint Council.

(xi) The worker-members on Joint Councils should function as representatives of the workers.

(xii) The question of giving minimum percentage of wages, or of income, or of profits, for welfare work to the Joint Council, should be settled at the level of the undertaking.

1. ILC sub-committee on workers' participation 1st meeting, 1.5.

(xiii) Whether the tenure of the Chairman of the Joint Council should be fixed or not, should be decided by local agreement.

(xiv) All necessary facilities for the work of Joint Councils should be provided by the employers.

(xv) Decisions in the Joint Councils should be arrived at by agreement.

Draft Model Agreement Regarding Establishment of JMC[1]

The Tripartite Committee approved the Draft Model Agreement regarding establishment of the Joint Councils of Management.

It was unanimously agreed that, to begin with, participation should be confined to the level of the undertaking. The following criteria for selection of the undertaking were agreed :[2]

(i) The undertaking should have a well established strong trade union.

(ii) There should be a willingness among the parties, viz., employers, workers and the unions to try out the experiment in a spirit of cooperation.

(iii) The size of the undertaking in terms of employment should be at least 500 workers. The representative of the Ministry of Railways suggested that a few units with less than 500 workers might be tried in the pilot stage to make it easier to watch the impediments and rectify them. It was agreed that three or four such units might be taken up in addition to those contained in the agreed list.

(iv) The employer in the private sector should be a member of one of the other leading employers' organisations. Likewise, the trade union should be affiliated to one of the central federations; and

(v) The undertaking should have a fair record of industrial relations.

List of Industries/Undertakings where the JMC Scheme is to be introduced[3]

The sub-committee approved a tentative list of industries and the number of units in each industry to be initially covered by the scheme of joint management councils. The employers' representatives agreed to give, in consultation with local labour unions, and within a month, a list of undertakings where the scheme could be promoted.

1. ILC Sub-committee as workers' participation 1st meeting, 1.4.
2. ILC Sub-committee or age 1st meeting, 6 Aug., 1957, 1.1.
3. ILC Sub-committee Meeting on WP 1st meeting, 1.2.

Panel of Experts and Holding of a Seminar[1]

The sub-committee approved the suggestions made in an office note as regards the constitution of a panel of experts and the calling of a seminar. It was agreed that there should be a promotion unit, or squad, for giving on-the-spot guidance to various joint councils. It was emphasised that in the initial stages of a new and vital experiment like this, overall guidance and coordination should come from the centre. But, at a later stage it might be appropriate to transfer the task of guidance and coordination to the states. It was pointed out that the government should spare its officers to function as experts. The employers' and workers' organisations would furnish a list of experts (about 10 on each side) who had knowledge of handling day-to-day labour problems at the unit level.

It was decided that a tripartite seminar on this subject should be organised under the auspices of the Ministry of Labour. The experts, on the aforesaid panel of experts, should also participate in the seminar.

Statutory vs. Voluntary Arrangement[2]

While there was a general agreement, in principle, with the basic idea of workers' participation in management, there was some discussion whether it should be implemented through legislation or by mutual agreement between employees and employers of selected industrial establishments. The employers representatives wanted that they should be given a period of two years to operate the scheme on voluntary basis. If the voluntary experiment did not succeed, the government might bring in legislation.

The employees' representatives were not in favour of the idea of leaving the matter to the initiative of the employers. They felt that in order to avoid any delay in the implementation of the scheme, an appropriate legislation was necessary.

There was some discussion regarding the method of selecting the workers' representatives. One of the workers' representatives suggested that the representative union, recognised under law, might be taken into consideration for the purpose.[3]

After some discussion it was decided that a small Sub-committee of four persons each from the employers' group and the employees'

1. ILC Sub-committee Meeting on WP 1st meeting, 1.3.
2. 15th Session, Report of the Study Group on Workers' Participation in 1st Management, 15.1.
3. 15th Session, Report of the Study Group on Workers' Participation in 1st Management, 15.1.

group and the government should be set up immediately to consider the details regarding the scheme of worker's participation in management. The Committee, however, accepted the main recommendations contained in the Report of the Study Group :

(i) The main functions of the councils may include provision of means of communication, improvement of working and living conditions, improvement in productivity, encouragement to suggestions and assistance in the administration of laws and agreements. It may be desirable to consult the councils regarding matters like alterations in standing orders, retrenchment, rationalisation, closure, reduction in or cessation of operations, introduction of new methods, procedures for engagement and punishment. They may also have the right to receive information about the general economic situation of the concern, the state of the market, production and sales programmes, organisation and general running of the undertaking, circumstances affecting the economic position of the undertaking, methods of manufacture and work and the annual balance sheet and profit and loss statement and connected documents and explanations, and such matters as may be agreed to by employers and employees.

(ii) It would be preferable to exclude wages and bonus and individual grievances from the purview of joint bodies but otherwise the list of functions should be flexible enough to be settled by joint consultation between the management and the representative trade union.

(iii) To reduce the danger of apathy, councils of management may be entrusted with some administrative responsibility, such as administration of welfare measures, supervision of safety measures, operation of vocational training and apprenticeship schemes, preparation of schedules of working hours and breaks and of holidays and payment of rewards for valuable suggestions.

(iv) There should be a strong self-confident trade union closely connected with the machinery of participation and with a reasonably clear separation of functions. It would be advisable to devise some methods for closely associating the trade unions in the selection of workers' representatives.

(v) It is necessary to enlist the willing cooperation of management at the middle and lower level such as junior managers, supervisors and foremen.

(vi) Joint consultation should be 'inbuilt' and for this purpose the government should provide advisory service on personnel management on the lines of the British Ministry of Labour.

(vii) While the government should accept leadership for organising a sustained educational campaign for creating the necessary atmosphere, it should not be made a departmental affair. But effort should be made to build up a tripartite machinery of direction by utilising employer's organisations, trade unions, non-official bodies, etc.

Some Instances of Workers' Participation in Management

The representative of the A.I.M.O. revealed that the Bombay Mills Ltd., the Malleable Iron & Steel Castings (P) Ltd., and the Devidayal Cable Industries (P) Ltd. had already implemented the scheme and agreed to send details to the Ministry. A few instances of dispute between labour and management on the issue of Joint Council of Management were also mentioned. It recommended that the good offices of the Panel of Experts, maintained by the government, should be used to settle those differences. A list of panel members should be circulated to all the participating units.[1]

Recent Deliberations on Workers' Participation

The Conference agreed in principle to the implementation of the scheme of workers' participation in management in the public, private and co-operative sectors, at various levels, including board level. The question whether this scheme should be voluntary or should be implemented by legislation, as also the modalities for its implementation, were left to be considered by the Standing Labour Committee. The Committee also took into account the framework and the outline of the scheme which had been proposed in the agenda papers.[2]

(i) It was felt that the envisaged statutory framework should be flexible enabling the government to introduce the scheme in a phased manner beginning with the establishments above a certain size.[3]

1. ILC Sub-committee, 4th meeting, 4.2, 19 Sep. 1958.
2. 28th Session, 28.6.
3. 29th Session, 29.2.

(ii) The mode of representation of 'workmen' should be on the basis of the decision taken at the National Seminar in the establishments in which a majority of 'workmen' were members of trade unions. In other cases, as well as in respect of representation of workers, other than 'workmen,' the representation should be decided by direct secret ballot. Dismissed employees whose cases were sub-judice should be made eligible for participation.

(iii) The participation should be on equal basis between workers and employers. However regarding participation at the Board level there was difference of opinion. Workers' representatives felt that the strength of workers should be 50 per cent of the total strength of the Board. The employers' representatives felt that, to begin with, representation of workers on the Board should be confined to only one representative each of 'workmen' and workers other than 'workmen.' The majority of the state ministers were of the view that this should be confined to 25 per cent, while the Labour Minister of West Bengal felt that it should be 50 per cent.

(iv) Question, relating to participation in equity should be kept separate from the proposed statutory scheme.

The employers' representatives expressed their opposition to the Workers' Participation Bill.[1] They, instead, suggested a bipartite participatory mechanism. The workers' representatives, on the other hand were in favour of a legal framework.

It was decided that the Standing Labour Committee would further discuss the Bill and the amendments suggested by various quarters as well as the report of the Parliamentary Committee.

1. 32nd Session, 32.26.

13

CONTRACT LABOUR

Abolition of Contract Labour was emphasised mainly in the 19th and 20th Sessions of the ILC. It suggested for compliance of the Supreme Court Judgements in Standard Vacuum Refining Co. of India Ltd. v. Their Workmen on the abolition and regulation of contract labour.

Regulation and Abolition of Contract Labour[1]

The Conference expressed its serious concern on the exploitative situation being faced by contract labour. It felt that contract labour should be abolished wherever feasible. If abolition of contract labour was not feasible, satisfactory working conditions should be ensured by enforcing the following terms :

1. The regular work of the establishment, i.e., work which was ordinarily part of the work of the principal employers, should, as far as possible, be done by the principal employer, with the labour directly engaged by them.

Contract labour should not be engaged in the type of work referred to in the Supreme Court Judgement in Standard Vacuum Refining Co. of India Ltd. v. Their Workmen, 1960(2) I.U.J. 233-1960. C. 948-18, i.e. if,

(a) work is perennial and goes on continuously;
(b) work is incidental and necessary for the work of factory;
(c) work is sufficient to employ a considerable number of regular workmen; and
(d) work is being done in most concerns through regular workmen.

2. Where it was not possible to dispense with contract labour in

---

1. 19th Session, 19.7.

the work referred to above, standard rates of wages should be fixed either through legislation or by the terms of the contract. The principal employer should either make payment of the wage directly or should be responsible for ensuring payment by the contractor as per the fixed rate.

However, the employers' representative did not accept the above suggestions.

3. For workers, other than those mentioned in (1) above (inspection services), the principal employer should be responsible for providing essential amenities, such as drinking water, lavatories, urinals, washing arrangements, rest rooms, canteens, creches and first aid, if need be, on terms which may be regulated by the terms of the contract.
4. For other benefits such as leave, holidays with pay, temporary housing, minimum wages, overtime, weekly rest-day, payment on termination of service etc., the contractor should be held directly responsible.
5. It was felt that legislation was necessary to enable the effective implementation of the above mentioned measures.
6. There was also a necessity for adequate inspection machinery to ensure effective enforcement of this legislation and other labour laws applicable to contract labour.

Several complaints were made that the principles regarding the abolition of contract labour generally agreed to were not being observed. It was emphasised that those principles should be strictly adhered to by all the parties.[1]

There was also an agreement that reports on the progress of abolition of contract labour in the private and public sectors should be obtained periodically.

It was again observed that legislative action was necessary. The Chairman said that a Draft Bill incorporating the principles of the Supreme Court judgement would be drawn up and circulated to all the parties concerned.

Some of the workers' representatives pointed out that the information regarding action taken on tripartite conclusions, was in many cases inadequate because many state governments had not sent their replies. It was, therefore, stressed that the state governments should be prompt in furnishing the requisite information.

1. 20th Session, 20.2.

14

UNORGANISED LABOUR

The Indian Labour Conference deliberated over the marginalised sections of the workforce like child labour, women labour as well as domestic servants. It sought to meet the problems of child labour through rationalisation of various protective laws, vocational training and education. It however suggested exclusion of agriculture and plantation labour, which otherwise constituted the largest segment of child labour, from the purview of the legistations as far as child labour was concerned. Regarding the age of employment. For women labour it suggested proper employment opportunities, training facilities, better amenities at the workplace and minimum standards on maternity benefits. To regulate the service conditions of domestic servants, it proposed to set up a special employment office in Delhi as a pilot project.

CHILD LABOUR, WOMEN LABOUR AND DOMESTIC SERVANTS

Child Labour[1]

Rationalisation of Protective Laws and their Implementation

The Conference discussed the problem of child and women labour and felt the necessity of proper training, and other suitable measures as well as elimination of child labour, rationalisation of various protective laws and their implementation. In this regard the following specific recommendations were made :

(i) Inspection services, including medical inspectorate, should be reinforced for better implementation of protective legislation.

(ii) Protective laws should be rationalised by providing for a

1. 14th Session, 14.5.

uniform minimum age of 14 for employment, uniform hours of work, rest interval, weekly rest-days and non-employment at night, i.e., between 7 p.m. and 6 a.m.

Exceptions

The provision regarding the age of employment need not at this stage apply to agriculture and plantation labour.

Vocational Training and Education

The state government should be requested to provide for such general and vocational training and education to children before they attain the age of employment as may be practicable in the respective states.

Comprehensive Legislation on Child Labour[1]

It was felt that there should be total elimination of child labour. The employers' and employees' representatives agreed on the need for elimination of child labour and pledged their cooperation for eradicating it.

The assurance of the employers' representatives included not only the child labour directly employed by them but also contract labour.

The Conference supported the proposal for a comprehensive legislation on child labour. It was, however, of the view that the problem arising out of socio-economic compulsions was difficult to be tackled merely by legislation. It felt that one of the ways for effectively dealing with the problem was to improve the economic conditions of the families which by force of circumstances had to send their children to work. In view of the concern expressed in the Conference, it was felt that Industrial Tripartite Committee should be set up at the central and state levels in respect of those industries where the incidence of child labour was high. Those committees should not only lay down the policies but also monitor the implementation of the schemes/programmes taken up in this regard.

The Recent Concern[2]

Trade unions should be more extensively involved in the implementation of schemes for elimination of child labour. The child labour elimination schemes under implementation should also be brought under tripartite review. The Child Labour Advisory Board

1. 28th Session, 28.10.
2. 32nd Session, 32.24.

should meet more regularly. Special incentives for parents of children removed from employment should be provided. The state governments should be empowered to prohibit employment of children in non-hazardous occupations as well (outside the scheduled hazardous employments and processes), keeping in view the local circumstances.

Woman Labour[1]

There was an agreement for creating proper employment opportunities for women, their training facilities, and better amenities at the work place.

Maternity Benefits[2]

It was decided that the central government should draw up minimum standards on maternity benefits and recommend them to state government for adoption either by an enactment or by revision of the existing laws.

Domestic Servants

The Conference was of the opinion that legislative measure for the regulation of service conditions of domestic servants was not feasible.[3] In this regard, the proposal to set up a special employment office in Delhi was unanimously approved. It was thought that the experience gained from the working of this scheme in Delhi might provide the basis for further action with respect to domestic servants.

As regards the composition of the Advisory Committee, as contemplated in the pilot scheme, it was felt that besides the government representatives, central organizations, representing domestic workers and their employers should also be on the Committee.

It was also decided that the Labour Welfare Officers and others connected with the administration of the scheme should collect data in respect of working hours, holiday facilities, rates of remuneration, dates on which salary was normally paid, period of employment and other privileges available so that further course of action might be planned on the basis of the collected data.

The Conference took the following decisions : (i) a special employment office should be set up in Delhi and a pilot scheme

1. 13th Session, 13.4.
2. 13th Session, 13.8.
3. 17th Session, 17.3.

started to deal with the registration and placement of domestic servants. This office should function on the same lines as any other employment exchange and be administered by the Directorate-General of Employment and Training; (ii) there should also be an Advisory Committee consisting of the Director of Employment and Training, one representative each of employees and employers, a social worker and a Member of Parliament.

The welfare of domestic servants should be entrusted to a Labour Welfare Officer to be appointed by the Delhi Administration.

15

ILO CONVENTIONS AND RECOMMENDATIONS

Opinion varied on the question of adopting some ILC Conventions and Recommendations. The government was of the opinion that some of the conventions and recommendations conflicted with the national laws and that their incorporation in the national laws would create difficulties in implementation. But the workers' representatives were in favour of necessary changes in the laws, rules and procedure so that they were in conformity with the conventions and recommendations.

The ILO Questionnaire

There was a discussion on the ILO questionnaire pertaining to various conventions for adoption. The questionnaire was related to the following :[1]

(i) Organisation of Labour Inspection in Industrial and Commercial undertakings.
(ii) Employment service organisation.
(iii) Draft conventions on social policy in non-metropolitan territories.

The Conference noted the views expressed on different items in the questionnaire and on the provisions in the proposed convention.

The Chairman observed that if the Government of India was reluctant to adopt a convention or a recommendation, it was not because they felt that the convention or the recommendation was wrong or undesirable. But beacause the condition was not conducive for their ratification.

The ILO questionnaire relating to the following subjects was discussed :[2]

1. 8th Session, 8.4.
2. 9th Session, 9.5.

(i) Fair wages clause in public contracts.
(ii) Protection of wages.
(iii) Freedom of association and protection of the right to organise.
(iv) Application of the principles of the right to organise and to bargain collectively.
(v) Collective agreement.
(vi) Conciliation and arbitration.
(vii) Cooperation between public authorities and employers and workers' organisations.
(viii) Vocational guidance.
(ix) Revision of the conventions concerning night work of women and young persons.

However, there was no specific decision on the subject.

Review of the ILO Conference Committees[1]

The Chairman said that he would consider the formation of a small tripartite committee to consider implementation of various ILO conventions.

Proposal for Conventions and Recommendation on the Agenda of the 38th Session of the International Labour Conferance[2]

(i) *Vocational Rehabilitation of the Disabled* : It was felt that the recommendation was too wide in its scope and it would be difficult to implement it in a country like India. If possible the scope of the recommendation should be limited to industrial disablement.
(ii) *Vocational Training in Agriculture* : It was agreed that such vocational training as was practicable within the resources of the country, should be made available for agriculturists.
(iii) *Welfare Facilities for Workers* : The need for welfare facilities was accepted. It was pointed out that welfare facilities were already being provided either under legislation or on a voluntary basis. Wherever deficient, such facilities should be improved.

It was agreed that the ILO proposals should be supported by the Indian delegation subject to the above limitations.

1. 13th Session, 13.1.
2. 14th Session, 14.10.

Report of the 8th Session of the Committee on Conventions[1]

(i) The Conference took note of the report of the 8th session of the Committee on Conventions.

(ii) Workers' representatives felt that Conventions No. 87 and 98 should be ratified and implemented without delay. But, according to the Union Labour Secretary, the ratification of those conventions would conflict with certain national laws and rules. He said, the laws, rules and practices in each country should conform to its own national policy. The workers' representatives suggested that necessary changes should be made in the laws, rules and practices to make feasible the ratification of those conventions. The Maharashtra Minister for Labour, suggested that there should be no change in the rules and practices relating to government servants' associations.

(iii) The Conference recommended that action should be expedited on ratification of Convention No. 115 and the progress in the matter should be reported in the next session.

1. 27th Session, 27.2.

16

CODE OF DISCIPLINE, EFFICIENCY AND WELFARE

A high standard of discipline was considered the prerequisite for higher productivity as well as for effective participation of workers in management. It was against this background that ILC deliberated over Code of Discipline, Efficiency and Welfare. Prompt attention to grievance, conciliation, arbitration were considered to be the suitable mechanisms for ensuring healthy industrial relations.

The review of the Code of Discipline indicated that in many cases the Code was violated by employers. There were complaints that in many cases employers refused to recognise unions, refer disputes to arbitration etc. It was also pointed out that even some Employing Ministries had violated the Code.

Regarding Code of Efficiency and Welfare, workers' representatives were generally of the view that the time was not yet appropriate for introducing it.

Widespread indiscipline in offices and factories engaged the attention of the Conference during its 15th session. The Chairman expressed the view[1] that indiscipline had assumed a serious proportion. He said, without a high standard of discipline there was no prospect of either improved productivity or any effective participation of workers in management. For both higher productivity and better discipline conditions would have to be created which *inter alia* required a sense of security of employment, prompt attention to grievances, a fair deal in all matters, free latitude for organisation, a practical recognition of the status of the workers and consideration for their well-being in human terms.

1. Extracts from Chairman's speech, 15th Session, July 11-12, 1957.

The Chairman appealed to the Conference to address itself to the problems with greatest earnest and sense of urgency and evolve a 'code of behaviour' in the enforcement of which the employers and the various organisations of the workers would give unqualified cooperation.

The report of the Sub-committee on Discipline,[1] as adopted by the Conference, was as follows[2] :

(i) There should be no strike or lockout without notice;
(ii) No unilateral action should be taken in connection with any industrial matter;
(iii) There should be no recourse to 'go slow' tactics;
(iv) No deliberate damage should be caused to plant or property;
(v) Acts of violence, intimidation, coercion or instigation should not be resorted to;
(vi) The existing machinery for settlement of disputes should be utilised;
(vii) Awards and agreements should be speedily implemented;
(viii) Any action which disturbs cordial industrial relations should be avoided.

The Sub-committee also recommended that the following matters might be further studied :

(i) Uniformity in wages, service conditions and other benefits in the same industry in an area;
(ii) Need for long-term settlements, avoidance of dilatoriness and speedy settlement of industrial disputes;
(iii) Sanction against employers or unions violating any of the principles mentioned in the preceding paragraph;
(iv) Proper definition of 'unfair' labour practices such as interference in trade union activities, etc.; and
(v) The question whether curtailment of production, consequent on closure, would amount to an act of indiscipline.

The Sub-committee considered that a Works Committee at the unit level would be a useful agency to deal with matters relating to discipline and recommended setting up of such committees wherever they did not exist and the appointment of similar committees at the local, regional and central levels.

It was agreed that a standing tripartite committee should be set

1. See Appendix XXII for the text of the Code of Discipline in Industry.
2. 15th Session, 15.7, July 11-12, 1957.

up and that it should meet in a fortnight's time to consider the matters mentioned in the report, as well as other suggestions.

Sufficient publicity should be given to the contents of the agreement on discipline in industry by bringing them to the notice of employers and workers. The 'employers and workers' organisations should adopt resolutions endorsing the principles and ways should be devised for disseminating the information widely.

The observance of the principles agreed to would be ensured by a top-level tripartite committee mentioned above and a number of committees at lower levels coming down to the works committees.

CODE FOR DISCIPLINE IN INDUSTRY

The Sub-committee agreed that the Code drawn up by it should be sent to the Standing Labour Committee or the Indian Labour Conference for approval. The Code should be widely publicised and resolutions supporting the Code should be adopted by employers' and workers' organisations. The Members of the Sub-committee agreed to send in their suggestions for evolving (i) a satisfactory grievance procedure, and (ii) an appropriate machinery for ensuring the implementation of the code. The Labour Ministry undertook to circulate a note on current position about grievance procedures.

The Chairman laid emphasis on the importance of a machinery to ensure effective implementation of the provisions of the Code. He felt that thought should be given to work out the strategy for making the Code effective and that any machinery set up to supervise the implementation should not be allowed to degenerate into a mere conciliating body. He also felt that all complaints regarding lapses in implementing the Code could not be handled at the top level. It might, therefore, be necessary to have regional committees or local committees. The issue whether there should be official or non-official chairman for these committees, was left to be decided later.

Implementation Machinery[1]

(i) It was decided that besides fixing responsibility for violations of the Code, Implementation Committees should, wherever necessary, bring the contending parties across the table to reduce tension. They may also work for out-of-court settlement of the industrial dispute pending in courts, with

1. 19th Session, 19.9, October 9-10, 1961.

the consent of the parties.

(ii) It was agreed that complaints should be dealt with at appropriate levels. Complaints relating to the state sphere should invariably be made to the concerned implementation machinery. The central organisations agreed to issue instructions to their members in this respect.

(iii) The central organisations agreed to give their own assessment of the position while forwarding replies of their members to the implementation machinery.

(iv) It was agreed that for the purpose of defining the word 'industry' in Clause 3 of the Criteria for Recognition of Unions, the classification of industries used by the Labour Bureau, Simla, would be adopted, and 'industry' would mean 'any business' trade, undertaking, manufacture or calling of employers, including any calling, service, employment, handicraft or industrial occupation or a vocation of workmen.

(v) It was agreed that the word 'local area' occurring in Clause 3 of Criteria for Recognition of Unions, would be defined by the concerned appropriate government.

(vi) It was decided that state government would take suitable steps to improve and strengthen their implementation machinery for ensuring prompt disposal of complaints made to them, if possible, within two months.

Amendment of the Code of Discipline[1]

The Conference suggested the following lines of amendments of the Code of Discipline for imposing restrictions on hunger strike :

(i) Hunger strikes should be avoided by all means. It was not, however, considered necessary to amend the Code for the purpose of banning hunger strikes. The workers' representatives also agreed to discourage hunger strikes as a means of settling disputes. It was suggested that in extreme cases when the workers had exhausted all other means of redressal of grievance, strike should be preferable to hunger strike.

(ii) The central and state governments should take all possible steps to ensure that workers and unions were not compelled to resort to hunger strike out of sheer desperation.

1. 20th Session, 20.3, August 7-9, 1962.

Review of Working of Code of Discipline[1]

(i) There were frequent references to cases of refusal by the employers to (a) recognise unions, and (b) agree to refer disputes to arbitration. It was agreed that a full note summarising the points and suggestions made in the Conference in this regard should be prepared and circulated to all concerned.

(ii) The Conference also reiterated the position that recognition of unions was one of the basic ingredients of the Code, and failure to recognise the unions which satisfied the criteria for such recognition as laid down in the Code, should be considered a serious violation of the Code.

(iii) As regards arbitration, it was agreed that readiness to refer disputes to arbitration was an important requirement of the Code. If conciliation failed, arbitration would be the next normal step, except in cases where the employers for some valid reasons preferred adjudication, such reasons being creation of new rights having wide repercussions or those involving large financial stakes. However, the reasons for refusal to agree to arbitration must be fully explained by the party concerned in each case, and the matter brought to consideration by the implementation machinery concerned.

(iv) To assist employers and trade unions, central and state governments would constitute, in consultation with the Central Employers' and Workers' Organisations, panels of arbitrators and make the list of names available to the parties. The government would also fix a ceiling on the fees which could be charged by the arbitrator, per case and per day.

(v) Minor disputes might be referred to a single person for arbitration. If cases were more complicated, each party would nominate one arbitrator, and the two arbitrators could select an umpire, whenever necessary. The services of the presiding officers of Industrial Tribunals might be made available for the purpose of arbitration.

Different views were expressed about the effectiveness of the Code of Discipline.[2] Some thought it had worked well while others felt that in the absence of proper sanctions and the non-acceptance of

---

1. 20th Session, 20.3, August 7-9, 1962, see Appendix XXIII for conclusions of the seminars on the working of the Code of Discipline.
2. 24th Session, 24.3, July 29-30, 1966.

the Code by some Employing Ministries, there were frequent violations of the Code, making it an ineffective instrument.

Some of the workers' representatives suggested a comprehensive review of the process of identification of bargaining agent and promotion of collective bargaining and incorporation in the law the principles of the Code of Discipline.

The Chairman observed that in his opinion the Code had worked fairly well and had a salutary effect on industrial relations. There might have been instances of violations here and there. The solution was not to do away with the Code, but to remedy the situation and seek to improve its working. As for the comprehensive review of the Industrial Relations Law, he said that he was also thinking about this for some time and had felt that the Trade Union Law called for some major amendments. The organisations should continue to ensure compliance with the requirements of voluntary instruments like the Code of Discipline and the Industrial Truce Resolution. Some proposals had been made in this regard in the memorandum on the subject.

CODE OF EFFICIENCY AND WELFARE

While there was a general agreement between the various representatives for realisation of the objectives behind the proposed Code of Efficiency, the consensus was for detailed discussion in the light of the needs of the industry and the employees. The introduction of the Code of Efficiency at that stage would still be premature. Attempts should instead be made to implement the Code of Discipline fully and whole-heartedly by both the employers and the employees and all impediments in the implementation of the Code of Discipline should be removed.[1]

It was suggested that the question of trying out the Code of Efficiency on a pilot basis in selected units should be considered. And the other related matters, like production, productivity, efficiency, existing efficiency schemes etc., should be discussed in a seminar. All available material on these subjects should be collected and made available to the participants to enable them to have a full discussion. For this purpose it was decided that a small committee consisting of Shri V.K.R. Menon, Shri B.N. Datar, Shri P. Chenasi Rao, Shri S.C.C. Anthony Pillai and a representative of the West Bengal Government should be constituted. The main function of this committee would be

1. 5th Meeting, Tripartite Committee, 8 Dec. 1959, 5.1.

to prepare the background material for the proposed seminar.

The Conference further discussed the adoption of a Code of Efficiency. The INTUC representatives were in favour of such Code. But the AITUC representatives were opposed to the idea of having any code on the ground that workers had not yet secured their due share in the gains of productivity. The representatives of HMS and INTUC, while appreciating the spirit behind the Code, felt that the time was not yet appropriate for introducing it.[1]

The employers' representatives pleaded for some time to study the implications of the proposals contained in the Report of the Tripartite Committee.

It was finally decided that a Tripartite Committee should be set up to discuss the matter further. The committee would meet after three months and formulate proposals for consideration of the Conference. Meanwhile the employers' and workers' representatives would study the Report.

The AITUC representatives observed that they would not participate in the committee. The Chairman, however, hoped that in the intervening three months, the AITUC would reconsider their position.[2]

1. 19th Session, 19.1.
2. 5th meeting, 8 Dec., 1959, 5.1, tripartite committee.

17

NEW ECONOMIC POLICY AND LABOUR

The New Economic Policy resulted in the renewed emphasis by the ILC on employment related issues. It deliberated over employment generation, training, retraining, redeployment, absorption of surplus labour, National Renewal Fund, BIFR etc. It also emphasised improvement of productivity and quality. The workers' representatives were of the opinion that there was a need for a comprehensive industrial relations laws. Social Clause which became an important issue in the context of international trade was a new item of the ILC agenda.

Ramanujam Committee

It was observed that the Government of India had, before it the considered views of the Central Trade Union Organisations, the Central Employers' Organisations and the state governments on the recommendations of the Ramanujam Committee. The Conference felt that it would be more useful to discuss the matter after the Government of India's own views in this regard were known. The Chairman assured that the drafts of the proposed Industrial Relation and Trade Union Bill would be prepared, keeping in view the ideas and suggestions expressed by all the parties and the changes that had since taken place both inside and outside the country. Chairman offered to have a discussion on the matter with select group of representatives of parties present in the Conference.[1]

NTC Mills

It was suggested that the recommendations of the Tripartite Committee on the N.T.C. Mills should be implemented immediately.[2]

1. 30th Session, 30.4.
2. 31st Session, 31.4.

New Industrial Policy

On the consequences of the New Industrial Policy, the Chairman referred to the assurance by the Prime Minister that it would not lead to any human distress and the legitimate interests of labour would be protected.[1]

Retraining and Redeployment in the Context of Structural Adjustment

In regard to retraining and redeployment, necessitated by the structural adjustment, the Conference felt the necessity of the identification of labour for such retraining and redeployment, and a scheme for industry-wise and occupation-wise redeployment. It also expressed the view that the government should identify the agency for retraining and indicate the time gap between identification of labour for retraining and their redeployment. It also wanted the modalities to be worked out for redeployment of labour from one unit to another unit.

The Conference felt that the constitution and the functioning of the National Renewal Fund should be reviewed so that it truly served the purpose of industrial renewal and regeneration and creation of employment opportunities. Representation should be given in the administration of the National Renewal Fund to employers' and workers' organisations. Priority should be given to training, retraining, vocational counselling and guidance for redeployment of workers affected by the rationalisation process. Investments should also be made by drawing on appropriate sources of finance for the rehabilitation of the rationalised enterprises.

It was felt that implementation of the training programmes should be undertaken within the framework of a well thought out plan. This was accepted by the state governments and trade unions of employers and workers. The training centres should be organised on a decentralised basis, taking into account the scope for using existing training centres in different parts of the country and down to the industrial establishments at district levels. The training infrastructure available with the industrial enterprises themselves should also be pressed into service for training and retraining. The training should also be in skills relevant to actual employment potential.

The Conference, acknowledging the positive correlation between education, skill formation and population control felt that the central and state governments should give high priority in allocation of

1. 30th Session, 30.4.

resources for elementary and vocational education. And the organisations of employers and workers should give full support for promoting elementary and vocational education through their constituents. The governments and the social partners should pay special attention to the education of women workers.

In the context of structural adjustment, the Conference suggested that vocational training system in the country should be reorganised. In specific terms the measures suggested were :

(a) Identification of skills needed in the present-day context by industrial enterprises and for self-employment.
(b) Designing of courses, syllabi and curricula, relevant to such identified skills in the labour market.
(c) Modernisation of the infrastructure of vocational training institutions.
(d) Institutionalised arrangements for interaction between the vocational training institutions, standard-setting bodies like the state and central councils of vocational training and the industry.
(e) Reorganisation of the employment exchanges to bring together job seekers and employers to their mutual advantage with promptitude.

Vocational Training

The Conference felt that there was a growing need for modernisation of the vocational training system. The vocational training courses should have more practical orientation and special emphasis should be placed on multi-skilling the trainees. In this connection it was suggested that the agenda for restructuring of the vocational training system should first be discussed in the National Council for Vocational Training (NCVT) and then brought before the Standing Labour Committee.

Absorption of Surplus Labour

For absorption of surplus labour if any, and for maximizing capacity utilisation, the Conference suggested diversification and broad- basing by working the units round the clock and on all days of the week.[1]

Comprehensive Industrial Relation Law

The Conference expressed its serious concern at the low productivity

1. 30th Session, 30.6.

of Indian Industries. It felt the necessity to improve the Industrial productivity upgrade the quality and make the products internationally competitive.

The Conference also decided to strive for improvement in discipline and attitude to work at all levels. It also decided that bipartite efforts to improve productivity and quality should be institutionalised.[1]

Improvement of Productivity and Quality

The workers' representatives said that it was a matter of concern that despite discussions in the various tripartite for a including the Indian Labour Conference over the years and despite efforts on the part of successive governments, a comprehensive industrial relations law had not become a reality. They said that in the present scenario of vast changes in the socio-economic front, the Central and State Governments and the social partners should come together for a comprehensive Industrial Relations law.[2]

While fully recognising that productivity of economic enterprises as a whole was of paramount importance, a need was felt to promote it through.[3]

(a) Broadbasing and diversification of production through full capacity utilisation and other means.
(b) By adopting suitable measures and practices for achieving higher levels of output and to produce goods and services of high quality which would enhance the competitive edge for the country's enterprises.

National Renewal Fund

The Conference felt that the constitution and the functioning of the National Renewal Fund should be reviewed so that the Fund truly served the purpose of regeneration and creation of employment opportunities. Representation should be given, in the administration of the National Renewal Fund to employers' and workers' organisations. Priority in the use of resources of the Fund should be given for training, retraining, vocational counselling and guidance for redeployment of workers affected by rationalisation. Side by side with training, retraining and counselling of workers, concurrent

1. 30th Session, 30.7.
2. 31st Session, 31.3.
3. 31st Session, 31.5.

investments should also be made by drawing on appropriate sources of finance for the rehabilitation of the rationalised enterprises.[1]

Employment Generation

The present employment scenario in which organised sector employment had become stagnant and the agrarian sector was not absorbing more job seekers, effective action should be taken in pursuance of the report of the NDC Committee on employment to create more job opportunities in the economy as a whole and to protect existing levels of employment to the maximum possible extent.[2]

The Economic Reforms Process should be geared to expansion of employment opportunities by evolving an employment policy which would arrest the loss of job opportunities and provide suitable rehabilitation package for sick industries.[3]

To provide protection against job losses in the wake of exit policy, it was felt necessary to examine scope for introduction of unemployment insurance.[4]

The Conference suggested that detailed studies should be undertaken on employment potential of various sectors of economy. It was particularly felt necessary to study employment potential in agro-based industries. Special measures including employment reviewing the existing laws and amending them, where appropriate, steps should be taken to augment employment opportunities for women.[5]

Working Conditions in Export Processing Zones

The Conference suggested that in view of growing employment in export processing zones, consequent to trade liberalisation, there was a need for detailed study of the working condition so as to ensure full protection to the workers under the various labour laws.[6]

Social Clause, Child Labour and Bonded Labour

The Conference fully endorsed the resolutions of the 32nd session of the Standing Labour Committee in respect of the social clauses, abolishing child labour and bonded labour.

It was suggested that in this regard government and other social

1. 31st Session, 31.11.
2. 31st Session, 31.20.
3. 31st Session, 31.21.
4. 32nd Session, 32.18.
5. 32nd Session, 32.20.
6. 32nd Session, 32.4.

partners should initiate follow up action.[1]

It was considered necessary that Trade Unions and employers were included in the National delegation to the World Summit for Social Development.[2]

Industrial Sickness

The growing sickness of industrial units was viewed with concern. It was felt that immediate preventive steps should be taken to go into the causes of sickness and effective remedial action initiated to combat it. Emphasis should be laid on quick measures for rehabilitation and revival of sick units. A Standing Committee should be set up to monitor the problem of sickness in industries and also to undertake in-depth study of individual cases of closed sick units as well as units identified as potentially sick.[3]

The Conference generally welcomed the Sick Industrial Companies (Special Provisions) Bill, 1905 which was introduced in Parliament. It, however, suggested that government might consider amending it to bring within its purview the sick industrial units and also the potentially sick units to prevent the latter from closing down. The Conference also felt that labour should be fully represented on the Board and the state governments should also have their representation.[4]

The Conference was of the opinion that there was a crying need for speedy and orderly investigation into the rehabilitation of Sick Industrial Enterprises registered with the BIFR.[5] In this regards the following measures were suggested :

(a) Review of the working of the BIFR so far and suggestion for changes, if necessary.

(b) Creation of adequate number of benches of the BIFR on a zonal basis.

(c) Hearing by BIFR benches to be so organised as to enable sittings in different places to suit, to the extent possible, the convenience of the parties called for hearing.

(d) Appointment of Members of the BIFR with adequate professional expertise in handling matters relating to structuring and restructuring of industries, management and industrial relations with trade union experience.

1. 31st Session, 31.19.
2. 31st Session, 31.17.
3. 28th Session.
4. 28th Session.
5. Text of Footnote.

(e) Simplification of the BIFR procedure and making it statutorily time-bound.

(f) Registration of an enterprise with the BIFR under the Sick Industrial Companies Act should not result in cessation of fund flows from the financing institutions until a decision was taken on rehabilitation.

(g) Wherever rehabilitation proposals had been approved, the government should ensure flow of funds for such rehabilitation. Wherever joint revival packages was submitted, those packages should be given full support by government and financial institutions.

Financial support for jute mills restructured on cooperative basis should be extended without delay.[1]

The BIFR should be restructured with experts from the areas of management and labour. The BIFR procedures should be simplified to avoid delays in the restructuring of sick enterprises. The inordinate delays in winding up and liquidation proceedings should be cut down by simplification of the legal process.[2]

Detailed and comprehensive studies of sickness in industrial enterprises should be undertaken for evolving appropriate remedial and pre-emptive measure.[3]

1. 32nd Session, 32.11.
2. 32nd Session, 32.12.
3. 32nd Session, 32.13.

Appendices

APPENDIX I

SPEECH OF Shri P.A. SANGMA, UNION MINISTER OF STATE FOR LABOUR, 31ST SESSION OF THE INDIAN LABOUR CONFERENCE (NEW DELHI, JANUARY 3, 1995)

Honourable Dr. Manmohan Singh, our esteemed Finance Minister, my colleague Shrimati Krishna Sahi, Honourable Minister of State for Industry, Ministers in charge of Labour and Employment in the States, Ms. Karavasil, Director, International Labour Organisation, New Delhi. Representatives of Employers and Workers, and officials from the Ministries and the States,

It gives me immense pleasure to welcome all of you to this Thirty-First Session of the Indian Labour Conference. This Conference synchronises with the lapse of about three years since the introduction of economic reforms. Economic Reform has its labour dimensions. In very simple terms, economic reform involves optimal use of factors of production including labour so that resources are efficiently used. Inefficient use of resources causes structural imbalances in economies. In the past, we opted for protection in several spheres of our economy–protection for the domestic industry, within the domestic industrial sector, for small scale industries, for labour, for the capital market and so on. Such protective strategy was also needed as a measure of welfare. Over the last four and a half decades, with the help of this protective strategy, it has been possible for us to develop infrastructure for agriculture, industries and services in a significant way. Nonetheless, protection has brought in its wake certain inefficiencies in resource use which we cannot any longer afford on account of globalisation and market competition. For more than a decade now, over hundred countries in the world have had to go in for economic reforms and liberalisation. Different countries have had different degrees of success. Higher the initial protection of the economies, the more difficult has been the process of liberalisation. Nonetheless, liberalisation is being continued by them. Certain South-East Asian and East Asian countries have been able to achieve significant degree of success. Even China has now opted for "socialist market economy." We cannot, but continue our reform, we have, under the cautious guidance of our Prime Minister and the Finance Minister carried forward the reform measures steadily. There is indeed a broad consensus in the country in favour of the reforms. This is also reflected in the new Industrial Policy of the Government of West Bengal. In order to carry the reforms further in the long term interests of the people of the country, the Government, the employers and the workers should come together and agree on the extent, intensity and pace of reforms including in the labour front.

The Labour Minister, keeping in view the social dimensions of economic reforms, has taken several important measures. Some of these measures are : enhancement of minimum wages in forty employments; amendment to the payment of Gratuity Act to make all employees eligible for gratuity irrespective of wage levels; introduction of amendment to the Employees' Provident Fund Law to provide for a Pension Scheme; a vigorous drive for collection of social security dues; decision to provide significantly enhanced social security benefits in the area of occupational health and safety etc.

In the context of economic reforms, one of the principal problems faced in the labour front is restructuring of sick and declining enterprises.

6. In the country as a whole, according to the Reserve Bank of India, there are about 2.5 lakh sick industrial enterprises (September, 1992). The Bank credit outstanding from them is of the order of about Rs. 10,000 crores. Textiles, Engineering, chemicals and Iron and Steel are the industrial sectors where sickness is of a high order.

Resources made available through the budget (in the case of Public Sector Enterprises) and through Commercial Banks and Financial Institutions are obviously inefficiently used in these enterprises. This should be a matter of serious national concern for which solutions have to be found through the reform process. The objective of the reform, no doubt, should be to save the inefficiently used resources and divert them for generating productive employment. In this context, we cannot also afford to forget that there are very compelling alternative demands on these scarce resources i.e., for health, nutrition and elementary education for the weaker sections of the society.

The investment in 237 Central Public Sector Enterprises (1992-93) is of the order of Rs. 1.5 lakh crores. About 2 million employees are engaged in these enterprises, the investment per employee being of the order of nearly Rs. 7 lakhs. About 40 per cent of the total investment and 38 per cent of employment in the Central Public Enterprises is accounted for by the Energy Sector (Coal and Lignite, Power and petroleum). These are in the monopoly sector of

Government.

Dependence on captive markets, surplus manpower, disproportionate on-loading of loan capital, weak marketing, weak product mix and high under-utilised capacities and fixed costs, unviable pricing structures, time over run in establishment of projects and entry into prima facie unviable areas are amongst the important causes for the low performance of the Central Public Sector Enterprises.

Fully taking into account the concerns of labour in the context of economic reform, since November, 1991, I have also been extensively involving the employers' and the workers' representatives in tripartite deliberations on the general status of major manufacturing industries and on the rehabilitation of sick public sector enterprises. I have had as many as eight meetings of the Special Tripartite Committee and thirteen meetings of the sectorial Industrial Tripartite Committees. The Tripartite recommendations on the rehabilitation of public enterprises is given considerable weight by the Group of Ministers as well as the Cabinet. The Group of Minister has already recommended revival of seven out of twenty two cases of Public Sector Enterprises presented to them. Other cases are under various stages of consideration. The turn around strategy for N.T.C. Mills unanimously approved through the tripartite mechanism is an example of meaningful collective effort at restructuring a declining enterprise.

More important than tripartite deliberations on rehabilitation of Public Sector Enterprises is the need for bilateral settlements at the enterprise level for the management of labour redundancies and rehabilitation. There are examples of successful management of labour redundancies at the enterprise level in the Pubic Sector itself. One example is N.T.C Mills, Coimbatore.

In any case, I would assure you all that the Prime Minister, Finance Minister and the Minister for Industries leave no stone unturned, if it is only for saving employment and preventing distress.

The Board for Industrial and Financial Reconstruction established under the Sick Industrial Companies Act should be seen as an expression of the Parliament's own concern about the inefficient use of capital and labour whether it be in the Public or Private Sector. The Board has come to be criticised as blocking rehabilitation of enterprises. But in fairness to them, I should go on record that they have demonstrated a high degree of sensitivity to examine fully the scope of revival of sick enterprises. They have recommended revival of public enterprises in nearly 30 per cent of the cases (i.e., in respect of 463 units out of a total of 1602 units registered with them).

In the context of economic reform, the industry often demands "level playing ground". Labour, on the other hand demands "social safety." What do these demands mean? They only mean demands, respectively for industry protection and labour protection. Protection does not go hand in hand with liberalisation because liberalisation itself is meant to dismantle protection which breeds inefficient use of resources. And economies characterised by protection and inefficient use of resources cannot compete and survive in a globalizing world.

While the industry would want protection for itself in terms of "level playing ground," it keeps demanding removal of the so- called "restrictive" provisions in labour laws which are, in fact, meant to protect labour.

Labour, while demanding continuance of the protective provisions in the labour laws in terms of "social safety," does not always realise that such protection involves costs for the industry which has implications for its competitiveness.

The dilemma of economic reform, in one respect then, is one of reconciling the conflicting interests of market competition and of protection for industry and labour; and of reconciling the conflicting concerns for securing the commercial viability of productive enterprises and of saving employment and working conditions in such enterprises. How are these conflicting interests and concerns to be reconciled?

According to me, the employers and workers themselves, on a bipartite basis, have to and can, find solutions. The two sides should shed their traditional, mutually adversarial approaches. The two sides cannot be cannibalistic, one on the other. In specific terms :

(i) Employers and workers should themselves review the industrial and labour laws, and identify and agree to give up scores of legal provisions and practices which cause diseconomies in production.

(ii) They should agree to reorient the legal provisions to enhancing productivity, because increased productivity alone can improve competitiveness and render improved labour protection sustainable and feasible.

(iii) Employers should, individually and collectively, invest on enhancing the employability of their workers through their training and retraining in fast changing technologies and skills needed in the employment market.

(iv) Innovative job-saving practices should be evolved by mutual agreement between the employers and workers to meet the crisis like economic recession. For example, in countries, like Germany, France and Japan workers have shared jobs. That is, in order to avoid layoff and retrenchment, workers have agreed for reduced working time in a week or month with proportionate wage-cuts. Measures of this nature would no doubt, call for transparency in the entrepreneurial and management practices of the employers.

Low productivity of the Indian Economy as a whole (Agriculture, Industry and Services included) should be a matter of serious concern too for all of us. Over the period of four decades from 1950-90, labour productivity per worker at 1981 prices has increased only at an annual average of Rs. 5.4 per annum, Based on purchasing power parity, our labour productivity is one of the lowest amongst the Asian nations—slightly over 3200 US $ (1990). Japanese labour productivity is more than ten times Indian productivity. The productivity of the Republic of Korea is almost three times that of India. Thailand, Sri Lanka, Pakistan and Philippines have registered more than double our productivity. We trail behind Bangladesh as well. This is indicative of an overall work culture on the part of the managements and workers which needs to be drastically improved, apart from the need for modernising our processes of production. In a quick interaction by the Labour Ministry with Central Public Sector Enterprises, it has been found that majority of them do not have productivity linked wage structure. This depressing scenario of productivity should be changed.

Coming to the employment scenario, growth of population by itself has been contributing to growth of the labour force in the country. In fact, the growth of labour force has been increasing at a faster rate than that of population (2.5 per cent per annum as against 2.1 per cent). We do have schemes and programmes, and we do make substantial investments for enhancing the pace of demographic transition, but in vast parts of the country we are not achieving the desired results. Trade Unions of employers and workers can make significant contributions to create awareness amongst the working people to adopt the Small Family Norm. While there is all round agreement on the need for population control, unfortunately, when it comes to formulating specific measures, we run into difficulties.

Recently, when the Labour Ministry wanted to amend the maternity Benefit Law to confine benefits to two children, the trade unions of workers could not reach a consensus on the matter. I am sorry to say that it was looked upon as a measure to cut down labour benefits. The most populous country in the world namely, China is vigorously implementing the norm of one child per family. In our political system, no doubt, such vigorous measures may not be feasible. But I would strongly call upon to the unions of workers that they should reconsider their position and give support to the Government. In at least creating legal disincentives against Maternity Benefit for unlimited number of children.

We have built up a good infrastructure of Vocational Training Institutes all over the country. These institutions provide training for technicians at the basic, advanced and supervisory levels. We have over 2600 ITIs with a seating capacity of 4 lakhs. But nearly one-fourth of the Vocational Training Institutions is not affiliated to the National Council for Vocational Training (NCVT). This is an indication of the fact that these non-affiliated institutions do not measure up to the vocational training standards prescribed by the Government of India. We offer vocational training for technicians in 63 trades. Some of these trades may need to be given up on account of their irrelevance to job market requirements. Training systems for other trades have to be modernised. In order to improve vocational training system in the country, we have been implementing a World Bank aided Project with an outlay of Rs. 451 crores for the Eighth Five Year Plan and with the participation of 28 States/UTs. But there have been slippages under the project in civil construction, equipment purchase and introduction of new courses. I would call upon all the Ministers in the Indian Labour Conference in charge of employment to intervene personally and give this vital scheme very high priority.

Resources have also been offered by the Government of India to the State Governments to undertake flexible training programmes, utilising the existing infrastructure of vocational training institutes. The training infrastructure of major Public Sector Enterprises can also be used for the purpose. These programmes would be particularly relevant for those who seek new job opportunities after having taken voluntary retirement from declining industries which are undergoing rationalisation. I would specially request the State authorities to make a success of these programmes.

Our employment exchanges, I should candidly say, require to be given a totally new orientation. They cannot fulfil any social purpose by merely being institutions for registering job seekers and advising their names for placements. They should become dynamic institutions in assessing job market requirements, providing counselling to job seekers according to their qualifications, experience and expectations and according to the needs of the employers. The employment exchanges should also facilitate guidance and counselling for self-employment according to the job market needs. All this would be feasible only by close interaction with the industry. I hope that this Conference would come out with meaningful recommendations in regard to this matter.

I shall now conclude, calling upon the various concerned Ministries of the Government of India, the State Governments, the employers and the working people represented in this Conference to resolve that they would, in co-ordination, eliminate inefficiencies in resource use; thereby achieve competitive economic growth; make training for skill development relevant to the world of work; and facilitate distribution of growth equitably by creating enhanced job opportunities.

Thank you and *Jai Hind.*

CONCLUDING STATEMENT OF LABOUR MINISTER (31st Session)

I want to conlude by saying that I had a very pleasant interaction with all State Labour Ministers, my trade union colleagues, the representatives of the employers and the officials of the State Governments and Central Government over the last two days. Though the agenda for the Conference was structured to cover amendments of I.D. Act exempting certain categories of services/employment from the purview of the I.D. Act, Social Security for unorganised sector, Restucturing the Vocational Training and Employment Exchanges and discussion on the participation of the workers in the Management Bill, 1990, deliberations were held on all aspects directly related to working class. Useful suggestions have been received in respect of the problems of sick industry, enhancing the scope of social security to unorganised sector, making the mechanism of tripartism more effective, elimination of child labour, restructuring of vocational training and employment exchanges etc. which will be examined and action will be taken to make them effective, wherever found feasible.

I have also agreed to have a Review Committee of ILC which will review the progress of implementation of the decision taken in the deliberations. Regarding the proposals to exempt certain categories of services/employments from the purview of the I.D. Act, a decision has been taken to postpone its consideration to the next SLC meeting and will be included as a part of the comprehensive amendment of the I.D. Act. Problems relating to the Beedi industry arising out of certain concessions granted to mini cigarettes have also been discussed. I propose to hold discussion with representatives of workers, employers and Governments on this subject at a later date.

On the issue of restructuring employment exchanges, certain suggestions have been made by representatives of employers, which I have agreed to discuss in the next SLC meeting with representatives of Trade Unions, State Governments and Employers.

APPENDIX II

SUMMARY RECORD OF THE DISCUSSIONS IN THE THIRTY FIRST SESSION OF THE INDIAN LABOUR CONFERENCE HELD IN NEW DELHI ON 3-4 JANUARY, 1995

The 31st Session of the Indian Labour Conference was held at Vigyan Bhawan, New Delhi on 3-4 January, 1995 under the Chairmanship of Shri P.A. Sangma, Minister of State for Labour. The composition of the Committee and the Conference was inaugurated by Dr. Manmohan Singh, Finance Minister. Smt. Krishna Sahi, Minister of State for Industry and Ms. Mira Seth, Member, Planning Commission also addressed the Conference on 3-1-95 and 4-1-95 respectively.

2. Based on the recommendations of the Standing Labour Committee made in its 32nd Session held in New Delhi on 27-10-94, the following items constituted the Agenda of the Conference :

(i) Confirmation of the Minutes of the 30th Session of Indian Labour Conference.

(ii) Action taken on the conclusions of the 30th Session of Indian Labour Conference.

(iii) Industrial Relations in the context of economic reforms (including rehabilitation of sick industries, social security and improvement in productivity).

(iv) Employment and vocational Training.

(v) Any other item with the permission of the Chair.

The Conference, with the permission of the Chairman, also discussed the Resolutions of the 32nd Session of the Standing Labour Committee.

3. The Conference selected the following three participants as Vice-Chairmen of the Conference :

(i)	Shri. Santi Ranjan Ghatak Minister-in-charge Labour Department, West Bengal	Representing State Governments
(ii)	Sh. G. Sanjeeva Reddy, President, Indian National Trade Union Congress	Representing Workers
(iii)	Shri A.S. Kasliwal, Council of Indian Employers	Representing Employers

4. Shri S. Gopalan, Labour Secretary, welcomed the distinguished guests and other delegates and thanked them for sparing time to participate in the Conference. While welcoming the Finance Minister, he stated that his advice on management of industrial relations in the present context of employment issues would form a proper guideline for meaningful deliberations. He also stated that the Minister of State for Industry had always given serious attention to the labour aspects of management of industries, particularly when matters of rehabilitation of Industry were being taken up for consideration. He further stated that the views which would be expressed by the delegates from the State Government and from the workers' and employers' organisations would be very valuable as they were well aware of the labour management issues at the grassroots level.

5. Shri P.A. Sangma, Chairman welcomed the Finance Minister, Dr. Manmohan Singh, Minister of State for Industrial Development, Mrs. Krishna Sahi, Labour Ministers of States and delegates from State Governments, workers' and employers' organisation and other participants and wished them a happy and prosperous new year. He described the Conference as a good occasion to review the situation arising out of the new industrial policy and economic reforms being implemented in the country. He thanked the employers' and workers' representatives for maintaining industrial harmony during the last three years. He observed that economic reforms had been more or less accepted by the country and these reforms would continue to be carried on. He referred to the problems of industrial sickness, increase in population growth and in the labour force, the decline in the rate of productivity in the country and generation of employment in the coming years. He pointed out that there were limits to protection demanded by both workers and industries and this might not go hand in hand with liberalisation, as liberalisation itself was meant to dismantle protection which bred inefficiency and ineffective use of resources. He brought to the notice of workers' representatives the stand taken by some of them and womens' organisations to opposing amendment to the Maternity Benefit Act restricting the applicability of benefits for only two children. He wanted a revision of this stand. He also requested the delegates to seriously discuss the problem of low productivity of workers and industries and to make suggestions for the upgradation of skill and training of the workers.

6. In his inaugural address to the Conference, the Finance Minister, Dr. Manmohan Singh thanked the Chairman for giving him an opportunity to address the Conference and hoped that the

Conference would assist in finding meaningful solutions to the formidable challenges that the country was facing. He emphasised the following points :

(i) The objective of all economic activities was to contribute to human happiness and it was only an integrated, contented and socially cohesive society that could help to realise cherished national objectives. The only way to eradicate poverty from the country was to ensure that the economy grew and expanded, and an environment was created in which the economy could grow faster. During the 1980s, there was a visible dent in poverty and the Indian economy was required to grow much faster in order to make more significant impact on poverty during the coming years. There could be no radical solution to the problems of social and economic management if the fiscal system was not well managed. If the country did not have a siutable macro economic system, if the country's balance of payments was not well managed and the fiscal system was not effectively managed, there would be retardation and social disorder.

(ii) The need of the day is to provide to the population, a decent quality of social services, health, education, roads, drinking water, irrigation etc. The present policy of the Government is neither anti-labour nor anti-poor. Government should take care of only those areas which it is best suited to handle. People should be empowered to help themselves. Government will take care of areas such as education, health, anti-poverty programme, rural development, irrigation, roads and drinking water and the like.

(iii) The Government would not neglect the public sector. They would encourage the public sector to grow wherever the public sector was viable and profitable. During the last three years, PSUs such as Coal India and the Steel Authority of India have improved their performance and they were now able to finance their large investments out of their own resources. Such enterprises would get full support and encouragement from the Government. There were enterprises which required capital restructuring. The Government would take a positive approach regarding this requirement in order to enhance their image and enable them to improve their productivity. In a number of cases, Government had written off a substantial part of capital that those enterprises owed to the Government in order to enable them to begin afresh and to move to a higher growth path. For sick units, Government would do everything which was in its power to rehabilitate them wherever rehabilitation was possible. In cases where the enterprises could not be revived, it was better to create fresh employment in areas where there was a demand for their products rather than supporting enterprises which had no potential for survival. In such cases the BIFR route had to be taken. Where closure became necessary, it would be ensured that the workers would not suffer. He felt that workers shall be encouraged to go in for retraining and redeployment, wherever a golden hands shake' was not acceptable to them. government had earmarked about Rs. 3000 crores during the last three years in the National Renewal Fund.

(iv) If inflation was not controlled, a rapid expansion of employment opportunities was not possible.

(v) Gainful employment could only come out of higher investment, taking full advantage of modern technologies so as to improve productivity and compete with others.

(vi) There was need to increase investment in the nation's education and health Sectors. The quality of training imparted by the training institutes needed to be upgraded every year. The educational system required to be changed so that equal opportunities could be provided for all. A great deal of investment was necessary in health care so that primary health care at affordable cost, became a reality in the country. Similarly huge investments were necessary in irrigation and in rural development etc.

(vii) Government needed to come out of those areas where facilities and infrastructure existed in the private sector to take care of the needs of business and industry.

viii) In the long run, collective bargaining on a bilateral basis had to become the principal instrument in the settlement of industrial disputes and industrial relations. It was a matter of pride that a free trade union movement was an integral part of India's democratic set up. The healthy growth of the trade union movement needed to be encouraged.

(ix) The industrial relation system in the country required major changes. Change in this area had been slow in coming and its absence tended to impede the growth of employment in the organised sector. The Conference needed to address itself to the task of appropriate changes in the system of industrial relations.

7. Smt. Krishna Sahi, Minister of State for industry stated that the new economic policy was in the interest of the workers, the industry and the country as a whole. She indicated that with the new economic policy, the country would certainly move on the path of progress. For this, she appealed for full support from the working class of the country. She assured the workers that the policy of the Government was to make the public sector enterprises self-reliant and consequently to enable them to protect the interests of the workers.

8. Ms. Mira Seth, Member, Labour and Employment, Planning Commission, in her address to the Conference, stated that the employment situation in the country had to be viewed in its proper historical perspective. She informed that during the Eighth Plan, there was a need to create employment opportunities for 58 million people and that could be achieved with a growth rate of 8 per cent per year and employment growth rate of 4 per cent per year. She stated that because of the country's resource situation, it would be possible to achieve a growth rate of 2.8 per cent per annum with a GDP growth rate of 5.6 per cent per year. It was, however, visualised that employment might grow slowly in the initial period and pick up later on. She also informed that during the first two years of the Eighth Plan, the growth rate has been 3.9 per cent per year and the employment growth rate had been about 2 per cent per year. She appealed to the State Governments and the Central Ministries to lay emphasis in their Annual Plans on employment generation and to make funds available to sectors which had high employment potential. The Planning Commission has been laying emphasis on greater social security measures and labour welfare measures in the unorganised sector. During the first two years of the Eighth Plan, additional funding for welfare purpose had been given to the Ministry of Textiles to look after the workers in the handloom and handicrafts sector. The Labour Ministry had also been requested to evaluate the functioning of Industrial Training Institutes.

The Conference noted the action taken on the conclusions of the 30th Session of the Indian Labour Conference. Some workers' representatives expressed concern over the delay in implementation of the conclusions of the last conference and desired that such delays should be avoided as these undermined the importance of the Indian Labour Conference.

9. The views and remarks of some State Governments were as follows:

A. RAJASTHAN

(i) The State Government had declared a new Industrial Policy thereby encouraging big industries to set up their units in the state, and seeking to remove all hurdles coming in the way of setting up big industries. Necessary steps had been taken to enhance productivity and to improve industrial relations in the States.

(ii) The Factories Act had been amended. About 5000 small factories had been excluded from inspection provisions.

(iii) The Central Government should provide resources to help the State Government to open labour courts in all districts of industrial importance.

B. WEST BENGAL

(i) The State Governments were not aware of the contents of the draft proposals for the amendments to the Industrial Disputes Act, 1947 and the Trade Unions Act, 1926.

(ii) The proposals for enhancement of eligibility ceiling for payment of Bonus from Rs. 2500 to Rs. 3500 and from Rs. 1600 to Rs. 2500 for computation of bonus might not be enough to satisfy the aspirations of the workers in general. The wage ceiling under the ESI Scheme needed to be increased from Rs. 3000 to Rs. 5000 p.m.

(iii) The National Renewal Fund had not been made available for State Public Sector Units and Private Sector. The NRF should also be utilised for retraining and redeployment of surplus labour and employment generation. A survey should be undertaken to find out the pattern of utilisation of compensation money received by the workers and their employment pattern after retirement.

(iv) The Central Government should take effective steps for liquidating PF and ESI arrears.

(v) The Central Government may bring the Minimum Wages Act under the 9th Schedule of the Constitution of India for its effective enforcement. The Central Government should consider providing funds for the purpose of recruitment of more Minimum Wage Inspectors and for their transport on duty.

(vi) the Central Government may formulate a comprehensive self-employment scheme for generation of employment.

C. ORISSA

(i) During the preceding four year period of 1990 to 94, there was a perceptible decline in the loss of mandays as compared to the last ten years. A judicious, just and proper management of all forces was essential for maintaining healthy industrial relations. It was the business of the Government machinery to be just and fair and maintain a balance in industrial relations.

(ii) Multiplicity of Trade Unions was certainly not in the interest of the working class. There should be only one union in one industry and, if possible, there should be one union for a group of industries.

(iii) Industrial unrest in the state had shown a downward trend after the introduction of economic reforms in the State.

(iv) The concept of the National Renewal Fund should be suitably expanded to meet the objective of rehabilitation of workers who face redundancy.

(v) The Orissa legislature has made legislative provisions to make non-payment of minimum wages a cognizable offense. An amendment to the provision of the Minimum Wages Act under which recovery of wages cannot be carried out without recourse to the judiciary with a complaint against the employers, needs to be considered.

(vi) The Government and Society at large are required to take adequate steps to give justice to unorganised labour and child labour.

D. HARYANA

(i) Small industries employing less number of workers should not be excluded from the provisions of labour laws.

(ii) A notification whereby the inspecting authorities are not to inspect small units and are to inspect the medium and big units only once in a year or on receipt of information of grave violation of labour laws or on receipt of a complaint from labour, had been issued by the State Government.

(iii) The new economic reforms introduced by the Central Government has had no effect on the labour relations in the State.

(iv) There is a large labour force in the unorganised sector in the

State. Huge resources are needed for extending the benefits of social security schemes to this class of workers.

(v) In big industries in the State, bipartite agreements between the trade unions and employers have helped in maintaining industrial relations and in the increase of productivity and in improvement of product quality in the State.

(vi) In the light of the new industrial Policy and the liberalised economic policy, the employment and training institutes need to pay much attention towards guiding the unemployed youth about self-financing schemes and other ways and means of employment.

E. ARUNACHAL PRADESH

The overall industrial relations in the State had been peaceful. The trade union movement in the state had just begun and a number of trade unions had been registered under the Trade Unions Act. The new industrial policy and the economic reforms introduced by the Central Government have had hardly any adverse impact on existing industries and the working class in the state.

R. PONDICHERRY

There had been no perceptible trend of workers getting thrown out of employment due to technological changes in the context of economic reforms launched by the Government of India. There was no incidence of bonded labour in the Union Territory. Child Labour practice was negligible in the State.

Views expressed by representatives of employers' organisations :

(i) The path of confrontation should be given up and united efforts to solve problems, which the country is facing, needed to be taken. Employer-employee relationships needed to be based on the concept of "Social partnership."

(ii) Adequate emphasis should be given to education in the country.

(iii) Care should be taken to ensure that populist measures do not impede economic growth.

(iv) Government needed to encourage Small Scale Sector by giving special preference to this sector in all matters including labour laws. The workers' trade unions should also cooperate in this sector.

Views expressed by the delegates representing workers' organisations :

(i) The National Renewal Fund had been mainly utilised for the voluntary retirement scheme. The Government had not taken action to institutionalise a system of training of redundant and idle workforce even in Government establishments.

(ii) The Government was taking negative attitude in BIFR sessions which pave the way for winding up of sick units.

(iii) The Government needed to come out with a clear-cut policy on financial support that sick PSUs would receive from Government and Public Sector Banks and Financial Institutions.

(iv) The private corporate sector had reaped profits taking full advantage of the de-regulated market-oriented economy, but it had not helped to generate employment.

(v) The Small Scale Sector had been hit hard by the New Economic Policy. Almost all protection including concessions on account of duty and tax had been withdrawn under the New Policy. The result had been that a large number of Small Scale Industrial units had gone sick/weak.

(vi) The voluntary Retirement Scheme had contributed to aggravation of unemployment problem. A vast majority of workers who had opted for voluntary retirement were having difficult times and their standard of living had gone down considerably.

(vii) The country was confronted with unemployment problem. Though the Government was giving a major thrust to self financing schemes for employment generation, that was not adequate to tackle the alarming rate of unemployment in the country.

(viii) With the introduction of the New Economic Policy, the problem of joblessness and unemployment had increased. The drive for privatisation, financial de-regulation and liberalisation of trade in the name of achieving higher growth, greater flexibility had not consistently delivered higher growth.

(ix) The question was not only to find jobs for the unemployed, but also to protect the jobs of lakhs of employees facing the prospect of loss of employment.

(x) The Government should consider setting up an Industrial

Workers Rehabilitation Fund to be funded by the Employers and Government. The employers' freedom to restructure the workforce should to be linked to their Social security obligations towards workers.

(xi) The role of Employment Exchanges should become that of employment and training promotion centres. For this, it was essential to link the Employment Exchanges with the Industrial Training Institutes and other vocational training centres. This would provide scope for improving the employability of the job seekers during the waiting period.

(xii) It had been agreed by the Government that the draft bills on the Trade Unions Act and the Industrial Relations would be discussed with the Trade Unions. This had not been done.

(xiii) Interest on the provident fund should be given at the rate of 13 per cent. Keeping in view the inflationary trends, the limit of exemption of income tax should be raised to at least Rs. 50,000 from the next year.

(xiv) The trade unions should be associated both at the National level and the State level in the Advisory boards for employment exchanges or the employment promotion centres and also with regard to vocational training at national and state levels. Training programmes had to be related to the job requirements of the industries.

The delegates desired that the resolutions of the 32nd Session of Standing Labour Committee should be placed before the Conference for discussion. Accordingly, with the permission of the Chairman, a copy of the resolutions of the Standing Labour Committee was circulated to all members of the Conference. The resolutions were discussed in detail. The Conference endorsed the resolutions adopted by the Standing Labour Committee and resolved that the Government and social partners should take further follow up action on these resolutions.

A Committee headed by Shri S. Gopalan, Labour Secretary drafted the resolutions of the Conference. The draft resolutions were discussed in detail by the delegates in the Conference and it was left to the Chairman to finalise the resolutions giving due consideration to the views expressed by the delegates in the Conference.

The conference ended with a vote of thanks to the Chair.

APPENDIX III

SUMMARY RECORD OF THE DISCUSSIONS IN THE 32ND SESSION OF THE INDIAN LABOUR CONFERENCE HELD IN NEW DELHI ON 23–24 NOVEMBER, 1995

The following were the items of the Agenda of the Conference.

1. Confirmation of the Minutes of the 31st Session of Indian Labour Conference.
2. Action taken on the conclusions of the 31st Session of Indian Labour Conference.
3. Proposal to exempt certain categories of services/employment from the purview of the I.D. Act—amendment of Section 2(j) of I.D. Act, 1947.
4. Social Security for Unorganised Labour.
5. Restructuring of Vocational Training.
6. Restructuring of Employment Exchanges.
7. Discussion on the Participation of Workers' in Management Bill, 1990.

Shri S. Gopalan, Secretary, Labour welcomed the Labour Minister, Shri G. Venkat Swamy, Minister of Rural Areas and Employment, Dr. Jagannath Mishra, Representatives of the employers' organisations, workers' organisations, State Governments, Union Territories and Central Ministries and Departments. He also, introduced Mr. William Brett, Vice Chairman of the ILO's Governing Body and the Chairman of the Workers' Group who was a distinguished guest to attend the Conference. Shri Gopalan also stated that the Ministry could not arrange a meeting of the Standing Labour Committee (SLC) prior to the ILC as the dates suggested for the SLC were not convenient to some constituents. He stated that this would not be taken as a precedent and every effort would be made to convene a meeting of the SLC before every Session of the ILC.

Secretary, Labour explained that a Bill to give legislative back up to the workers' Participation in Management Scheme was introduced in Parliament in 1990. Several Members of Parliament and others suggested amendments of the different Sections in the Bill. Many of the amendments suggested related to the scope and coverage of the Scheme as well as the procedure for participative arrangements. Since those were very extensive and the Ministry wanted to consider it in detail, the Bill was referred to the Standing Parliamentary Committee on Labour and Welfare for examination and report. The Committee asked for concrete suggestions from the Government and, as such, the Ministry of Labour proposed the item for discussion in the ILC with a view to having a detailed examination and obtaining a consensus. Similarly, Section 2(j) of the Industrial Disputes Act, 1947 was amended in 1982 defining 'industry' for the purpose of the ID Act and the revised definition excluded certain categories of establishments from the purview of the Act. The Ministry of Labour wanted to provide Alternative Grievance Redressal Mechanism for those excluded categories, However, attempts to provide Alternative Grievance Redressal Mechanism could not be achieved due to various reasons and the revised definition was, therefore, not notified. The Ministry had been approached by NDDB, Khadi & Village Industries, Employers' Organisations, etc. to notify the revised definition of 'industry' excluding certain categories of establishments. Hence the subject was included for discussion in the ILC. Social security for the unorganised labour was under consideration of the Ministry. Similarly, the need to restructure vocational training and the employment exchanges had also been felt. Therefore, those three items had also been included for discussion in the ILC.

Shri G. Venkat Swamy, Minister for Labour, in his inaugural address mentioned all the important developments that had taken place after the last Session of the ILC. The Fifth Conference of the Labour Ministers of Non-Aligned and Other Developing Countries was held in Delhi from 19-23rd January, 1995 and the Conference adopted the Delhi Declaration. The Declaration resolved to undertake programmes for horizontal co-operation in the various socio-economic spheres having implications for labour and employment, to seek guidance from ILO labour standards for taking action at the national level by such country as considered appropriate to its socio-economic conditions without any form of coercion, to eliminate child labour in a time-bound manner, giving immediate priority to elimination of child labour in hazardous employments. India had been entrusted the responsibility for co-ordination in the follow up action. He also stated that India's effective leadership in arguing against the mechanism and pitfalls associated with the "Social Clause" played a key role in cautioning other member countries of the ILO who gradually veered to agree with Inia's stand. He informed the ILC that the Government had recently taken two major decisions to benefit the working class— one, to provide for pension for provident fund subscribers and the other, to ensure protection and welfare for construction workers. In furtherance of the Government's objective to extend coverage and improve the benefits of social security it had been decided, inter alia, to enhance the minimum amount of compensation payable under the Workmen's Compensation Act, 1923. He stressed the importance of enhancing the level of competence of skilled workers and technicians and also the need to evolve appropriate training systems. He also felt that employment services should provide necessary data and feedback which could help in planning the training needs. The employment services, in addition to its placement functions, should also guide the job seekers on vocational programme. He also explained the circumstances for suggesting a discussion in the ILC on Section 2(j) of the ID Act. He stated that under the recently launched programmes to eliminate an estimated number of 2 million child labour engaged in the hazardous occupations, an estimated number 1.5 lakhs children had so far been enrolled in special schools where necessary amenities were made available to them apart from monthly stipends. He sought the co-operation of employers, workers, and State and Union Territory Administrations to make this programme a grand success. Referring to the recent mine accident in Dhanbad area, he informed the Conference that a Court of Inquiry had been set up to determine the causes and circumstances leading to the accidents with a view to prevent recurrence of such incidents in future. He thereafter invited the delegates to actively participate in the discussions and benefit the Conference by their suggestions and observations on various agenda items.

Later, the Conference observed one minute's silence in memory of the workers killed in the recent mine accidents.

Dr. Jagannath Mishra, Minister for Rural Areas and Employment stated that vocational training was an essential element in the process of non-formal education. In the larger context of national development, vocational training should receive utmost importance for employment generation, higher productivity and overall growth of the economy. He pointed out that in the area of rural development and anti-poverty programmes vocational training formed an integral part of self-employment programmes. He highlighted the necessity for training before a self-employment project could be taken up. Though facilities for vocational training had been made available by and large in most parts of the country, the quality of the training required to be improved. In fact, the standard of training institutions itself was required to be upgraded by properly equipping them, staffing them and by up-dating the syllabi to make it relevant to new technologies. He informed that the Ministry of Rural Areas and Employment was supporting the State Governments in strengthening the training infrastructure and opening mini-ITIs at Block levels. It would be desirable to go into the question of upgrading the quality of those institutions. He also felt that the faculties of most of the training institutions were unable to keep up with the technological changes because of lack of exposure. Therefore, training of trainers should also receive adequate attention. He suggested that the private sector should be involved in this effort and the State Governments should take the lead since training institutions came directly under their purview. He also stressed the importance of the application of science and technology for rural areas and the consequent need to restructure vocational training. He observed that despite India's large scientific, technical and manpower pool, the application of science and technology in rural areas could not be achieved. In this context, he referred to the commendable work done by voluntary organisations for dissemination of improved technologies with financial support from CAPART. He suggested that the effort should be expanded considerably and a strong network of training institutions should be developed throughtout the country.

Shri G. Sanjeeva Reddy, President INTUC (Workers' Group), Shri K.K. Kanoria, President AIOE (Employers' Group) and C. Gurunath, Labour Minister, Karnataka (States) were elected as Vice Chairmen of the Conference.

Shri Sanjeeva Reddy congratulated the Labour Minister for declaring government's intention not to have an 'Exit Policy.' He also thanked the Labour Minister and the Ministry for fulfilling the commitments made on issues like bonus, slab DA and pension. He thanked the Minister for agreeing to modify the pension scheme. He felt that the Government had not given adequate attention to creation of more jobs. Sickness in industry had been growing and unemployment was on increase. He stated that the functioning of the BIFR was far from satisfactory and there should be a labour Member in BIFR. The decisions of the BIFR had also not received sufficient attention for their implementation. He felt that no useful service except data collection was being done by the employment exchanges. He suggested that trade unions should be actively involved in implementing child labour abolition scheme and programmes. The proposal to modify Section 2(j) of the ID Act and to notify it without an Alternative Grievance Redressal Mechanism would not be in the interest of the workers and as such the proposal should be withdrawn. Since the manufacturing activities in many major units had shifted to small units, social security schemes for the unorganised sector should receive urgent attention. He also suggested that vocational training should be modernised by introducing new course and by providing better equipment. Though there was a need for some modification in the Workers' Participation in Management Bill, the scheme should be made applicable to public as well as private sector units. He also pleaded for measures to avoid strikes in banks and coal mines.

Shri A.B. Bardhan, AITUC drew the attention of the Conference to the threat of strikes in banks, jute industry, coal mines, etc. He asked the Labour Ministry to take adequate measures to avert strike in those sectors. He said that the enabling Bill providing for pension scheme should be allowed to be passed but the pension scheme should be revised after consulting trade unions. He also felt that the Construction Workers Bill in its present form would not be adequate to meet the aspirations of the workers and a revision of the legislation should be carried out after studying the laws adopted by the State Governments of Karnataka and Tamil Nadu. He emphasised that tripartism should be given due importance in dealing with the problems relating to labour. The decisions of the ILC should be implemented with all sincerity. Issues such as environmental matters and macro-economic policies had a direct bearing on labour and, therefore, the workers should be consulted on those issues as well. He suggested that the Finance Minister and other concerned Ministers should be invited to attend the ILC Sessions. He also asked the Conference to consider the various points raised in the written submission by the AITUC.

Shri I.P. Anand, Employers' representative, complimented the Government for its constructive approach to the problems of child labour and for launching the massive programme for elimination of child labour. The objective of labour participation should be to increase production and productivity and participation should initially be at the shop-floor level. He argued that increased productivity and competitiveness would generate employment and enhance wages. He suggested that ordinances should not be resorted to as a matter of routine and tripartism should be given its due importance in decision-making processes.

Shri A.S. Kasliwal stated that Employers had all along been demanding notification of Section 2(j) of ID Act as amended in 1982. They would not welcome any further amendment to Section 2(j). He referred to the decisions to raise the bonus ceiling to Rs. 3500 and stated that it should not have been done with retrospective effect. He also felt that workers' participation should be restricted to shop-floor level and the participants should be the employees of the units. However consultation would be a better option. Referring to the functioning of the BIFR, he suggested that a via media should be found between closure and payment of idle wages.

Shri Krishna Moorthy Hooda, Labour Minister, Haryana stated that the recently introduced pension scheme was a good step and the State Government would welcome it. He felt that workers' participation in management should be decided on the basis of secret ballot. He also supported social security for unorganised agricultural labour. He suggested that the Central Government should consider extending financial support to State Governments for programmes meant for abolition of child labour.

Shri U. Purohit, HMS stated that labour policy of the Government of India had been influenced by multinational companies and foreign countries. HMS was totally opposed to the notification of Section 2(j) of the ID Act. He felt that the goal of full employment by the year 2000 AD was not realistic unless attention was paid to agro-based industries. HMS was for the pension scheme, but the scheme should be based on a consensus arrived at through consultations with trade unions. A comprehensive national labour law would be required to protect the interests of the workers. The Bonus Act should be totally changed and there should be no ceiling for bonus. The functioning of the BIFR was far from satisfactory. The lukewarm approach of the Government to vocational training was evident in the budget allocation for the purpose. He suggested that a Tripartite Committee should be constituted to consider agricultural workers' problems. He was of the opinion that Government should ratify all ILO conventions. He condemned the callous attitude towards bonded labour. He felt that the existing workers' participation scheme put the entire responsibility for productivity on labour alone. He suggested that the Child Labour Advisory Board should meet regularly.

Shri Sabir Shaikh, Minister for Labour, Maharashtra, welcomed the workers' participation in management scheme and suggested that workers should participate in trade also. Considering the size of the workers in the unorganised sectors, highest priority should be accorded to protect their rights and to ensure social security for them. He suggested for construction of hospitals for beedi workers. He was of the opinion that Section 2(j) of the ID Act should not be notified without Alternative Grievance Redressal Mechanism. He also wanted uniform rate of minimum wages to be made applicable all over the country.

Shri S. Malhotra, Director, JK Corporation suggested that economic realities of the country should be kept in mind while formulating labour policies. Indian industry should try to improve productivity and competitiveness in order to compete with multinational companies and foreign companies in the context of the ongoing economic reforms. Many countries in Asia had become India's competitors and in those countries the labour cost continued to be less. Threat of strike should be avoided and the workers should try to fulfil their obligation also. He welcomed the pension scheme and suggested that its implementation should be improved and perfected.

Shri Shanti Patel (HMS) stated that economic liberalization had caused closure of units, retrenchment and unemployment. He wanted transparency in the implementation of workers' participation in management scheme and also suggested that workers should be represented even at the level of Board of Directors. He felt that the public sector units had no functional autonomy to negotiate with the workers and settle matters. He stressed the need for a comprehensive industrial relations law. He was of opinion that the National Renewal Fund could not achieve anything except voluntary retirement in public sector units. The working of Industrial Tribunals had been affected by large scale vacancies. He wanted the government to consider the memorandum of HMS circulated in the meeting. The Bonus law should be amended and no ceiling should be fixed.

Shri Prabir Chakravorty, employers' delegate suggested for revival of the sick industrial units. He stressed that tripartism should be given its due importance and ordinances should not be resorted to as a matter of routine.

Dr. M.K. Pandhe (CITU) stated that many important decisions affecting the working class had been taken without consulting the trade unions. He wanted the Government to ratify the ILO convention No. 127 concerning Maximum Permissible weight to be carried by one person. He pointed out that the decisions of the special Tripartite Committee had not been implemented and the meetings of the committee had not been convened regularly. He suggested that some space should be provided in the Labour Ministry to enable the workers' organisations to consult among themselves. He felt that the programme to abolish child labour in hazardous industries by 2000 AD would be difficult unless the programmes could be formulated, implemented and monitored properly involving the trade unions. He suggested that minimum wages should be raised as a measure to reduce child labour. He was also in favour of abolishing the bonus ceiling as it would deny bonus to the majority of workers. He suggested that a meeting of trade unions and the Bureau of Public Enterprises should be called to discuss the DA formula. He was also of the view that functioning of the BIFR had not helped revival of the sick units. In his opinion the goal of full employment by 2000 AD would be far from achievable. He said that the CITU wanted the pension scheme for workers but they would not accept the scheme in the present form. It should be made voluntary. He stated that workers should not be denied their basic rights in the name of setting up Export Promotion Zones. He pleaded that Government should take measures to avoid strikes in the banking, insurance, jute and mining sectors. He wanted the Government to take measures immediately to implement the NTC agreement.

Shri N.M. Barot, NLO said that the BIFR had not achieved its objective and it had been issuing only winding up orders. He suggested that the public distribution system should be made available for the benefit of the workers. He wanted to explore the possibility of monthly deduction towards bonus. He welcomed the pension scheme and felt that constructive suggestions should be considered for revision. Corruption in provident fund offices should be looked into. Many units had defaulted in payment of gratuity. He suggested convening a special conference to discuss the industrial sickness. He felt that the amount under the NRF had not been properly accounted for. He suggested that unemployment insurance should be considered as a social security for all types of unemployment. ITIs should be strengthened with modern equipments and infrastructure and by adopting new tools and technologies. He also suggested the government to consider introduction of a minimum wage applicable all over the country.

Shri S.R. Sengupta (UTUC) felt that the public distribution system should be strengthened. He suggested that an implementation committee should be set up to monitor the decisions taken by the ILO. He was of the opinion that the child labour issue should be considered and examined in the context of the socio-economic conditions obtaining in the country. He expresed the view that the proposal to notify Section 2(j) was the violation of ILO standards. He said that the managements of many units including the NTC had been flouting the agreements.

Shri C. Gurunath, Minister for Labour, Karnataka suggested that the path followed by Kerala and West Bengal should be adopted in addressing the various labour issues. He suggested that ITIs should be strengthened by introducing new trades and by providing better infrastructure. The possibility of obtaining assistance from foreign countries to improve the quality of vocational training should also be explored. He felt that involvement of District Collectors directly with the implementation of child labour elimination programmes would not be effective unless they could get proper guidance at state level and from the workers' organisations.

Shri A.S. Sinha, UTUC (LS) stated that one would like to welcome the pension scheme but it should be funded entirely by the Government and the employer. He did not find any benefit for workers in the Workers Participation Schemes, as the means of production would not be control of workers. His apprehension was, that if the present proposal to amend the I.D. Act excluding certain categories of establishment was accepted, the excluded categories would be enlarged in future. He said that a comprehensive legislation on agricultural workers was promised long ago but it could not be fulfilled by the Government so far. He sought the Government intervention to avoid the proposed jute mill strike.

Shri C.M. Krishna, Employers' representative, stated that none of the suggestions of the employers were included in the Workers' Participation in Management, Bill, 1990. He was of the opinion that involvement would not come by legislation since Indian Industry was facing competition from multi-national and foreign companies. Government should trust Indian Industry and should have faith in bipartism. He suggested that Section 2 (j) of the I.D. Act as amended in 1982 should be notified immediately.

Shri R.S. Mardolkar, Labour Commissioner, Goa felt that the Child Labour Abolition and Prohibition Act and Bonded Labour System. Abolition Act should be studied and the loopholes in the legislations should be removed. A schedule should be attached to the Child Labour Prohibition and Abolition Act prohibiting employment of children listed in the scheduled industries. He also wanted amendment in the Factories Act to make flexible arrangement for their working hours. He felt that NCVT should be asked to make suggestions for restructuring vocational training in the country. The views of the Directors of Employment Exchanges on reorganising the Employment Exchange should be considered before the matter is placed before the ILC.

Shri Gurdev Singh, Labour Secretary, Rajasthan suggested that the need for a suitable legislation for the purpose of recognition of trade unions. He also said that multiplicity of trade unions had led to industrial unrest in many sectors. Since the unorganised sector absorbed 92 per cent of the work-force, social security for them was necessary.

Shri D.D. Shastri, TUCC, stated that tripartism should be encouraged at the state level also and expressed concern that the recommendation to this effect made in the last meeting of the ILC had not been responded to by the State representatives. Sickness in industry should have been on the agenda for this Conference as it had resulted in retrenchment and unemployment. He was opposed to the notification of Section 2(j). He suggested that trade Union should be involved in the programme for elimination of child labour. The abolition of child labour should be linked with abolition of poverty. He also suggested that the BIFR should be reorganised through inclusion of workers' representatives. He also felt the need for restructuring the Employment Exchanges.

Shri Sen, CII said that training should receive utmost priority for skill development and skill upgradation. Training was also an important input for a higher productivity. He suggested the adoption of the German practice of dual training "initial training," followed by "shop floor training."

Shri Subrato Mukherjee, Vice President, INTUC, welcomed the Pension Scheme as it would benefit the workers in the long run. He suggested that the share of profit of workers should be protected by law. He requested the Central Government and the State Governments to pay special attention to protect the jute industry. The huge arrears on account of Provident Fund, Gratuity and ESIC should be realised from the employers.

Shri A. Gandhiraj, Labour Minister, Pondicherry stated that an alternative mechanism for redressal of grievance of excluded categories of workers should be created before notifying the definition of industry under the I.D. Act. He suggested that the vocational training system which was restricted to conventional trades only, should be modernised. He sought for directives from the Central Government for preparing separate registers of SC/ST candidates in the Employment Exchanges in view of the recent decision of the Supreme Court that SC/ST benefits should not be admissible to migrant workers. He suggested that the Central Government should bring a legislation to identify the negotiating agent in view of the multiplicity of trade unions in an industry. He welcomed the Pension Scheme as it would provide security of jobs and reduce rush to government jobs. He suggested that the law should be changed to permit women to work after 10 P.M.

Shrimati Rukmani Haldia, Joint Secretary, Ministry of Textile, informed that the Cabinet had approved the proposal to sell the surplus land available with the sick NTC mills and the funds of the order of Rs. 2000 crores so generated would be utilised for the modernisation of the mills. Clearance of the BIFR had been sought for the proposal.

Labour Commissioner, Tamil Nadu, stated that for the Welfare Fund for Building Workers should be collected at source and should be first adjusted in the states itself instead of going to the Consolidated Fund of India. He expressed grave concern that the mini cigarette had captured over 20 per cent of the Beedi market and had severely affected the Beedi workers. He suggested that the Central Government should prepare Audio visual films on vocational training and make them available to the states. He also suggested for computerisation of the employment exchanges.

The Principal Labour Secretary, West Bengal stated that the State Government felt the need to appoint a Committee to monitor the implementation of the decision of the Indian Labour Conference. He stated that the Jute Corporation of India should be activated to solve the problems of Jute Industry. On inquiry from the Chairman, he informed that meetings with Jute workers were being held at the state level to prevent the strike situation.

The Workers' representatives suggested that there should be a Committee to monitor the implementation of the decisions of Indian Labour Conference. In this regard it was also suggested that the Standing Labour Committee should meet more frequently as it would monitor the action taken on the decisions of the tripartite meetings. They also felt that the practice of holding tripartite discussion on labour matters at the state level should be revived as was decided in the 31st Session of the Indian Labour Conference. After discussions, the Chairman agreed to form a Tripartite Review Committee for monitoring the implementation of the decisions of the Indian Labour Conference.

Item 3 : Proposal to exempt certain categories of services/employment from the purview of the I.D. Act—amendment of Section 2 (j) of I.D. Act, 1947.

The Workers' representatives were against the proposal to grant exemption to any categories of services/employments from the purview of the I.D. Act. They felt that it would go against the spirit of ILO conventions.

The employers' representatives stressed the need to notify the revised definition of 'industry' under the I.D. Act passed by the Parliament since long ago. It was however decided to postpone that item and to place before the next SLC meeting alongwith it the proposed amendments to the I.D. Act.

Item 4 : Social Security for Unorganised Labour.

Shri Barot stressed the need for social security measures covering accidents and death etc. before bringing up legislation for agricultural workers.

Shri Ganguly stated that the Government should provide social securities to all sections of unorganised sector workers like beedi, handlooms, powerlooms, brick-kilns and home workers etc. He felt that steps such as land reforms, need-based wages, compulsory education to children, abolition of contract labour and unemployment benefits should be given greater attention. He informed that in one district of Kerala, 40,000 beedi workers had been organised and they were running a factory on a cooperative basis. He suggested that this should be taken as a model to organise the unorganised workers in other parts of the country.

Shri Purohit congratulated the Government for bringing legislation for building and construction workers and the elimination of sweepers from all over India. He stated that benefits of the Pension Scheme, Provident Fund, ESIC etc. should be extended to all unorganised workers.

Shri Kashyap suggested for exploring the possibilities for raising funds for extending social security benefits to unorganised workers.

Item 5 : Restructuring of Employment Exchanges.

The CITU representative pointed out that most of the workshops of ITIs were not functioning due to inadequate supply and maintenance of equipments. He suggested that new training technology and new skills should be introduced. Skill development of women should also receive importance. Training of trainers should be done on a continuous basis. He also supported suggestion for factory level training.

Shri Barot suggested to have a fresh look at the vocational training programme. He felt that employers, workers and governments should give adequate importance to vocational training to enhance the employability of the workforce.

Shri B.D. Joshi, AITUC, also supported the suggestion to restructure the vocational training programme and suggested that vocational training should be linked to employment.

Shri I.P. Anand stated that the vocational training programme should be further streamlined and felt that the setting up a council would not serve any purpose.

The Labour Minister later agreed to place the subject of restructuring vocational training as an agenda for the next meeting of the Standing Labour Committee.

Item 6 : Workers Participation in Management Bill, 1990.

Shri B.D. Joshi, AITUC, suggested that the Workers' Participation in Management Bill, 1990 should be adopted quickly. He said that the proposed scheme should be a participative scheme and it should not be converted into a mere consultative machinery.

A Committee headed by Shri S. Gopalan, Labour Secretary, drafted the conclusions of the Indian Labour Conference and placed them before the Conference for consideration. The conclusions were approved by the Conference except some reservations from CITU, TUCC and UTUC (LC) about the Pension Scheme.

In his concluding remarks, the Labour Minister stated that though the agenda of the Conference was structured to cover specific items, deliberations were held on all aspects directly related to labour. He further acknowledged the valuable made in the Conference suggestions in respect of the sick industries, social security for unorganised labour, tripartism, child labour, vocational training and employment exchanges etc. He agreed to the proposal for a Review Committee of ILC for reviewing the progress of implementation of the decisions taken in the Conference.

The Conference ended with vote of thanks to the Chair.

APPENDIX IV

*SPEECH OF UNION MINISTER OF LABOUR **SHRI M. ARUNACHALAM,** (Union Minister of State for Labour, 33rd SESSION OF THE INDIAN LABOUR CONFERENCE, NEW DELHI, OCTOBER 24-25, 1996*

Distinguished members of the Indian Labour Conference, Secretary, Labour, Labour Ministers from the States, senior officials of the Ministries/Departments of Government of India and the State Governments, other participants, ladies and gentlemen.

It gives me immense pleasure to welcome all of you to this 33rd session of the Indian Labour Conference, the highest tripartite consultative machinery available in the Ministry of Labour. We are in the midst of a festive season and I extend to all of you my warm and cordial greetings on this happy occasion.

We had received letters of request from few distinguished members for changing the schedule of the meeting as it clashed with the festive season. We have also received letters of request from some members suggesting change of items in the agenda and inclusion of new items which were not listed earlier. I would like to avail of this opportunity to clarify that while personally I have the highest regard for suggestions emanating from members who have distinguished themselves in the field of labour for many years, we were handicapped in changing either the schedule of the meeting or the items in the agenda which are fixed sufficiently in advance. I would, therefore, crave the indulgence of those members who had made such requests to kindly bear with us and to cooperate fully for smoothly transacting the business of the meeting even though attending the meeting for them in the midst of a festive season might have caused some amount of inconvenience and dislocation.

As you are aware, the dates of both the ILC and SLC are fixed in the previous meetings and these are time bound operations. Prior to this meeting of the ILC we had a meeting of the Standing Labour Committee on 13-9-96 and the outcome thereof has already been indicated in the notes circulated for this meeting. As you are further aware, a tripartite review committee was set up on 4-5-95 on the recommendations of the SLC. I am happy to share with you that this body has already met thrice this year on 23-2-96, 13-7-96 and 16-8-96. The working of this Committee will prove to be of immense value in implementing the dicisions taken by the ILC.

The ILC being the apex tripartite consultative machinery is expected to give broad directions in the matter of formulation of labour policy and programmes. As the Labour Secretary has already mentioned in his welcome address over the years the ILC has set the pace and tone of many such important policies and programmes which are of interest and relevance to labour. The change of Government in the Centre took place in June, 1996 and with change of Government there have been certain changes in the labour policies and programmes outlined in the Common Minimum Programme launched in middle of June, 1996. The Common Minimum Programme had attempted to strike a balance between a high rate of economic growth through maintaining a high level of production and productivity in the interest of generating larger and wider avenues of employment to meet the acute unemployment situation on the one hand and protecting and safeguarding the irreducible barest minimum needs and interests of the working class and in particular the workers in the unorganized sector. The areas of priority emphasized in the Common Minimum Programme which are of interest and relevance to labour are :

(i) Eradication of child labour in all occupations and industries.
(ii) A comprehensive law guaranteeing minimum wages, fair conditions of work, group insurance etc. for agricultural workers.
(iii) A new law to deal with industrial sickness and revamping of the BIFR.
(iv) Better enforcement of labour laws.
(v) Recognition of trade unions through secret ballot.
(vi) Participation of workers in the management of public sector enterprises.
(vii) Imparting technical and vocational skill to encourage self-employment.
(viii) Retraining and redeployment of employees of public sector enterprises.

I need hardly emphasise that we in the Ministry of Labour are fully committed to the ethos, culture and philosophy of tripartism. No major policy decisions in this Ministry have ever been taken without taking the three social partners (including the State Governments) into confidence and without obtaining a workable consensus on various issues. As recommended by the last session of the Indian

Labour Conference, we have been impressing on the State Governments to revive the practice of holding tripartite consultations at the State level also. I had personally taken up this matter with the State Government and I am happy to share with you that as a result of these efforts the tripartite consultative machinery has been revived in 15 States. The response from others is awaited. I urge the representatives of Governments of these States who are present in the Conference to take immediate steps for revival of such bodies. This will be engaging my close personal attention and intervention.

In the wake of the dicisions taken in the meetings of the Special Tripartite Committee and Tripartite Review Committee on measures to remove industrial sickness and restructuring of BIFR, Secretary, Labour has met the Chairman, BIFR twice to share with him the anxiety and concern of the Honourable members represented in these committees and to pay due attention to protect and safeguard the workers' statutory dues while going in for implementation of revival packages or even liquidation proceedings although the latter is always avoidable. He has also poverty, addressed demi officially Secretaries of about 15 departments like Chemicals, Fertilizers, Civil Aviation, Civil Supplies, Coal, Telecommunications, Food, Mines, Petroleum and Natural Gas, Power etc. to share with them the anxiety and concern expressed by the members on the plight and predicament of rationalised, displaced and retrenched workers, prompt settlement of statutory dues and redressal of their genuine grievances. Such actions have already evoked some positive response from Secretaries of several Ministries/Departments. While industrial sickness is an endemic problem with many CPSUs and revival of sick CPSUs is the principal mandate of BIFR, industrial sickness can be pre-empted by close and constant monitoring and surveillance on the part of all concerned. Since workers' interests are closely intertwined, I would like to assure all members of this August body that we in the Ministry of Labour will spare no stones unturned to prevent sickness and to ensure revival of sick industrial undertakings where sickness is inevitable through a coordinated approach and through dialogue and discussion. I am also happy to share with you that Secretary, Labour along with others had extensive discussion with Secretary, Department of Banking in regard to removal of industrial sickness and creation of a more vibrant structure as alternative to BIFR which will be alive to the needs of workers and their genuine interests.

The workers engaged in construction industry had remained neglected for long. These workers have now been covered under a comprehensive law giving them legal protection which covers areas of service conditions, occupational safety and health and welfare. The Act also provides for setting up a Welfare Fund by levying and collecting cess on the cost of construction incurred by the employers. This Fund will be used exclusively for the welfare of the workers engaged in the construction industry numbering about 9 million.

Child labour is a social evil and cause for serious concern for all of us and embarrassment of the country. The Common Minimum Programme of the present Government clearly states our objective of total elimination of child labour from all occupations. The programme for identification and elimination of child labour from hazardous employment has already been launched in some selected areas of the country. The need is to enlarge the coverage of this programme and speed up the pace of its implementation.

It should be simultaneously borne in mind that children go to work and not to school on account of social, economic and cultural compulsions. Elimination of Child labour will be possible only if children can be withdrawn from work and can be put to special schools where in addition to learning and acquiring the basic and minimum levels of learning functional literacy, they can also acquire other skills such as communication skill, vocational skills, managerial and entrepreneurial skills so that they can become productive members of the society after crossing the threshold of childhood.

Since parental poverty, parental illiteracy and parental unemployment are at the root of existence of the child labour problem it will be possible to effectively deal with the problem of elimination of child labour only by a composite and multi pronged approach and strategy which takes congnisance of eradication of parental poverty, parental illiteracy and parental unemployment.

Simultaneously, there are lot of fads, taboos and obscurantist ideas in the minds of poor and illiterate parents about the need for importance of sending their children to school which also need to be removed.

Finally none of this will work until and unless we have created a learning society which values and prizes literacy, unless we have created a congenial and functional environment in the schools which facilitates enrolment, retention, participation and acquisition of learning. Without all these we will not be able to generate confidence in the minds of the parents about the relative value and importance of education which is so sadly wanting today. Evidently this task cannot be attended to by Government alone. This will have to be supplemented in a big way by the NGOs who have the urge, inclination and the commitment to provide need based an relevant education in an unorthodox and unconventional manner to create the desired impact.

I am happy to inform you that India has recently ratified ILO Convention 147 concerning minimum standards in merchantships. The Convention brings together several other ILO instruments and calls for a commitment to the implementation of basic standards of merchant shipping. With this, the number of Conventions ratified by India will be 37 and India will be 34th country to ratify this convention.

I attach special importance to this meeting today. Our Government is committed in no uncertain terms to uphold the interest of and cause of poor and deprived in general and of workers in particular. This acquires special significance in the context of the uncertainties and apprehensions arising out of the changes triggered of by the economic reforms and globalisation. I would like to urge the participants to take up for consideration the agenda items and to hope that the Conference will take final decisions on the items some of which have been on the agenda for a long time. With these words I hereby declare the 33rd session of the Indian Labour Conference open and invite to take up for consideration the agenda items.

APPENDIX V

SUMMARY RECORD OF THE DISCUSSIONS, THIRTY-THIRD SESSION OF THE INDIAN LABOUR CONFERENCE HELD IN NEW DELHI ON 24-25 JANUARY 1996

The 33rd Session of the Indian Labour Conference was held at Parliament House Annexe on 24th and 25th October, 1996 New Delhi under the Chairmanship of Shri M. Arunachalam, Union Minister of Labour. The composition of the Conference and the list of persons who attended the session are given in Annexure-I and Annexure-II respectively.

2. The following items constituted the Agenda for the 33rd Session of the Indian Labour Conference :

(1) Confirmation of the Minutes of the 32nd Session of Indian Labour Conference
(2) Action taken on the Conclusions of the 32nd Session of Indian Labour Conference held on 23-24 November, 1995
(3) Modernisation and re-organisation of Employment Exchanges
(4) Modernisation of Vocational Training System
(5) Floor level minimum wages for unorganised employment
(6) Recognition of trade unions through secret ballot
(7) Amendment to the I.D. Act, 1947 including notification of Section 2 (j) of the I.D. Act
(8) The Bill of Workers Participation in Management

3. Dr. L. Mishra, Labour Secretary, welcomed the participants of the Indian Labour Conference. He mentioned the role played by the Indian Labour Conference in assisting the Ministry of Labour in setting the pace and tone of labour policy in all important areas; in helping to bring legislative enactments and their implementation for the protection and welfare of workers; and in contributing to adoption of large number of international labour standards by way of ILO Conventions and Recommendations. He hoped that Indian Labour Conference would continue to be a torchbearer of the highest traditions and standards of tripartism in the field of

formulation of labour policy and programmes in future also.

4. Shri M. Arunachalam, Labour Minister also extended his greetings to all the participants of the Indian Labour Conference. The salient points made by him in his inaugural address were as under :

   (1) It was not possible to change the schedule of the meeting and to make changes in the agenda items as requested by some members as the schedule of the meeting and items in the agenda were fixed sufficiently in advance.

   (2) A tripartite review committee was set up on 4-12-1995 to review the implementation of the recommendations of the Indian Labour Conference. This committee had met on 23-2-1996, 30-7-1996 and 16-8-1996.

   (3) The Common Minimum Programme of United Front refers to a number of points concerning labour and it will be this Ministry's endeavour to fulfil these commitments to the cause of the working people.

   (4) The Ministry of Labour has been impressing upon the State Governments to revive the practice of holding tripartite consultations at the state level. As a result of these efforts, tripartite consultation has been revived in several states.

   (5) Elimination of child labour would be achieved by associating all persons and organisations having the sensitivity to the issue of the commitment to fight this practical.

   (6) India is continuously endeavouring to upgrade labour standards and has recently ratified ILO Convention 147 concerning minimum standards in merchant ships.

5. The following three participants were elected as Vice-Chairpersons of the 33rd Session :

(i) Shri Shanti Ghatak, Labour Minister, Government of West Bengal	:	Representing State Governments
(ii) Shri G. Sanjeeva Reddy President, INTUC	:	Representing Trade Unions
(iii) Shri Gopalkrisha CIF	:	Representing Employers

General Discussion

6. Trade Union representatives stated that they were not consulted in the matter of deciding the Agenda of the Conference. Though the listed items for discussion were important, there were many urgent problems of workers and those issues should also have been included in the Agenda for discussion. The conclusions of the 32nd Sessions of the Indian Labour Conference have not been implemented fully and the concerned Ministries/departments have not given due importance to the Conference as well as its conclusions. They also expressed disappointment that Union Ministers In-charge of various employing ministries as well as Finance and Planning Ministers are not attending the Conference.
7. Representatives of some of the Trade Unions were of the View that the new economic policies of the government have failed to solve the problems of the working class. These policies have led to decline in employment opportunities. More and more production and manufacturing activities have shifted from the organised sector to the unorganised sector through contract labour. Prices of essential commodities have also been rising simultaneously only to worsen the conditions of workers. The present economic policies have benefited the rich alone, while the workers have been left to bear the burden. Therefore social partners in the Conference should reject the wrong economic policies and accept the swadeshi model of economy.
8. Some workers' representatives were of the views that BIFR should be suitably restructured. They also suggested that workers representatives should be included by reconstituting the BIFR, and it should facilitate revival of sick units rather than becoming an instrument for closure of industries.
9. Trade Union representatives felt that government should look into the root cause of sickness in industries. There should be a policy under which sickness could be arrested right in the beginning itself. The real sufferers of sickness in industries were workers and the financial institutions which have given loans. Responsibility should be fixed on those persons who were responsible for mismanagement, misplanning, transfer of money and other malpractices leading to sickness in industry. It should be ensured that sickness was not induced

deliberately to facilitate privatisation. Financial assistance should be made available from National Renewal Fund for the rehabilitation of sick units. The issue of sale of surplus land available with sick NTC mills has not been solved in Maharashtra because of difference of views between the Central Government and the State Government. This problem needs to be looked into.

10. It was also stated by workers' representatives that ceiling limit for the eligibility for bonus has been enhanced in case of workers in Ports and Docks and Railways this should be done for all categories of workers. They also suggested that there should be no disparity between Government. Employees and workers employed in industry etc. for the payment of gratuity. The ceiling of gratuity should be enhanced from Rs. 1 lakh to Rs. 2.5 lakhs for individual workers also. The Trade Union representatives' pointed out that different wage ceilings existed for various benefits under different labour laws. Ministry of Labour should, therefore, prepare a paper on wage ceiling with a view to removing the existing disparity.
11. Trade Union representatives stated that 681 industries in Delhi would be closed on environmental grounds as a result of the judgment of the Supreme Court. Thousands of workers employed in these industries would face difficulties. Government should look into this problem. They also pointed out that commercialisation has been taking place in social sectors like education and health etc. Therefore, the workers employed in these areas should not be allowed to be taken out of the purview of the I.D. Act.
12. It was further, suggested that Minimum wages should be reviewed and revised periodically and automatic indexations should be allowed. A declaration should be made by the Government that no existing facility under the ESI would be curtailed to any employee who was already getting that facility.
13. The employer representatives states that the current policies of the Government have helped to achieve growth rate of 12 per cent in industrial production and 7 per cent in G.D.P. Lockouts were not a result of unilateral action taken by the employers. Managements were compelled to lockout because of labour agitation like go slow to work, obstructions to

delivery of finished goods or violence etc.

14. The representative of CIE stated that in the light of international competition and globalisation of economy both the social partners should work together. The existing rigidity in attitudes would not serve any purpose in the present day world. Unrealistic demands, would give rise to more sickness, more unemployment and more poverty. The management should be given the right to manage. The trade unions should be depoliticised in the best interest of the country.
15. Employers representatives pointed out that Social Clause would be used by some countries to introduce non-tariff barrier and thus to cripple the economy of the developing countries and as such all social partners should oppose it. It was, therefore, suggested that Indian delegation to the Ministerial Conference of WTO in December, 1996 in Singapore should be a tripartite delegation.
16. Labour Minister, Goa stated that the Central Government has already adopted policies and programmes for economic liberalisation, structural adjustment, trade liberalisation etc. Keeping in view of all these developments, there is a need to have a new labour policy. Therefore, Government should have a fresh look at all the old industrial laws existing in the country and suitable amendments/modifications in these laws should be carried out, wherever necessary.
17. Minister of Labour, West Bengal stated that the State Government has passed several amendments to laws like the Payment of Gratuity Act and the Payment of Wages Act. The Presidential assent to those enactment are, however, still pending.
18. Labour Minister, Maharashtra stated that the Contract Labour (Regulation and Abolition) Act, 1970 should be amended to facilitate absorption of contract labour. A provision should be made to the effect that even if the contract is terminated or came to an end, the contract workers should be given employment by the contractor.
19. Some of the observations/suggestions made by the members in the General discussion relating to the specific items of the agenda of the Conference have been incorporated in the succeeding paragraphs under the specific items.

Item No. 1 : Confirmation of the minutes of the 32nd Session of the Indian Labour Conference.

20. The minutes were confirmed.

Item No. 2 : Action taken on the conclusions of the 32nd Session of Indian Labour Conference.

21. Action Taken Report on conclusions of the 32nd Session of the Indian Labour Conference was placed before the Conference for discussion. Action Taken Report on some pending conclusions of the 31st Session held on 3-4 January, 1995 was also placed before the Conference for consideration. The Conference noted the action taken as mentioned in the Action Taken Report. A summary of important observations/suggestions made in the Conference is given below :

22. The response received from various State Governments on the conclusions of the ILC to revive the practice of holding tripartite consultations at the state level was noted. It was also observed that the machinery set up by some State Governments was not truly tripartite in characters and their meetings were not being convened on a regular basis. The workers' representatives requested the Labour Minister to write again to the State Governments requesting them to revive the practice of holding tripartite consultations at the state level, by constituting truly and appropriately representative tripartite Bodies and by holding their meetings on a regular basis.

23. The workers' representatives pointed out that there were violation of labour laws in some Export Processing Zones in the country. The Chief Labour Commissioner (Central) informed that the concerned Regional Labour Commissioners (Central) had been instructed to take with them representatives of trade unions the time of inspection, and similar instructions had been conveyed to the State Labour Commissioners. An employer representative stated that permitting a union leader to accompany the Government inspecting authority would be bad in principle.

24. Concern was expressed over the posts of Presiding Officers of CGIT-cum-Labour Courts, lying vacant for long and the resultant delay in disposal of cases in the CGITs. Secretary (L) informed that the terms and conditions of appointment offered to the Presiding Officers had not been very attractive and the issue of salaries and other entitlements of Presiding Officers of CGITs had been taken up with the Fifth Pay

Commission and the issue of tendency in Labour Courts was being monitored at various levels.

25. The workers' representatives unanimously requested the Government to remove the ceiling limit for the eligibility of bonus. They expressed the view that the removal of ceiling limit for the eligibility of bonus would have no financial implications on the part of employers and, therefore, there should be no hurdle in removing the ceiling limit. Representative of CIE stated that the issue of bonus should not be tampered with piece-meals and the whole issue of reviewing the Bonus Act should be examined de novo.

26. The workers' representatives stated that the revised DA formula had not been implemented in some of the Public Sector Undertakings. The representative of SCOPE clarified the difficulties in implementing the revised DA formula. He said that there were different interpretations in different industries. The workers' representatives also raised the issue of non-payment of DA in sick units. Trade Unions representatives wanted the Labour Ministry to convene a meeting of representatives of the concerned Ministries including Ministries of Finance and Industry, Deptt. of Public Enterprises and the Central trade unions to discuss the issue of DA and the issue of functional autonomy to be given to the public sector enterprises.

27. The Chairman clarified that all recommendations made in the last conference, on matters relating to Economic Reforms, industrial restructuring and social dimensions were referred to the concerned Ministries for necessary action. The representative of the Department of Industrial Development informed the Conference that three studies on industrial sickness in India were conducted in the past and their reports were circulated amongst the concerned organisations. The workers' representatives expressed their concern over the delay in implementation of the Turn Around Plan for revival of sick mills of NTC even after it was approved by the Cabinet. Secretary (Labour) agreed that a meeting of Ministries of Labour, Finance and Textiles and the concerned State Governments and the trade unions would be arranged to expedite a decision on this issue. The members also expressed their concern over non-payment of wages and bonus to workers in sick establishments.

28. Central Provident Fund Commissioner informed the Conference that keeping in view the suggestions received from various parties, the Pensions Scheme had been modified. He also informed that as on 23-10-1996, 88005 beneficiaries have been sanctioned pension and no establishment had asked for any exemption under Section 29 of the Act. So far, he also informed the Conference that the vigilance machinery of the Employees Provident Fund Organisation had been activated. The representatives of some trade union organisations expressed the view that many establishments had asked for exemption from the Pension scheme but no exemption was granted and they also asked for the review of the Pension Sheme. CIE representative stated that the review of the Pension Scheme should be undertaken only after a period of about five years from its introduction. Regarding Gratuity, the workers' representatives demanded that the ceiling of Gratuity for workers should be raised from Rs. 1 lakh to Rs. 2.5 lakhs as in the case of Central Government employees. Some workers' representatives felt that the scope for introduction of unemployment insurance should be explored so as to give protection against job losses.
29. Trade Unions representatives stated that the workers had never been consulted in the matter of framing the environmental standards. They also expressed their concern over the closure of establishments under the orders of the Supreme Court as the workers were the real sufferers. Labour Minister, West Bengal stated that the technology for environment was very expensive and not upto the mark.
30. Concern was expressed in the conference over the slow progress in elimination of child labour. There was a general consensus over the issue that sincere and effective steps should be taken to deal with the problem of child labour. Workers' representatives demanded that central trade union organisations should be involved in monitoring the implementation of National Child Labour Projects. Labour Secretary clarified that the United Front Government was committed to the abolition of child labour in all employments, occupations and processing whether hazardous or non-hazardous, and necessary steps would be initiated in that direction. He also suggested that a composite approach taking into account parental poverty, parental illiteracy, parental

income and parental employmental was needed.

Item No. 3 : Modernisation and Re-organisations of Employment Exchanges

and

Item No. 4 : Modernisations of Vocational Training System

31. The Chairman placed various points as listed in the Agenda Note for consideration of the Conference.
32. The President, INTUC stated that the Standing Labour Committee in its last meeting had discussed those two items in details and had made a number of recommendations. He requested the Labour Ministry to take effective steps to implement those recommendations of the Standing Labour Committee.
33. Representative of BMS made a number of suggestions to improve the performance of vocational training institutions. He recommended the adoption of German system of imparting practical education periodically. He also suggested that training institutions should be equipped with updated machinery, vocationalisation should start from Class VIII onwards leading to vocational courses at higher secondary level, well-trained teachers on full time basis only should be employed, books in Hindi and in regional languages at reasonable prices should be made available and representatives of industry and trade unions should be given representations in policy making bodies. He also supported the proposal to set up Skill Development Fund provided it was monitored by a tripartite machinery.
34. The representative of HMS suggested that the workers affected by the restructuring of industry and business should also be given access to training facilities in vocational training centres and the Government should support the training projects, with credit facilities for the beneficiaries, so that they could use their acquired skills for self-employment.
35. A representative of AIMO stated that employment exchanges should be computerised to up-grade the data base to match the demand. He emphasised that the objective of the employment exchanges should be conducive to industrial growth and not contrary to industrial growth. He advocated an idea that there should be a central body for coordination

and monitoring the functioning of all the employment exchanges in the country. He also suggested that all enactments and institutions connected with Employment Exchange policy should be combined under one umbrella and that should be a tripartite and autonomous body.

36. The representatives of the confederation of Indian industries (CII) said that vocational training should be given as much importance as was being given to primary education; vocational training should be made available at the door steps by opening training centres in small towns; the vocational centres should not only train the people for employment in industry but also for self-employment; and teachers of vocational centres should be exposed to industry.

37. CIE representative stressed that the present approach to impart vocational training should be stepped up with active participation of both workers and employers. He supported the idea of adoption of German training model with such changes as were suitable to the requirement of Indian industry.

38. Representative of SEWA stated that the problem of unemployment could be solved if suitable steps were taken to impart right type of vocational training to the workers in the unorganised sectors including nursery, forestry, horticulture, food processing etc. She requested the Government to evolve a national policy on home based workers which should provide for their employment, working conditions, wages, identity cards, social security and welfare etc.

39. Mr. Werner Blenk, Director, ILO office New Delhi thanked the Chairman for inviting him to attend the Conference. In his address to the Conference, he stated hat vocational training was a major ingredient in the fight against unemployment; vocational training was an investment for future generation; and investment in vocational training prepared the young to find them a place in society and in labour market and to contribute to the society. He emphasised the need for involvement of workers and employers in the upgradation of vocational training. He assured that the ILO would provide all possible assistance in that field, if required.

40. The views expressed by the State Government on these two items are summarised below :

    (1) Employment Exchanges have been computerised totally in Goa. A Manpower Development Cell has been set up in the

state which has devised the schemes to make available the trained manpower to industries to suit their requirement. There is a need to find out the reasons for delay in implementing the Skill Development Projects undertaken by the Government of India. Goa has demanded financial assistance through World Bank Project for a woman ITI in Goa which should be considered favourably.

(Goa)

(2) All employment exchanges should be computerised on war footing. The volume of Live Register should be kept within a manageable position. The existing provision of renewal of Employment Exchange Registration Card after three years may be dispensed with. The applicant may be deleted automatically from the Live Register after attaining the age of 40 years in case of general categories and of 45 years in case of registrants belonging to SC or ST. The proposal for making the Employment Exchanges as nodal agencies for all self-employment schemes of the Government both Central and State will be more effective. It is necessary to bring the employment situation of the unorganised sector under the purview of the Employment Market Information. The employers in the private sector should be compelled to discharge their statutory obligations properly and timely about the submission of reports/returns etc. A provision should be introduced to ensure that those people who are recruited by them should at least be registered. They should also intimate the exchanges the details of registration of those who have been employed by them. The importance of vocational guidance and proper counselling at the stage of School Education needs to be given topmost priority. The introduction of audiovisual aids for proper training of the concerned personnel will increase the efficiency of the programme of vocational guidance. There is also a need for periodical employment bulletins in the regional languages. The Central Government should give financial aid to the State Governments for the restructuring and modernisation of the Employment Exchanges.

(West Bengal)

(3) Just renaming the Employment Exchanges as the Employment Promotion Centre will not achieve the desired object. It should be followed up with modernisation and technical support. The Employment Exchanges deserve to be restructured to meet the requirements of the situation emerging out of unemployment.

(Tripura)

(4) The name of Employment Exchanges may be changed to Employment Promotion Centres. The Employment officers should be given necessary training for providing better service to private sector employers. They should be deputed for training/seminars arranged by ILO/UNESCO in foreign centres. Arrangements should be made for organising Rojgar Melas and Special training programmes viz. "Interview Technique." Employment Exchanges should also be authorised to sanction loans to the needy registrants of Employment Exchanges. Central Government should formulate a scheme to provide such Audiovisual Aids alongwith Cassettes/overhead projects so as to have uniformity.

(Maharashtra)

(5) Employment Deptt., Haryana has set up 17 Private Sector Bureau with relaxed conditions of registration and sponsoring. As a result, the figure of private sector employment through Employment Exchanges has increased. Every week, the unemployed youth of specific category are called in one Employment Exchange of each district alongwith the District level loaning Agencies. The unemployed are motivated for self-employment ventures and followed up for banking finance. During the last two years, 98 self-employment loaning camps have been organised in which 62290 applicants were given loan amounting to Rs. 114.61 crores.

(Haryana)

(6) Under a self-employment scheme in Manipur, 10 per cent of the unit cost is provided by the Department, 15 per cent by the entrepreneur and 75 per cent by the Bank. The scheme is regarded as the best Government sponsored

scheme in terms of success and recovery of loans.

(Manipur)

(7) Employment Exchanges in Punjab have taken a shape of NODAL AGENCIES in the matter of self-employment. However, it has not been possible to raise suitable employment on regular basis.

(Punjab)

(8) An action plan for each state for generation of employment should be prepared keeping in view the geographical and economical conditions of the state with the help of the experts of national and international level. Under the Self-Employment Scheme, Central Government may provide financial help, to bear the burden of seed money, in case of economically weaker individuals.

(Rajasthan)

(9) The Employment Exchanges (Compulsory Notification of Vacancies) Act, 1959 and the Rules framed thereunder have become largely obsolete and consequently the role and relevance of the employment organisation appears to be declining. These need to be amended suitably.

(Orissa)

(10) Appropriate action is required to be taken for amendment of the Employment Exchange (Compulsory Notification of Vacancies) Act, 1959 and Rules to provide for compulsory recruitment through employment exchanges and to make employment exchanges registration compulsory for an applicant for any job. Provisions for stringent punishment to the defaulting employers should be made.

(Assam)

(11) There should be a high level enquiry into the utilisation of funds under the World Bank Project. There should be proper Rules to control the functioning of private vocational training centres as they are engaged not in proper training but in minting money. German training model with suitable changes may be adopted. Vocational

training should be linked with employment.

(Andhra Pradesh)

Item No. 5 : Floor Level Minimum Wages for Unorganised Employment

41. The President of Bhartiya Mazdoor Sangh stated that there were wide disparities in the minimum wages in different states which caused the flight of industry from one state to another state. This was highly undesirable and could be checked only by reducing the disparities considerably, if not totally abolishing them. In this context, he mentioned that some states had already linked minimum wages to the variable dearness allowance, while other states were hesitant to implement the scheme. Finally, the concept of National Minimum Wage should be made applicable not only to the scheduled employments notified under the Minimum Wages Act but to the entire unorganised sector in any corner of the country.
42. The General Secretary of CITU states that the criteria for determination of minimum wages which were laid down in 1957 had not been implemented by the states so far. Even the Supreme Court Judgment given in 1991 and its directions are yet to be implemented by the states. He also felt that all minimum wages must be fixed above the poverty line. In fact, this was announced in the Indian Labour Conference of 1988 but the states have yet to implement the decision. He also felt that the irreducible minimum wage to be paid to the workers should be Rs. 50 per day and this rate must be revised periodically. He also recommended that the provisions of Social Security and Pension Scheme must also be implemented in the unorganised sector.
43. The representative of UTUC (LS) felt that the concept of National Minimum Wage was very relevant and must be implemented. Further, there should be no list of scheduled employment and all workmen in the unorganised sector must be covered under the Act. Finally, the principle of fixation of minimum wages for the workers must be governed by the Supreme Court Judgment of 1991.
44. AITUC representative stated that the National Minimum Floor Level Wage should be brought under the purview of Schedule IX of the Constitution so that the employers could

not litigate on the notifications issued in that regard.

45. The representative of HMS also stated that the National Minimum Floor Level Wage should be brought under Schedule IX of the Constitution.

46. CIE representative clarified that the employers were against the concept of national level minimum wages at that stage. He mentioned that as labour was in the Concurrent List of the Constitution, views of the State Government must be ascertained. Further, he felt that the initiative on the issue must come from the side of the State Governments.

47. The views of State Government on this item were as follows :

(1) In spite of clear guidelines given for revision of minimum wages in different scheduled employments, the State Governments have failed to revise the wages on time. The State Government suggests an amendment to the Minimum Wages Act which should prescribe that the workers in any scheduled employment shall be paid at the rate of floor level minimum wages, in case the rates fixed or revised by the State Government or Central Government, in any scheduled employment, are less than the floor level wages.

(Goa)

(2) There should be no rate of minimum wage below the poverty line and this should be linked to Consumer Price Index to compensate the workers against the rise in cost of living.

(Maharashtra)

(3) The recommendations of National Commission on Rural Labour for floor level of minimum wage should be adhered to.

(Punjab)

(4) It is necessary to bring parity in the minimum wage at the regional and national level. It will reduce the migration of workers from one state to the other and from one part to the other. Central Government should make efforts in this direction and meet the costs on this account, if any.

(Rajasthan)

(5) The concept of floor level minimum wages is not in the

interest of the working class. In that event, the floor level minimum wages are likely to become the minimum wages for the workers in different employments. The minimum wages should be such as would take care of the basic needs of the workers. This is likely to vary from state to state and from place to place within a state. The guidelines/ norms for fixation of rates of minimum wage should be the same for all states. It will check the flight of workers from one state to the other and the industry in one state will not flourish at the cost of the other states. A policy may be evolved for inclusions of employments in the Schedule of the Minimum Wages Act. The Minimum Wages Act should be included in Schedule IX of the Constitution.

(West Bengal)

48. During the discussion, the Concept of National Floor Level Minimum Wage was also clarified. It was explained by Secretary (Labour) that the Floor Level Minimum Wages refers to the subsistence wage which was essential for keeping the body and soul together. This was advocated by the National Commission on Rural Labour in their Report given in 1991. The methodology used for determining the National Minimum Floor Level wage was explained in the Conference. The National Commission on Rural Labour had worked out a figure of Rs. 20 per day as the Floor Level Minimum Wage, based on the cost of living index of the year for agricultural workers at 802 in 1990. It was explained that if the figures were extrapolated, then at 1996 prices, the Floor Level Minimum Wage would come to approx. Rs. 35 per day (where the CPI for agricultural workers had gone up to 1431).

49. There was a consensus that no minimum wage for any occupation should be fixed below the minimum subsistence wage of Rs. 35 per day at 1996 prices.

Item No. 6 : Recognition of Trade Union through secret ballot and Amendment to the I.D. Act

50. The President, INTUC stated that in a meeting held earlier at INTUC office, all trade unions had unanimously suggested that a bipartite Committee should be set up to examine the issue of recognitions of trade unions through secret ballot. He,

therefore, suggested that the issue may also be examined by the Bipartite Committee which would be set up to consider amendments to the Industrial Disputes Act, 1947.

51. Representatives of some trade unions strongly emphasised that the issue should be finalised in the Conference itself as it was the commitment of the United Front Government. They, however, wanted that if the issue was to be referred to a Bipartite Committee, the report of the Bipartite Committee must come within a month.

52. The representative of the CIE stated that the Trade Union Act was very relevant to the Industrial Disputes Act. Therefore, both the items should be linked together and examined by the Bipartite Committee.

53. The views expressed by the State Government on the issue were as under :

(1) The proposal for determination of representative character of trade unions through secret ballot is a step which deserves appreciation. For this purpose, the modalities to be adopted needs to be finalised soon.

(Tripura)

(2) The State Government of West Bengal is in favour of mechanism for recognition of trade unions through secret ballot. The State legislature had passed the Trade Unions (West Bengal) Amendment Act, 1983 making elaborate provisions for recognition of trade unions as bargaining agents. The Amendment Act received the assent of the President in November, 1992.

(West Bengal)

(3) Recognition of trade unions through secret ballot is the need of the hour. Considering the mushroom growth of trade unions, it has become necessary to curtail further growth of such trade unions in the interest of healthy relations between employers and employees. Suitable amendments may be made to the Trade Union Act, 1926 so as to ensure democratic functioning of the trade unions.

(Maharashtra)

(4) It is very essential to lay down some specific criteria for

recognition of trade unions of any establishment through secret ballot so that inter-rivalry of trade unions could be curved. The executive instructions may be followed in letter and spirit and subsequently the same may be given statutory shape.

(Haryana)

(5) An approach regarding determination of representative character of the trade unions through secret ballot is supported. The modalities to be adopted for secret ballot should be implemented by an executive order in the initial stage, and, if felt necessary, brought under legislation.

(Punjab)

(6) The proposal of recognition of trade unions through secret ballot is supported. There should be an amendment to the Trade Union Act for this purpose.

(Rajasthan)

(7) Government of Orissa has introduced the secret ballot system for verification of membership of trade unions by adopting 'Verification of Membership and Recognition of Trade Union Rules 1994'. The method has been successfully implemented in many industries in the State including the Rourkela Steel Plant which is the largest industry in the State.

(Orissa)

54. The views of various State Governments on the proposed amendment to the I.D. Act are summarised as follows :

(1) The Government of Goa opposes any amendment giving exemption to certain categories of employment from the purview of the definition of term 'Industry' contained in Section 2 (j) of the I.D. Act, 1947. This exemption should not be considered in the absence of alternative remedy made available to the exempted categories. There are no valid grounds for narrowing down the scope of definition of industry under the Industrial Dispute Act. There is, however, a case for enlarging its scope to cover other categories which are denied the protection of the I.D. Act.

(Goa)

(2) The State Government is unable to agree to the proposal to exempt certain activities from the purview of the I.D. Act keeping in view the nature of the activity and/or of number of persons employed. This will leave the workers totally at the mercy of their employers virtually without any remedy and will encourage the employers to keep the number of persons employed within ten. They will go in for contract labour, daily paid labour etc.

(West Bengal)

(3) The State Government do not feel any urgency to amend the I.D Act and at the same time, they do not have any serious objection to the proposed amendments.

(Tripura)

(4) The term "Industry" has undergone several changes from the year 1960 as a result of a number of court judgments. Therefore, this question should be considered in the light of the court judgments. In Maharashtra, a legislation known as Maharashtra Employees of Private Schools (Conditions and Services) Regulations Act, 1977 is in force. The Act provides for regulating the process of recruitment and also Tribunal for adjudication of the dispute arising out of dismissal of a teacher. It is, considered necessary to bring the teacher within the meaning of Section 2 (S) of the Act. The State Government should be the appropriate authority is the proper machinery to handle both the matters relating the Industrial Disputes Act, 1947 and also law and order problems. It is, therefore, not desirable to delegate certain powers of the appropriate Government to the authorities of the Central Government.

(Maharashtra)

(5) The State Government shall be the appropriate Government for the purpose of industrial disputes. The Government of India should be the appropriate Government in case of any such establishments as are wholly owned and controlled by the Government of India. The State Government does not agree to the amendments relating to special provisions of lay off,

retrenchment and closure. The existing provisions should be continued.

(Haryana)

(6) The Government of Punjab supports the proposal to exempt certain establishments from the purview of the Industrial Dispute Act, 1947. However, it would be better if some alternate remedies are made available to such categories of workers.

(Punjab)

(7) The proposal of exclusion of certain economic and welfare activities from the meaning of industry is agreed to. There should, however, be a separate law to ensure remedy against exploitation of workers, prevention of unrest, and smooth functioning of these activities.

(Orissa)

55. The Conference in the end recommended that a Bipartite Committee may be set up to formulate specific proposals for a Comprehensive Industrial Relations Bill and to consider the issue of recognition of Trade Unions through Secret Ballot. The following will be the members of the Bipartite Committee :

1. Shri G. Sanjeeva Reddy, President (INTUC)
2. Shri R. Venugopal, (BMS)
3. Dr. Shanti G. Patel, President (HMS)
4. Shri Pritish Chanda, President, UTUC (LS)
5. Shri K.L. Mahendra (AITUC)
6. Dr. M.K. Pandhe, General Secretary (CITU)
7. Shri S.R. Sen Gupta, General Secretary (UTUC)
8. Shri D.D. Shastri, President (TUCC)
9. Shri I.P. Anand (CIE)
10. Shri Prabir Chakraborty (AIOE)
11. Shri Arvind Doshi, Chairman (CII)
12. Shri C.M. Krishna (CIE)
13. Shri T.K. Bhaumik (CIE)
14. Shri Abhishek M. Singhvi (CIE)
15. Shri Jauhari Lal (CIE)
16. Shri Rammohan Bidawtka, Vice President, AIMO

56. The Committee would elect/nominate its Chairman/Alternate Chairman. The Committee will submit

its report within a period of three months.

Item No. 8 : The Bill of Workers' Participation in Management

57. The President, INTUC stated that the Bill of Workers' Participation in Management is already pending in Parliament. The Ministry of Labour has already received amendments to that Bill from members of Parliament, trade union organisations, employers organisations and other organisations. He requested Labour Minister to examine all the amendments received in the Ministry and place the Bill duly amended after taking into consideration the suggested amendments before the Parliament.

58. CIE representative stated that the employers should be given an opportunity of being heard before the amended Bill was placed before Parliament.

59. The views of the State Governments on the issue were as under :

(1) The views of the workers' group and the employers' group may be communicated to the State Governments so that the State can take them into consideration and submit suggestions.

(Goa)

(2) The participation of workers in management can be meaningful only if the workers have equal representation in the management at all levels including the Board level. The Workers' representatives should be selected by secret ballot. The workers' representatives should have access to all the accounts and documents of the unit. The views of State Government should also be taken into consideration.

(West Bengal)

(3) An attempt was made to introduce the scheme in the public sector undertakings but the response was not encouraging. It would be just and proper to have the say of representatives of employers on the issue before the Bill is amended suitably so as to avoid any misconception or misunderstanding.

(Maharashtra)

(4) The views of workers and employers may be considered

and taken into account before the proposed Workers' Participation in Management Bill is introduced in Parliament.

(Haryana)

(5) The Government of Punjab has no objection if the Bill is passed by the Parliament without making any amendment. However, before the Act is brought into force, a better understanding and congenial atmosphere should be created between the management and the workers.

(Punjab)

(6) The Workers' Participation in Management Bill is a welcome step. With this the climates of industrial relations will improve and the productivity will be increased. In the beginning, it should be tried in big public units and private sector undertakings employing more than 1000 workers and which are over five years old.

(Rajasthan)

(7) The scheme of workers participation in management should have statutory backing. Instead of involvement of unions, nominations should be by elections through secret ballot system.

(Orissa)

60. A Committee was constituted consisting of 4 representative each from Trade Unions, Employers Organisations and State Government to draft the conclusions of the Conference.

61. Shri Debandranath Sarangi, Secretary (Labour), Government of Tamil Nadu placed a Resolution on the elimination of Child Labour from all occupations and industries before the Conference. The Resolution was welcomed and adopted unanimously by the Conference. A copy of Resolution is at Annexure III.

62. Shri Divakar Dev, Additional Secretary, Ministry of Labour in his vote of thanks, thanked the Chairman, Labour Ministers of State Government, representatives of Central employers' and workers' organisations and all other participants. He thanked all those who contributed to the successful conclusion of the Conference. He specifically appreciated the work done by officers and staff who organised the Conference.

ANNEXURE I

33RD SESSION OF THE INDIAN LABOUR CONFERENCE
NEW DELHI : OCTOBER 24 - 25, 1996

COMPOSITION

CHAIRMAN	:	*Union Labour Minister*
GOVERNMENT GROUP		
Central Government	:	23 Seats
State Governments/Union Territories	:	32 Seats (one seat each)
EMPLOYERS' GROUP		
Council of Indian Employers	:	24 seats
All Indian Manufacturers' Organisation	:	4 seats
Confederation of Indian Industry	:	2 seats
		30 seats
WORKERS' GROUP		
India National Trade Union Congress	:	10 seats
Bhartiya Mazdoor Sangh	:	5 seats
Hind Mazdoor Sabha	:	3 seats
United Trade Union Centre (LS)	:	3 seats
All India Trade Union Congress	:	3 seats
Centre of Indian Trade Unions	:	3 seats
National Labour Organisation	:	1 seat
United Trade Union Congress	:	1 seat
Trade Union Coordination Centre	:	1 seat
		30 seats

ANNEXURE II

33RD SESSION OF INDIAN LABOUR CONFERENCE
(NEW DELHI - 24 - 25 OCTOBER, 1996)

LIST OF PARTICIPANTS

CHAIRMAN	:	Shri M. Arunachalam, Union Labour Minister
VICE CHAIRMAN (WORKERS' GROUP)	:	Shri G. Sanjeeva Reddy, President, INTUC
VICE CHAIRMAN (EMPLOYERS' GROUP)	:	Shri R.K. Somany, C.I.E.
VICE CHAIRMAN (STATE GOVERNMENT)	:	Shri Santi Ghatak, Labour Minister, Government of West Bengal

WORKERS' GROUP
INDIAN NATIONAL TRADE UNION CONGRESS (10 SEATS)

DELEGATE	ADVISER
1. Shri Subrato Mukherjee, MLA, Vice President, INTUC, 15/1, Garihat Road, Calcutta - 700019	1. Shri Gopeshwar, General Secretary, INTUC, 37, K. Road, Jamshedpur - 831001
2. Shri Ravi Arya, Organising Secy., INTUC, Plot No. 4, Block No. 37, Nehru Nagar East, Bhilai - 490022	2. Shri Ramesh Pandey, Secretary, INTUC, 4, Bhai Veer Singh Marg, New Delhi - 110001
3. Shri Tara Singh Viyogi, Vice President, INTUC, 20 Vikas Nagar, Gwalior - 474004	3. Shri Govind Rao Adik, M.P., Vice President, INTUC, 3, Kushak Road, New Delhi
4. Shri R.C. Khuntia, Vice President, INTUC, 5 RF 1, Unit 3, Bhubaneswar - 751001	4. Shri Raja Kulkarni, Secretary, INTUC, Tel - Rasayan Bhawan, Tilak Road, Dadar, Bombay - 400014

5. Shri Rajendra Pd. Singh,
Vice President, INTUC,
5, Chhachu Bagh,
Patna - 1

6. Shri Haribhau Naik,
Treasurer, INTUC
27/B, Bharucha Marg,
Fort, Bombay - 400023

7. Shri P.L. Subbiah,
Organising Secretary, INTUC,
621 Trichy Road,
Ramanathapuram,
Coimbatore - 641045

8. Shri N.M. Adyanthaya,
Organising Secretary,
Valentine, Jeppu Bappal,
1 Cross, Kankanady Post,
Mangalore - 575002

9. Smt. Renukadevi Barkataky,
President, INTUC, Assam Br.,
Panchbati, GNB Road,
Silpukuri,
Guwahati - 781003

10. Shri Ravi Arya,
Organising Secy., INTUC,
Plot No. 4, Block No. 37,
Nehru Nagar East,
Bhilai - 490022

5. Shri R.P. Mishra,
Secretary, INTUC,
4, Bhai Veer Singh Marg,
New Delhi - 110001

6. Shri S.L. Passay,
Secretary, INTUC,
4, Bhai Veer Singh Marg,
New Delhi - 110001

7. Shri S.S. Chouhan,
Org. Secretary, INTUC,
Sawan Ashram,
Delhi - 110007

8. Shri M. Raghuviah,
General Secretary, NFIR,
3, Chelmsford Road,
New Delhi - 110055

9. Shri Balwant Rai Kapoor,
President,
INTUC Punjab Branch,
852, Gate Khazana,
Amritsar (Punjab)

BHARTIYA MAZDOOR SANGH (5 SEATS)

1. Shri R.K. Bhakt,
President, BMS,
Ram Naresh Bhawan,
Tilak Gali, Paharganj,
New Delhi - 110055

2. Shri Hasu Bhai Dave,
General Secretary, BMS,
'Jignesh,' Shivam Nagar,
Near Ram Dham, Kalwad Road,
Rajkot - 360005

1. Shri Amar Nath Dogra,
Vice - President, B.M.S.,
5239, Ajmeri Gate,
Delhi - 110006

2. Shri Prem Nath Sharma,
Bhartiya Mazdoor Sangh,
Ram Naresh Bhawan,
Tilak Gali, Paharganj,
New Delhi - 110055

3. Shri K.J. Thakkar,
   Bhartiya Mazdoor Sangh,
   Shastri Pole, Kothi Char Rasta,
   Baroda - 390001
4. Shri R. Venugopal,
   Organising Secy., BMS,
   Ram Naresh Bhawan,
   Tilak Gali, Paharganj,
   New Delhi - 110055
5. Shri Paritosh Pathak
   3, Dharamdas Ganguly Lane,
   Shivpur,
   Howrah - 711102
   West Bengal

3. Shri Sukh Nandan Singh,
   Bhartiya Mazdoor Sangh,
   89, Alexander Road,
   Ambala Cantt - 133001
4. Shri S.S. Sharma,
   Bhartiya Mazdoor Sangh,
   42, Patel Colony,
   Sardar Patel Marg,
   'C' Scheme, Jaipur - 302001
5. Shri M.N. Jha,
   Bhartiya Mazdoor Sangh,
   Q. No. 147, Type - III,
   Sector - 1, BHEL,
   Ranipur - 249403, U.P.

HIND MAZDOOR SABHA (3 SEATS)

1. Dr. Shanti Patel,
   President, HMS,
   Sneh Sadan, B-II,
   Sitladevi Temple Road,
   Mahim, Bombay-400016
2. Shri A.D. Nagpal,
   Secretary, HMS,
   1181, Sector 43-B,
   Chandigarh-160036
3. Shri A. Subramanian,
   Vice President, HMS,
   2212, Trichy Road,
   P.O. Singanallor,
   Distt. Coimbatore - 641055 (TN)

1. Shri Arun Kumar,
   Research & Education Officer,
   H.M.S., 120, Babar Road,
   New Delhi-110001
2. Shri R.A. Mittal,
   Secretary, HMS,
   12-Chelmsford Road,
   New Delhi - 110055

UNITED TRADE UNION CENTRE (LS) (3 SEATS)

1. Shri Pritish Chanda,
   President, UTUC (LS),
   77/2/1, Lenin Sarani,
   Calcutta - 700013
2. Shri Sankar Saha,
   Secretary, UTUC (LS),
   77/2/1, Lenin Sarani,
   Calcutta - 700013

3. Shri Achintya Sinha,
   Secretary, UTUC (LS),
   77/2/1, Lenin Sarani,
   Calcutta - 700013

ALL INDIA TRADE UNION CONGRESS (3 SEATS)

1. Shri A.B. Bardhan,
   General Secretary, AITUC,
   Sadar,
   Nagpur-440001
2. Shri B.D. Joshi,
   Dy. General Secretary,
   24, Canning Lane,
   New Delhi - 110001
3. Shri K.L. Mahendra,
   Secretary, AITUC,
   103, Jambagh,
   Hyderabad-500001

1. Shri H. Mahadevan,
   Secretary, AITUC,
   664, 11th Cross, III Phase
   Bangalore
2. Shir D.L. Sachdev,
   Secretary, AITUC,
   D-197, Ganesh Nagar,
   Pandav Nagar Complex,
   Delhi-110092

CENTRE OF INDIAN TRADE UNIONS (3 SEATS)

1. Dr. M.K. Pandhe,
   General Secretary, CITU,
   15, Talkatora Road,
   New Delhi - 110001
2. Shri A.K. Padmanabhan,
   Secretary, CITU (Tamil Nadu)
   13, Mosque Street,
   Chepauk, Madras - 600005
3. Shri B.V. Raghavulu,
   Genl. Secretary, CITU (A.P.)
   N.V.B. Rao Smaraka Kendra,
   1-1-60/4, RTC 'X' Road,
   Musheerabad, Hyderabad-500020

1. Shri S. Suryanarayana Rao,
   V. President, CITU (Karnataka),
   No. 12, Thanappa Gardens,
   18th Cross, Sampangi Rama
   Nagar, Bangalore - 560027
2. Shri P.K. Ganguly,
   Secretary, CITU,
   15, Talkatora Road,
   New Delhi-110001
3. Shri S. Dev Roye,
   Secretary, CITU,
   15, Talkatora Road,
   New Delhi-110001

TRADE UNION COORDINATION CENTRE (1 SEAT)

1. Shri D.D. Shastri,
   President, TUCC,
   49C, Chitta Ranjan Avenue,
   Calcutta - 700012

UNITED TRADE UNION CONGRESS (1 SEAT)

1. Shri S.R. Sen Gupta,
   General Secretary, UTUC,
   249, B.B. Ganguly Street,
   Calcutta - 12

NATIONAL LABOUR ORGANISATION (1 SEAT)

1. Shri N.M. Barot,
   President, NLO,
   Gandhi Majoor Sevalaya,
   Bhadra,
   Ahmedabad - 382010

NATIONAL FRONT OF INDIAN TRADE UNION (OBSERVER)

1. Shri Upender Kumar,
   General Secretary,
   NFITU, Delhi Unit,
   E-12/D (MIG), Mayapuri,
   New Delhi-110064

SPECIAL INVITEE
NATIONAL CENTRE FOR LABOUR (NCL)

1. Ms. Renana Jhabavala,
   Secretary, NCL

1. Shri Ashok Choudhary,
   Secretary, NCL

EMPLOYERS' GROUP
COUNCIL OF INDIAN EMPLOYERS (24 SEATS)

1. Shri Prabir Chakravarti,
   Vice President, A.I.O.E.,
   Shri Annapurna Cotton Mills
   & Industries Ltd.,
   Amar Bhavan, IInd Floor,
   P-10, New Howrah Bridge
   Approach Road, Calcutta-700001

2. Shri M.K. Garg,
   Adviser, AIOE,
   Federation House,
   Tansen Marg,
   New Delhi-110001

1. Shri G.D. Maheshwari,
   Secretary, EFI,
   Phelps Building,
   9-A, Connaught Place,
   New Delhi-110001

2. Shri O.M. Solanki,
   Vice President,
   Swadeshi Polytex Ltd.,
   6th Floor, Hotel Samrat,
   Chanakyapuri,
   New Delhi - 110001

3. Shri C.M. Krishna,
President - Personel,
Crompton Greaves Ltd.,
1, Dr. V.B. Gandhi Marg,
Bombay-400023

4. Shri A.K. Barua,
Director-Personnel,
Pfizer Ltd., Express Tower,
Nariman Point,
Mumbai-400021

5. Shri Abhishek M Singhvi,
Sr. Advocate,
Supreme Court of India,
New Delhi - 1100491

6. Shri T.K. Bhaumik,
Vice President - Personnel,
BOC India Ltd.,
P-43, Taratala Road
Calcutta-700088

7. Shri B.C. Prabhakar,
Working President,
Karnataka Employers' Asson.,
135, Dr. A.R. Krishna Shastri
Road, (Surveyors' Street),
Basavangudi, Bangalore-560004

8. Shri Gopalkrishna,
Chairman & Mg. Director,
Rural Electrification
Corporation Ltd.,
Scope Complex,
Lodi Road, New Delhi-110003

9. Shri P.N. Singh,
Director, Personnel.,
Steel Authority of India Ltd.,
Ispat Bhawan, Lodi Road,
New Delhi-110003

10. Shri Gurdeep Singh,
Director, Personnel.,

3. Dr. V. Sreenivasan,
Executive Director (HRNM),
Dalmia Cement (Bharat) Ltd.,
15, Barakhamba Road,
New Delhi-110001

4. Shri L.B. Sinate,
Executive Director (Pers. & IR)
F.C.I., 15-20,
Barakhamba Lane,
New Delhi - 110001

5. Shri Michacl Dias,
Secretary General,
The Employers Asson, Delhi
13/16, W.E.A. Karol Bagh,
New Delhi - 110005

6. Shri B.P. Pant,
Deputy Secretary,
A.I.O.E., Federation House,
Tansen Marg,
New Delhi-3

7. Shri A.I. Bunet,
Director - Personnel,
N.H.P.C., Sector-13,
NHPC Office Complex,
Faridabad

8. Shri P.C.K. Ravindran,
ED (C&AS),
A.A.I., Rajiv Gandhi Bhawan,
Safdarjung Airport,
New Delhi-110001

9. Shri Prabhakar Rao,
Manager (Legal),
F.C.I. 16-20,
Barakhamba Lane,
New Delhi-110001

10. Shri K.C. Joseph,
General Manager (HR),

Indian Ailrlines Ltd.,
Airlines House,
123, Gurdwara Rakab Ganj Road,
New Delhi-110001

11. Shri Vineet Virmani,
Vice President,
EFI Nothern Regional Council,
15, Golf Links,
New Delhi-110003

12. Shri S. Niyogi,
Director (Personnel.),
Andrew Yule & Co Ltd.,
Yule House, 8, Dr. Rajendra
Prasad Sarani, (Civil Row)

13. Shri I.P. Anand,
Chairman,
Corporate Shivthana Centre,
16, Nizamuddin East,
New Delhi-110013

14. Shri Jauhari Lal,
Director, Personnel.,
O.N.G.C. Ltd.,
Jeevan Bharti Bldg.,
New Delhi-110001

15. Shri M.A. Hakeem,
Secretary General, SCOPE,
SCOPE Complex, Lodi Road,
New Delhi-110003

16. Shri G.P. Barua,
Executive Vice President,
Williamson Magor & Co. Ltd.,
4, Mangoe Lane,
Calcutta-700001

17. Shri I. Hussain,
E.D. (P.A.), BHEL,
Sirifort, New Delhi.

Indian Oil Corpn. Ltd.,
SCOPE Complex,
7, Lodi Road,
New Delhi-110003

11. Shri N.N. Singh,
Director (Persl.)
N.E.E.P.C. Ltd.,
Brookland Compound,
Lower New Colony,
P.B. No. 79, Shillong-793003

12. Shri Samir K. Das,
Vice-President, HRD,
Cooperative Mgmt. Office,
3rd Floor, JN Heredin Marg,
Mumbai-400038

13. Shri Indu Bhushan,
ED (Persl.),
IFFCO Ltd., 34, Nehru Place,
New Delhi-110019

14. Shri G.P. Srivastava,
General Manager (P & HRD),
Pawan Hans Ltd.,
Safdarjung Airport,
New Delhi-110003

15. Shri V.Y. Tamhane,
Secretary General,
The Bombay Millowners'
Association, Elphinstone
Bldg., 10 Veer Nariman Road,
Bombay-400001

16. Shri S.K. Nanda,
Secretary General, EFI,
Army & Navy Building,
148, M.G. Road,
Mumbai-400023

ALL INDIA MANUFACTURERS' ORGANISATION (4 SEATS)

1. Shri Ram Mohan Bidawtka,
   Vice President, AIMO
   (Mumbai Zone), Jeevan Sahakar,
   4th Floor, Sir P.M. Road, Fort
   Mumbai-400001
2. Shri G.D. Bagri,
   M/s Hindustan Circuits Ltd.,
   199/201, Moti Mansion,
   A.B. Kokhatkar Marg,
   Mumbai-400004
3. Dr. P. Asthana,
   Executive Director,
   AIMO, Jeevan Sahakar,
   4th Floor, Sir P.M. Road,
   Fort, Mumbai-400001
4. Shri K.K. Bhaiya,
   Secretary, AIMO
   Jeevan Sahakar,
   4th Floor, Sir P.M. Road,
   Fort, Mumbai-400001

CONFEDERATION OF INDIAN INDUSTRY (2 SEATS)

1. Shri Arvind Doshi,
   Chairman, CII Water Resource
   Management Committee &
   M.D., Premier Automobiles Ltd.,
   Lal Bahadur Shastri Marg,
   Kurla, Bombay-400070
2. Shri S. Sen,
   Senior Director C.I.I.
   23, 26, Institutional Area,
   Lodi Road, New Delhi-110003

1. Shri Deepak Roy,
   Dy. Director, CII,
   23, 26, Institutional Area,
   Lodi Road,
   New Delhi-110003

STATE GOVERNMENTS
ARUNACHAL PRADESH

1. Shri Morge Ete,
   Labour Commissioner,
   Government of Arunachal Pradesh,
   Naharlagun-791110

ASSAM

1. Shri N.C. Barua,
   Secretary (Labour),
   Government of Assam,
   'Secretariat,
   Dispur, Guwahati-781006

BIHAR

1. Shri Subhash Sharma,
   Labour Commissioner,
   Government of Bihar,
   Vikas Bhavan,
   Patna-800015

DAMAN & DIU

1. Shri Kiran Bhatia,
   Chief Inspector of
   Factories & Boilers,
   Government of Daman 8 Diu,
   Raj Bhavan, Dona Paula,
   Daman-396220

DELHI

1. Shri J.C. Negi,
   Dy. Labour Commissioner,
   Government of NCT of Delhi,
   15, Rajpur Road,
   Delhi

GOA

1. Shri Luizinho Faleiro,
   Labour Minister,
   Goa Secretariat,
   Panaji-403004

1. Shri J.K. Dadoo,
   Secretary (Labour),
   Goa Secretariat,
   Panaji-403004
2. Shri R.S. Mardolker,
   Labour Commissioner,
   Government of Goa,
   Junta House, 1st Floor,
   Panaji-403004

HARYANA

1. Prof. Ganeshi Lal,
   Labour Minister,
   Government of Haryana,
   Haryana Civil Sectt.,
   Chandigarh-160001

1. Smt. Kamla Chaudhry,
   Comm. & Secretary (Labour)
   Govt. of Haryana,
   Haryana Civil Sectt.,
   Chandigarh-160001
2. Smt. K.A. Arora,
   Director (Employment),
   Government of Haryana,
   Haryana Civil Sectt.,
   Chandigarh-160001
3. Shri R.R. Jowel,
   Labour Commissioner,
   Government of Haryana,
   Haryana Civil Sectt.,
   Chandigarh-160001

JAMMU & KASHMIR

1. Shri A.R. Mubaraki,
   Labour Commissioner,
   Government of
   Jammu & Kashmir,
   Secretariat,
   Srinagar

1. Shri K.R. Tak,
   Dy. Labour Commissioner,
   Government of
   Jammu & Kashmir,
   H.No. 1490, Gali Qasam Jan,
   Ballimaran, Delhi-110006

KARNATAKA

1. Shri Ramesh Kumar,
   Secretary (Labour),
   Government of Karnataka,
   M.S. Building,
   Bangalore-560001

KERALA

1. Shri K.K. Vijayakumar,
   Secretary (Labour),
   Government of Kerala,
   Secretariat,
   Thiruvananthapuram-695001

MADHYA PRADESH

1. Shri Ratnesh Soloman,
   Labour Minister,
   Government of
   Madhya Pradesh
   Vallabh Bhavan,
   Bhopal-462004

1. Shri Dilip Mehra,
   Labour Secretary,
   Government of
   Madhya Pradesh
   Vallabh Bhavan,
   Bhopal-462004

2. Shri L.K. Pandey,
   Dy. Labour Commissioner,
   Government of
   Madhya Pradesh,
   Secretariat,
   Indore-452001

MAHARASHTRA

1. Shri Sabir Shaikh,
   Minister for Labour,
   Government of Maharashtra,
   Mantralaya,
   Bombay-400032

1. Shri M.B. Gajare,
   Addl. Labour Commissioner,
   Government of Maharashtra,
   Commerce Centre, Tardeo,
   Bombay-400034

2. Shri D.T. Kumawat,
   PA to Labour Minister,
   Government of Maharashtra,
   Mantralaya,
   Bombay-400032

MANIPUR

1. Shri L. Tomba Singh,
   Labour Minister,
   Government of Manipur,
   Manipur Sectt., South Block,
   Imphal - 795001

2. Shri Babu Singh,
   Director (Craftsman Training),
   Government of Manipur,
   Manipur Sectt., South Block,
   Imphal - 795001

1. Shri Khokamani Singh,
   Director (Employment),
   Government of Manipur,
   Manipur Sectt., South Block,
   Imphal - 795001

MEGHALAYA

1. Shri S.K. Srivastava,
   Commnr. & Secretary (Labour),
   Government of Meghalaya,
   Rilang Building,
   Shillong - 793001

1. Shri W.S. Mawlong,
   Labour Commissioner,
   Government of Meghalaya,
   Rilang Building,
   Shillong - 793001

ORISSA

1. Shri Durga Sankar Pattnaik,
   Labour Minister,
   Government of Orissa,
   Bhubaneshwar-751001

1. Dr. K.J.S. Chatrath,
   Commnr, & Secretary (Labour),
   Government of Orissa,
   Bhubaneshwar - 751001

PONDICHERRY

1. Shri B.V. Selvaraj,
   Labour Secretary,
   Government of Pondicherry,
   Chief Sectt. Building,
   Pondicherry - 605001

PUNJAB

1. Shri Khushal Behl,
   Labour Minister,
   Civil Sectt.,
   Government of Punjab,
   Chandigarh-160001
2. Shri Jagpal Singh Sandhu,
   Labour Commissioner,
   Civil Sectt., 8th Floor,
   Government of Punjab,
   Chandigarh-160001
3. Shri Hardyal Singh,
   Addl. Labour Secretary,
   Civil Sectt., 8th Floor,
   Government of Punjab,
   Chandigarh - 160001
4. Shri Charanjit Bhatia,
   Asstt. Labour Commissioner,
   Civil Sectt., 8th Floor,
   Government of Punjab,
   Chandigarh - 160001

1. Shri K.S. Janjua,
   Prl. Secretary,
   Civil Sectt., 8th Floor,
   Government of Punjab,
   Chandigarh-160001

RAJASTHAN

1. Shri S.L. Sharma,
   Addl. Labour Commissioner,
   Government of Rajasthan,
   Deptt. of Labour,
   Jaipur - 302001

TAMIL NADU

1. Shri Debendranath Sarangi,
   Secretary (Labour),
   Government of Tamil Nadu,
   Secretariat,
   Chennai-600009

TRIPURA

1. Shri Keshab Majumdar,
   Labour Minister,
   Government of Tripura,
   Civil Sectt.,
   Agartala - 799001

1. Shri Om Prakash,
   Resident Commissioner,
   Tripura Bhavan,
   Kautilya Marg, Chanakyapuri
   New Delhi - 110021

UTTAR PRADESH

1. Shri Naginder Singh,
   Labour Secretary,
   Government of Uttar Pradesh,
   Secretariat,
   Lucknow-226001

1. Shri T.P. Pathak,
   Spl. Secretary (Labour),
   Government of Uttar Pradesh,
   Secretariat,
   Lucknow-226001
2. Shri S.K. Das,
   Labour Commissioner,
   P.B. No. 220, Kanpur-208001
3. Shri A.S. Jatav
   Addl. Labour Commissioner,
   Gaziabad, U.P.

WEST BENGAL

1. Shri Santi Ghatak
   Labour Minister,
   Government of West Bengal,
   Writers' Building,
   Calcutta - 700001

1. Shri V. Subramaniam,
   Labour Secretary,
   Government of West Bengal,
   Writers' Building,
   Calcutta - 700001

2. Shri T.K. Chakraborty,
   P.S. to Minister,
   Government of West Bengal,
   Writers' Building, Calcutta-700001

CENTRAL GOVERNMENT
LOK SABHA SECRETARIAT

1. Shri R.S. Mishra,
   Under Secretary,
   Lok Sabha Sectt.

MINISTRY OF AGRICULTURE

1. Shri I.K. Narang,
   Asstt. Commr. (Dairy),
   Deptt. of Animal Husbandry,
   Krishi Bhavan, New Delhi.

MINISTRY OF CHEMICALS & FERTILIZERS

1. Shri S.L. Ravidas,
   Dy. Secretary,
   Shastri Bhavan,
   New Delhi

1. Shri N.K. Agrawal,
   Indl. Advisor,
   Udyog Bhavan,
   New Delhi

MINISTRY OF COMMUNICATIONS

1. Shri Ram Singh,
   Under Secretary,
   Ministry of Communications,
   Sanchar Bhavan, New Delhi

MINISTRY OF DEFENCE

1. Shri V.K. Taneja,
   Dy. Adviser (Labour Welfare)
   Room No. 445, A Wing,
   A.H.Q., Ministry of Defence,
   Sena Bhavan, New Delhi

1. Smt. Meenakshi Seth,
   Jt. Director, D.G.O.F.,
   Ordnance Factory Board,
   10-A, Auckland Road,
   Calcutta - 700001

MINISTRY OF HEALTH & FAMILY WELFARE

1. Prof. K.B. Logani,
   Dy. Dir. General (Medical),
   D.G.H.S., Nirman Bhavan,
   New Delhi

MINISTRY OF INDUSTRY

1. Shri Sohan Lal,
   Director (I.D.),
   Ministry of Industry,
   Udyog Bhawan, New Delhi

MINISTRY OF PLANNING

1. Shri V. Nanda,
   E.O. (IR),
   Ministry of Planning

PLANNING COMMISSION

1. Dr. O.P. Sharma,
   Jt. Adviser (LEM),
   Planning Commission,
   New Delhi - 110001

MINISTRY OF POWER

1. Shri K.L. Verma,
   Under Secretary,
   Ministry of Power,
   Shrma Shakti Bhawan,
   New Delhi - 110001

MINISTRY OF RAILWAYS

1. Shri Neeraj Kumar,
   Ex. Director (T & MPP),
   Ministry of Railways,
   Rail Bhawan, New Delhi

1. Shri S. Seth,
   Addl. Member (MS),
   Ministry of Railways,
   Rail Bhawan, New Delhi

MINISTRY OF RURAL AREAS & EMPLOYMENT

1. Shri Avtar Singh,
   Jt. Director,
   Deptt. of Rural Employment &
   Poverty Alleviation,
   Krishi Bhawan, New Delhi

MINISTRY OF TEXTILES

1. Shri T.S. Randhava,
   Director,

1. Shri S.K. Keshava,
   Director,

Ministry of Textiles,
Udyog Bhawan,
New Delhi

Ministry of Textiles,
Udyog Bhawan,
New Delhi

MINISTRY OF URBAN AFFAIRS

1. Shri Y.P. Singh,
   Director (Works),
   C.P.W.D., Room No. 238-C,
   Deptt. of Urban Development,
   Nirman Bhawan, New Delhi.

SPECIAL INVITEES

1. Shri Werner K. Blenk,
   Director,
   Intl. Labour Organisation
   New Delhi

1. Shri A.S. Oberai,
   Director,
   South Asia Multidisciplinary
   Advisory Team (SAAT),
   International Labour
   Organisation

MINISTRY OF LABOUR

1. Dr. L. Mishra,
   Secretary (L)
2. Shri Divakar Dev,
   Addl. Secretary (L)
3. Shri D.K. Trehan,
   L.E.A.
4. Shri S.C. Sharma,
   CLC (C)
5. Shri Abhik Ghosh,
   DGE&T
6. Shri S.K. Sharma,
   D.G., ESIC
7. Shri A.P. Verma,
   Director, NLI
8. Shri R.S. Kaushik,
   CPFC
9. Shri G. Vaidyanathan,
   D.D.G., FASLI
10. Shri V. Mahajan,
    D.G.M.S.,
11. Shri P.M. Sirajuddin,
    Director
12. Shri V. Mahajan,
    D.G.M.S.
13. Shri P.M. Sirajuddin,
    Director
14. Shri D.S. Dagar,
    Director
15. Shri S.I. Siddiqui,
    Director
16. Shri Arvind Risbud,
    Director
17. Shri V.P. Yajurvedi,
    Welfare Commr., DGLW
18. Shri G.S. Sethi,
    Director, DGE&T

19. Smt. Ranjana Kale,
Dy. Secretary
20. Shri R.K. Rang,
Dy. Secretary
21. Shri S.K. Mukhopadhyay,
Jt. CLC (C)
22. Shri P.K. Padhy,
Jt. Director
23. Shri V.K. Sharma,
Addl. D.T.
24. Ms. Sudha Midha,
Joint Director
25. Shri S.N. Brohmo Chaudhry,
Joint Director
26. Shri G.R. Majhee,
Dy. CLC (C)
27. Shri T.C. Girotra,
Dy. CLC (C)
28. Shri H.C. Gupta,
Under Secretary
29. Shri Mitter Sain,
Dy. Secretary
30. Dr. R.S. Tiwari,
Asstt. Director
31. Shri G. Bhujbal,
Joint Director
32. Shri Anil Kapoor,
ALC (C), Delhi
33. Shri B.K. Gupta,
Insurance Commissioner
34. Dr. (Mrs) Shashi Prabha,
Medical Commissiner, ESIC
35. Smt. Naina Bakshi,
Asstt. Director
36. Shri David Mally,
ADX, DGET

ANNEXURE III

RESOLUTION OF THE 33rd SESSION OF THE INDIAN LABOUR CONFERENCE HELD ON 24th & 25th OCTOBER, 1996.

Whereas Article 24 of the Constitution stipulates that no child below the age of 14 years shall be employed to work in any factory or mines or engaged in any other hazardous employment, and Article 39 provides that the State shall direct its policy towards securing that children are given opportunities and facilities to develop in a healthy manner and in condition of freedom and dignity and that childhood and youth are protected against exploitation and against moral and material abandonment.

Having taken into account the aforesaid and noting the pace and progress of efforts directed towards the elemination of child labour hitherto at the Central and State levels.

We, the members of Indian Labour Conference affirm our wholehearted support to the commitment of the Government to eliminate the child labour in all industries and occupations and realising the need for accelerating the pace and progress in the elimination of child labour and providing a momentum to the ongoing efforts, resolved that the Government should provide strong administrative and adequate budgetary support on its own and also secure necessary support from the relevant international organisations for programmes in this behalf of elimination of child labour from all occupations and industries and that resources should be pooled from a variety of resources and integrated imaginatively and skillfully to secure the objective of convergence and synergy in implementation of elemination of child labour initiatives and efforts to make the entire process meaningful and create the desired impact.

ANNEXURE IV

CONCLUSIONS ARRIVED AT IN THE 33rd SESSION OF THE INDIAN LABOUR CONFERENCE (ILC) – (APPROVED BY THE DRAFTING COMMITTEE

1. The Conference noted that different wage ceilings exist for various benefits under different labour laws. Ministry of Labour should prepare a draft statement on wage ceilings and place it before the next Session of the Standing Labour Committee.
2. The Conference noted that a large section of the employees of the Public Sector Undertakings and Central Government have resorted to strike/served strike notice on the issue of wage ceilings fixed for payment of Productivity linked bonus and urged the Government to remove these wage ceilings as well as under the provisions of the Act. However, the employers' group urged a total review of the Bonus Act.
3. The Conference noted its concern over the delay in implementation of the Turn Around Plan for revival of sick mills of NTC even after its approval by the Cabinet. Therefore, Labour Ministry should convene a meeting of Union Ministries of Labour, Finance and Textiles and Trade Unions and the concerned State Governments to expedite a decision in the matter. In the meantime, Ministry of Textiles should take steps to pay wages in time and bonus before Diwali, 1996.
4. The response received from various State Governments on the conclusions of the ILC to revive the practice of holding tripartite consultations at the State level was noted. It was felt that though some of the Government have set up such Bodies at the State level, some of these Bodies are neither truly tripartite in nature nor do they hold their meetings on a regular basis. Therefore, Minister for Labour should again write to the State Governments to revive the practice of holding tripartite consultations at the State level by constituting truly and appropriately representative Tripartite Bodies and by holding its meetings atleast twice a year.
5. As decided at the 31st Session of the ILC immediate steps

should be taken by the Ministry of Labour to constitute a Bipartite Committee with a view to frame a comprehensive industrial relations law who will submit their report in 3 months time. The Bipartite Committee should consider proposal to amend the Trade Unions Act, 1926 and the question of recognition of trade unions through secret ballots on a priority basis and submit its recommendations within a month. As far as Workers Participation in Management is concerned, the Workers Group wanted the Ministry of Labour to come to an immediate decision. However, the Employers representatives reiterated their stand that workers participation is not feasible through legislation. Employers' views will be considered by the Labour Ministry before finalising the Bill.

6. For workers, the ceiling fixed for payment of gratuity under the Payment of Gratuity Act, 1972 is Rs. 1 lakh whereas it has been raised to Rs. 2.5 lakh in the case of Central Government employees. The disparity should be removed by raising the ceiling of gratuity to Rs. 2.5 lakh for workers.
7. Ministry of Labour should take steps to ensure the presence of Finance Minister, Industries Minister, Textiles Minister, Commerce and other concerned Ministers in the meetings of the ILC. The Conference felt that some Ministries of the Government of India are not giving the ILC Session due importance and are not deputing officers at the appropriate level to attend the Conference. The Ministry of Labour should convey the feelings of the Conference and request various Central Ministries to depute their senior officers not below the rank of Joint Secretary to attend ILC Session.
8. Labour Ministry should discuss with the Deptt. of Public Enterprises and other concerned Ministries the issue of variance in application of the revised DA formula in public sector enterprises and review the issue of non-payment of revised DA to sick PSUs employees and the status of wage revision in CPSUs taking help of SCOPE and Workers representatives.
9. The Government of India should include representatives of Central Trade Union Organisations and Employers' Organisations in the Indian Delegation to attend the Ministerial level meeting of the WTO in Singapore in December, 1996.

10. Representative of the Central Trade Union Organisations should also be associated/involved in monitoring of the implementation of National Child Labour Projects.
11. A National Floor Level Minimum Wage for unorganised establishments should be fixed taking into account the poverty line basis as well as the decisions of the Supreme Court.
12. Vocational Training Programme of DGE&T should be re-oriented towards improving the quality of vocational training and upgradation of skills. Employment Exchanges should be modernised and re-organised to function as an effective placement centre.
13. Trade Union representatives may also be involved when Central Industrial Relations Machinery visit the Export Processing Zones.
14. The conclusions reached in the ILC should be construed as matters of continuing importance until they are disposed of by appropriate follow up action; and such of the conclusions of the 32nd Session of the ILC which have not been so far implemented should be pursued including through review committee meetings.

APPENDIX VI

PROPOSALS ON LABOUR POLICY FOR INCLUSION IN THE THIRD FIVE YEAR PLAN AS APPROVED BY THE STANDING LABOUR COMMITTEE AT ITS 18TH SESSION

I. *Approach to Industrial Relations*

1. It was considered that strong trade unions, and enlightened employers and minimum intervention by Government constitute the basic elements of sound industrial relations.

2. The policy as laid down in the Second Five Year Plan which leaves adequate scope for the parties to come together on their own initiative for settlement of their differences and empowers Government to refer disputes to adjudication in the event of a breakdown, requires to be somewhat modified. The modification should envisage (a) strengthening the current emphasis on reaching bipartite agreements and tripartite conventions like the Code of Discipline on a voluntary basis and extending their coverage to both the public and private sectors, and (b) more intensive efforts at securing agreement for reference of disputes to voluntary arbitration.

3. The principles of voluntary arbitration agreed to at the 17th Session of the Indian Labour Conference (Madras, July, 1959) were reiterated. While noting the possible difficulties in operating these principles, the Committee recommended the following measures to secure increased recourse to voluntary arbitration:

(i) Voluntary arbitration in its present form does not bind workers who do not belong to a trade union which enters into an agreement with the employers. There should be an amendment of the relevant Act which will provide that the decisions reached in voluntary arbitration should have the same status as awards of Industrial Tribunals. Specifically, these decisions should be binding on all employees, irrespective of whether they belong to the union or not. In this connection the implication of the recent Supreme Court decision require to be examined while framing the proposed legislation.

(ii) There are certain restraints placed on the parties under the Industrial Disputes Act, 1947 when a dispute is referred to a

Tribunal. These should also apply to the parties if they take recourse to voluntary arbitration.

(iii) The Central and State Government should prepare in consultation with the employers' and workers' organisations, lists of suitable persons who would accept the responsibility of acting as arbitrators. These lists should be compiled on a regional and industry-wise-basis. The persons included in the lists should be such as would inspire confidence of the parties. It would, however, be open to parties to select an arbitrator out of these lists or even outside these lists.

(iv) The question whether persons who accept the responsibility to act as arbitrators should be paid or not, needed further consideration.

(v) Recognition of trade unions on the part of employers is a necessary prerequisite for the success of voluntary arbitration. While welcoming the progress made in this matter through the Code of Discipline, the Committee recognised the need to intensify efforts to secure a better working of the existing voluntary arrangements concerning recognition of unions.

(vi) the workers' representatives suggested that (a) representative of labour should have access to all information and records relevant to the dispute, (b) expenses incurred by both the parties in connection with an industrial dispute should be borne by the Industry, and (c) there should be nationalisation of audit for undertakings in the private sector. The employers' representatives did not however, accept these suggestions and agreed to inform Government of their reasons for non-acceptance.

II. *Industrial Relations Machinery*

1. The Machinery for Industrial Relations should consist of :

(a) Conciliation Officers;
(b) Arbitrators (Voluntary); and
(c) Industrial Tribunals.

2. Some criticism was voiced by workers' representatives regarding the functioning of the conciliation machinery, particularly in regard to (a) delays, (b) calibre of conciliation officers, (c) reluctance of employers to lay their cards on the table, and (d) employers' tendency to send junior officers in their establishments for conciliation proceedings with inadequate power for entering into a settlement.

Employers' representative, however, did not accept the criticism implied in (c) and (d). As regards the difficulties referred to in (a) and (b), the Committee felt that (i) the calibre of the conciliation officers needed improvement, (ii) there should be a provision for training-on-the-job as well as refresher training for conciliation officers, and (iii) adequate strengthening of the conciliation machinery was necessary.

3. Another difficulty experienced in conciliation was the absence of 'norms' for settling disputes. Over the last 10 years, sufficient judicial and other pronouncements have been made on industrial matters which will enable the evolving of such norms by tripartite committees as has been done in some States. This is a task to which Governments at the Centre and in the States should address themselves.

4. At present conciliation proceedings do not start unless there is a threat of strike. This association between threat to strike and conciliation requires to be removed in the interest of better functioning of the machinery. Conciliation in all cases should commence as soon as a dispute is referred to the officer concerned by either of the parties.

5. The adjudication machinery should be used sparingly in accordance with the principles agreed to at the 17th Session of the Indian Labour Conference.

6. The question of creation of a special cadre for industrial judges should be considered to secure higher status for judges appointed on Tribunals.

7. Opinion was divided whether the Labour Appellate Tribunal should be reviewed at this stage or not.

8. Workers' representatives urged that the enforcement Tribunal envisaged in paragraph 15 of the Chapter on Labour Policy and Programme in the Second Five Year Plan, should be set up.

9. Workers' representatives pointed out that in some cases retired judges of industrial tribunals secured employment with employers and stressed that this should be discouraged. Employers' representatives said that such instances were extremely rare.

10. The Committee also felt that there was need to provide for a Mediation Service for dealing with disputes in the early stages. The mediators could be brought in at a stage before a dispute comes to the surface and could be approached by employers and workers informally in any situation which may lead to a dispute.

III. *Trade Unions*

It was recognised that the conditions for the success of any industrial society were the existence of strong and healthy organisations of workers and employers. It was suggested that Government should consider the question of implementing the recommendation made in the Second Five Year Plan concerning certification of employers' associations as representatives of the industry in an area, where there association seek such certification. In addition, the following steps for improvement in the trade unions were suggested while reiterating the recommendations made in this regard in the Second Five Year Plan these were :

1. The election of collective bargaining agent was not favoured nor was the consensus of opinion in favour of any attempts being made for the present, to enlist in trade unions through systems comparable to 'union ship,' persons who did not desire to join the union.
2. The present position in the Code of Discipline in securing recognition on a voluntary basis should be given a further trial before changes are made in favour of legislation.
3. Workers' representatives urged that special leave and other facilities should be given to employees for appearing before the industrial relations machinery and courts. The employers, representatives pointed out that reasonable facilities were already being given in such cases.

IV. *Rationalisation*

While the policy on rationalisation outlined in the Second Five Year Plan and endorsed at the 15th Session of the Indian Labour Conference (New Delhi, July, 1957) was reiterated, it was suggested that Technical Committees should be set up at the Centre as well as in the States to ensure that rationalisation schemes were sound and were implemented according to agreed principles.

V. *Wages*

(i) Workers' representatives made a reference to the comments made by the Pay Commission concerning the norms for fixation of minimum wages, evolved at the 15th Session of the Indian Labour Conference (New Delhi—July, 1957). A suggestion was made that the policy enunciated by the said Conference regarding the need-based minimum wage, should be embodied in the Third Five Year Plan.

While noting the difficulties that stood in the way of full implementation at this stage of the norms recommended by the conference, the Chairman suggested and the Committee agreed with the suggestion, that the question of nutritional requirements for a worker and his family and the composition of the diet which is to provide the requisite nutrition, needed further examination at the technical level.

(ii) A point was made that wage differentials between skilled and unskilled workers, had narrowed down. While reduction of wide disparities in wages was a desirable objective, the question required to be considered from the point of view of the need for adequate incentives also.

(iii) Referring to the policy set out in the Second Five Year Plan that the aim of wage policy should be to evolve a wage structure with rising real wages, workers' representatives pointed out that, compared to the year 1947, real earnings of the workers had come down in the case of the skilled workers. It was felt that the matter required detailed examination.

(iv) It was urged that steps should be taken to ensure a more effective enforcement of the "Fair Wage Clause" to protect the interests of the workers concerned in the construction industry.

(v) It was suggested that Government should consider the question of adding to the schedule to the Minimum Wages Act, other employments where working conditions were bad and the workers, needed statutory protection.

(vi) A point was made that, whereas production had increased in recent years, real wages had not kept pace and that it was necessary that wages should rise with productivity. The existing knowledge in regard to (a) techniques for measurement of productivity, and (b) norms on the basis of which gains of productivity should be shared, was not adequate. It was, therefore, suggested that productivity studies should be undertaken in some selected industries to evolve such techniques, norms, etc. Securing of suitable technical assistance under the I.L.O. Technical Assistance Programme may also be explored in this connection. The programme of Productivity Studies should be drawn up in consultation with the National Productivity Council and a small Steering Committee, with which workers' and employers' representatives were to be associated, should be set up to deal with matters connected with the proposed studies.

(vii) Criteria should be evolved for ascertaining an industry's capacity to pay.

(viii) The employers' representatives suggested that bonus which was an uncertain element in the wage cost, should be done away with. After some discussion, it was agreed that the question was one of evolving some suitable norms so that the uncertainty associated with it was minimised. It was agreed that for this purpose a Bonus Commission which should go into the question and evolve some suitable norms, should be appointed. The other terms of reference of the proposed Commission should be decided by a small Tripartite Sub-Committee which should be set up for the purpose.

(ix) A number of Wage Boards had been set up in years and more were likely to be appointed soon. Some of the problems which the existing Wage Boards had to tackle were likely to be faced by Wage Boards which will be appointed in future. There was need to have co-ordination whereby the experience already gained and the essential data which could be compiled in advance) could be made available to these Wage Boards.

VI. Two general points mainly concerning employment but having a bearing on wages were also mentioned. These were (i) settlement of landless labour on lands available for distribution, and (ii) provision of additional employment opportunities to workers engaged in seasonal and casual employment.

VII. *Worker Participation in Management*

Worker Participation in Management scheme which has been operating successfully in some selected units, should be extended to as many establishments as possible. To intensify the drive for extension of the scheme, the existing arrangements at the Centre should be strengthened. Suitable machinery should also be created at the State level for this purpose.

VIII. *Workers' Education*

While it was agreed that the programme of workers' education should be intensified in the Third Five Year Plan, workers' representatives, felt that, apart from the current activity undertaken by the Central Board of Workers' Education, there was need for diversifying the workers' education programme and associating workers' representatives with it at various levels. Trade Unions could play an important role in this field. In considering such diversification, the Board should explore how far, in some of these diversified programmes, more effective use could be made of workers' organisations with suitable assistance from the Board.

Some of the workers' representatives pointed out that the question of management training in labour matters should also receive increasing attention.

IX. *Social Security*

(i) The consensus of opinion was in favour of the proposal made in the Memorandum that the integrated social security scheme recommended by the Study Group, should be implemented during the Third Five Year Plan, subject to such modifications as might become necessary as a result of consultations with the workers' and employers' organisations.

(ii) The Employers/representatives made a reference to the proposal concerning enhancement of the rate of contribution to the provident fund from 6¼ to 8½ per cent. After some discussion, it was agreed that Technical Committee which should recommend the industries where the proposed enhanced rate of contribution could be introduced straightway should be appointed. To begin with, the Technical Committee should undertake investigations in respect of the following 4 of the six industries initially covered under the Employees' Provident Funds Act, 1952 :

1. Cigarettes
2. Paper
3. Iron and Steel
4. Electrical, mechanical or general engineering products.

(iii) It was suggested that 'Family Planning' should be increasingly brought within the scope of the programmes under the Employees' State Insurance Scheme.

(iv) The workers' representatives suggested that while considering the question of implementation of the integrated social security scheme, recommended by the Study Group on Social Security, Government should also examine the question of introducing schemes relating to compulsory life insurance for industrial workers. The question of permitting workers to finance life insurance policies from the Fund under the Integrated Scheme should also be examined.

(v) The coverage of the Employees' Provident Fund Scheme should be extended to commercial establishments also.

X. *Working Conditions*

(i) Steps should be taken to ensure effective implementation of the existing statutory provisions concerning working conditions.

(ii) The Committee noted with concern that the rate of accidents has been on the increase during the last few years. It was urged that greater attention should be paid to the problem of *safety*, and workers and employers should extend their full co-operation in any programme intended to promote greater safety. There was need to study the problem in detail with a view to improving safety devices and promoting greater safety. It was suggested that relevant data regarding all aspects of safety should be collected, and analysed and the whole subject of safety discussed in a comprehensive manner in a Safety Conference which should be convened for the purpose. The proposed Conference should cover all industries/occupations other than mines.

(iii) While there was general agreement on the point that the system of *contract labour* should be abolished progressively, it was recognised that it may not be possible to do away with the system completely. It was urged that steps should be taken to implement the various recommendations made in the Second Five Year Plan regarding gradual abolition of contract labour, wherever feasible, securing for such labour, conditions and protection enjoyed by other workers, etc. Other suggestions made were (a) the programme of studies being undertaken, pursuant to the recommendation made in the Second Five Year Plan, to ascertain the extent and nature of the problem of contract labour, should cover coal mines and plantation also (b) workers' and employers' representatives should, as far as possible, be associated with these studies, and (c) agencies like co-operatives, should be encouraged to take up functions of contractors. Such co-operatives were functioning in a number of States. It was suggested that a study should be made of the experience gained in the working of such co-operatives with a view of eliminating possible malpractices in the functioning of these co-operatives.

XI. *Industrial Housing*

While noting the steps taken recently the Government by way of liberalising the procedures and the terms of assistance under the Industrial Housing Scheme, the Committee felt that the progress of the scheme so far had not been quite satisfactory and urged that steps should be taken to ensure speedy progress in future. The specific suggestions made in this connection were :

(i) The existing legislation in different States relating to land acquisition should be suitably amended, wherever not already done, with a view to eliminating procedural delays in acquisition of land, etc.,

(ii) the administration of the Departments of Co-operation in the States should be improved with a view to ensuring speedy progress so far as co-operative housing schemes are concerned,

(iii) there was need to study the problem of Industrial Housing in detail with a view to formulating steps for ensuring better progress of the Industrial Housing Scheme. It was suggested that relevant material relating to the various aspects of industrial housing should be collected and the views of the State Governments on how further progress can be made in the field of housing, obtained. Thereafter the whole subject of industrial Housing should be discussed in a comprehensive manner at the next session of the Indian Labour Conference.

XII. *Labour Research*

The organisations agreed to send their proposals concerning the programme for Labour Research during the Third Five Year Plan period.

APPENDIX VII

FIVE-YEAR LABOUR PROGRAMME

A brief summary of the programme is given below :

1. *Legislation*

(i) Revision of the Factories Act
(ii) Enactment of Health Insurance Legislation
(iii) Minimum Wages Legislation
(iv) Amendment of the Trade Unions Act
(v) Trade Disputes Legislation
(vi) Revision of the Workmen's Compensation Act
(vii) A Central Act for Maternity Benefits
(viii) A Central Act regulating conditions of work in Shops and Commercial Undertakings
(ix) Legislation for regulating conditions of work in Road Transport and other Services, viz Tramways and Motor Vehicles Plying for Passenger or Goods Traffic, Dock and Municipal labour
(x) Revision of the Mines Act
(xi) Legislation to replace the Ordinance constituting the Coal Mines Welfare Fund, and for providing dispensary service for Coal Miners
(xii) Revision of the Payment of Wages Act.
(xiii) Legislation for enforcing improvements in the working conditions in Plantations.

2. *Administrative Measures*

A. *Provincial*

(i) Expansion of the Factory Inspection Services
(ii) Organisation of an Inspectorate for enforcing legislation relating to the regulation of conditions of workers in Shops and Commercial Undertakings, Transport Services and Plantations, etc.
(iii) Setting up of an Administrative Organisation for prescribing and enforcing minimum wages in 'sweated' industries.

(iv) Conciliation and Adjudication Machinery
(v) Labour Welfare Organisation
(vi) Housing
(vii) Provision of medical service in connection with the Health Insurance Scheme
(viii) Extension of measures recently taken by the Central Government for the benefit of workers in road construction and building to similar categories in the Provinces, and
(ix) Co-operation between Central and Provisional Governments in regard to :

(a) collection and maintenance of statistics relative to cost of living indices and labour statistics;
(b) exchange of information regarding labour situation; and
(c) conduct of enquiry into earnings of agricultural labour.

B. *Central*

(i) Organisation of the Workmen's State Insurance Corporation
(ii) Organisation of the Chief Adviser, Factories
(iii) Expansion of the Mines Inspectorate
(iv) Constitution of Labour Bureau
(v) Conciliation and Adjudication Machinery for Central Undertakings and for Centrally Administered Areas
(vi) Administration of the Coal Mines and Mica Mines Welfare Funds
(vii) Organisation of training courses for candidates for appointments as Labour Welfare or Personel Relations Officers either under Government or private employers.
(viii) Machinery to co-ordinate the execution of Housing Schemes.
(ix) Organisation and expansion of Employment Exchange Services.

3. *Joint Measures*

(i) Study of wage and dearness allowance structure with a view to standardising occupational terms and wages and the determination of differentials in wage rate as between various occupations in an industry and the promotion of agreements for the payment of a fair wage to all workers.

(ii) Measures for securing a living wage to miners and plantation workers.

(iii) Study of administrative and financial aspects of Unemployment Insurance

(iv) Elimination and regulation of contract labour

(v) Reform of the system of recruitment with a view to the elimination of middlemen

(vi) Institution and expansion of schemes for imparting training to workers, including miners, with a view to improve their productive and earning capacity.

(vii) Standardisation, as far as possible, of terms of service and the evolution of fair conditions of service, particularly relating to security of tenure

(viii) Constitution of Joint Works Committee of employers and workers.

(ix) Constitution of Industrial Committee for Coal, Plantations, Jute, Cotton Textiles and Engineering Industries.

APPENDIX VIII

REPORT OF THE SUB-COMMITTEE ON THE CONSTITUTION OF TRIPARTITE ORGANISATION

We met at New Delhi on 25 May 1945 to consider the proposals[1] made in the memorandum, dated 24 February 1945. Opinions were received in advance sub-committee and these were also discussed.

1. We are of opinion that no change need be made in the constitution of the Tripartite Plenary Labour Conference. It should deal with all labour Subjects and should briefly be called "Labour Conference." Its composition should remain unaltered but, in nominating representatives of employers and employees, not represented through the recognised all India organisations, care should be taken that they are drawn from classes which are not substantially represented on those organisations and are by themselves truly representative of the interests concerned. We doing so, the aim should be to discourage separatist tendencies, and to accord representation to such interests (particularly in the case of employing interests) as cannot be affiliated to the all-India organizations, e.g. municipalities, port trusts, stevedore labour or any other interests which are essentially non-industrial in character. It is understood that railway unions, as a rule are affiliated either to the All India Trade Union Congress or the Indian Federation of Labour and are thus already represented in fact on the tripartite organisation. Handloom industry, both master weavers and men, can also organise and secure representation through the all India organization.

2. The Standing Labour Committee should maintain its present composition with the Honourable the Labour Member as the President. The Committee should, however, derive its power from the Labour Conference. The Committee should deal with specific general questions referred to it by the Conference for detailed examination and report, as also with matters on which Government may desire similar examination before fuller discussion at the Labour Conference. The latter cases will partake somewhat of the double-discussion procedure in vogue at the International Labour Organization. The

1. Same as those in the Chairman's Speech at the sixth session of the Indian Labour Conference.

recommendations and reports of the Committee should be made to the Conference except when the Conference itself directs the Committee to address them to Government or in cases of considerable urgency when to avoid delay Government may require early advice of the Tripartite Organization. It will be open to the Committee to advise that no action should be taken in the latter class of cases, pending a full discussion at the Conference—and, if in such a case, Government found necessary to take action before receipt of the Conference's opinion, it would not be open to Government to quote or rely on the opinion of the Standing Labour Committee. Sir Shri Ram (representative of employers) dissents from these views and considers that the recommendations, etc., of the Committee should invariably be addressed to Labour Conference, except in cases of extreme urgency. The expressions of opinion at the Standing Labour Committee should be treated as confidential.

4. We consider it would be difficult to set up a Labour Welfare Committee to deal with various labour subjects on an all-India basis. It is preferable to make a start with *ad hoc* committee on tripartite basis either for different industries or on a regional or all-India basis, according to requirements of each case. The aim should be ultimately to move towards the evolution of a single Labour Welfare Committee for all industries and regions in the light of the working of the *ad hoc* committee. We attach two lists on the 'terms and conditions of employment' and 'concrete questions relating to Labour Welfare, second of which in our opinion, is suitable for the selection of subjects on which *ad hoc* committees may be appointed as and when advisable. These lists are not exhaustive and may be amended or added to from time to time.

5. We understand that Government representatives meet together a day before the Labour Conference with a view to arrive at an agreed plan for discussions at the Conference. We consider that it might prove advisable for the different groups represented in the Labour Conference similarly to have a discussion among themselves before the Conference to exchange views, formulate group policy and to avoid repetitions of arguments at the Conference, to select speakers for the expression of their views. Government should make available to the all-India organisations concerned the names of persons appointed to represent independent employers and employees and should be prepared to make available if required a room for such group discussions.

H.C. Prior
A. Hughes
S.V. Joshii
M.A. Mirza
Shri Ram
R. Menzies
V.V. Giri
V.M. Tarkunde.

LIST I

Terms and conditions of employment

1. Recruitment—methods of
2. Wages-fixation and payment
3. Hours of work—limitations and exception's
4. Working conditions in regard to health and safety
5. Standing Orders and unfair practices
6. Holidays—paid and unpaid
7. Termination of employment
8. Combination and recognition

LIST II

Concrete questions relating to Labour Welfare

1. Housing-provision of and rent.
2. Health-in habitations
   (a) dietary
   (b) medical facilities
   (c) sanitary arrangement
3. Education—3 R's and vocational.
4. Other activities :

A—inside the work place
   (a) canteen
   (b) shelters for rest
   (c) creches

B—at home
   (a) physical culture
   (b) recreation
   (c) amusement

5. Co-operation.
6. Employment of welfare staff

APPENDIX IX

NOTE ON THE CONSTITUTION OF THE INDIAN LABOUR CONFERENCE AND THE STANDING LABOUR COMMITTEE

[Placed before the eighth session of the Indian Labour Conference, New Delhi, 21-22 April 1947]

The Indian Labour Conference and the Standing Labour Committee were constituted in 1942. According to the Constitution, the Conference was to consist of 44 representatives—22 representing Central, Provincial and State Governments. 11 represerrting employers and 11 representing workers. The Conference should meet at least once a year and its functions were "to advice the Government of India on any matters referred to it for advice, taking into account suggestions made by Provincial organisations of workers and employers recognised for the purpose of the Conference."

2. The Standing Labour Committee was to consist of 20 members—10 representatives of Government, 5 of employers and 5 of workers. The Constitution provided that the Committee :

"(i) should meet as often as it might be convened by the Central Government for the consideration of question that might arise before it; and

(ii) should advise Government on any matters referred to it by Government, but that copies of such advice should be forwarded to all members of the Plenary Conference upon any matters referred to it by that Conference."

3. At the next Labour Conference held in September 1943, it was decided that delegates might be accompanied by advisers. Provision was accordingly made that :

"(i) A delegate representing more than one Province or State may be accompanied by one adviser each from such Province or State other than 3 advisers; and

(ii) a delegate representing the Government of India may be accompanied by not more than his own;

(iii) each delegation representing employers and workers may be accompanied by advisers, not exceeding the number of delegates constituting the delegation."

The adviser may speak but not vote.

4. After some experience was gained of the working of the Conference, it was found that the Constitution needed certain changes. They are briefly as described below :

(i) It was felt that there was no clear-cut division of functions between the Conference and the Standing Labour Committee. It was not that one was a deliberative body and the other an executive body. Both were deliberative, and the subjects discussed by both were of the same nature.

(ii) There being no clear-cut division between questions and concrete problems, the discussion in the Conference, as well as in the Committee became too general to be of much use. Even concrete problems were treated as though they were general.

(iii) The provision relating to advisers also needed modification.

(iv) There was no machinery to undertake the task of examining special problems and reporting upon them.

(v) There was no machinery to study and advise on problems of labour welfare, industry by industry.

(vi) There was criticism from the employers side against the reservation of three seats, to be filled by nomination by Government.

(vii) The method of representation of labour was also said to suffer from the defect that among those who represented labour there were none who actually belonged to the working classes.

(viii) An analogy was also drawn between the I.L.O. and the Conference and it was claimed that the Conference both in its Constitution and procedure should be modelled on the I.L.O. and that it should have the right to decide its own agenda.

5. Dealing with the criticism that Labour Conference should be modelled on the I.L.O., the then Labour Member pointed out that the I.L.O. was an independent organisation created by an International treaty and that its Conventions and Recommendations placed definite obligations on Member State, failure to fulfil which involved certain international liabilities. Its constitution was regulated by itself and it has its own independent finance. The Indian Labour Conference, on the other hand, was not independent in the same sense as the I.L.O.

was. It was only an advisory body constituted to advise the Government of India on such matters as were referred to it for advice. It could not take decisions. On the questions of the right of the Labour Conference to determine its agenda, the then Labour Member said that Government could not surrender the right to frame the agenda for the Conference as the Conference was not a Legislature or any independent authority.

Certain suggestions were placed before the Sixth Labour Conference for consideration.

First, it was suggested the subjects should be divided into two categories, one dealing with general subjects, such as terms and conditions of employment, labour legislation, questions relating to social security and the other dealing with all concrete questions relating to labour welfare and administration of labour laws. Subjects in List I should be assigned to the Plenary Conference and a new body should be created, called the Labour Welfare Committee, which would consider subjects coming in List II.

Secondly, the Standing Labour Committee should cease to be a deliberative body, and that it should act as the agent of the Conference and perform such duties as may be assigned to it from time to time. It would normally report to the Conference, but it should be open to Government to refer to it any matter on which it needed advice urgently.

6. These proposals were remitted for consideration by a Committee which reported that "no change need be made in the Constitution" of the Plenary Labour Conference and that it should continue to deal with all labour subjects. Its composition should remain unaltered; but in nominating representatives of employers and employees, not represented through recognised all-India organisations, care should be taken that they are drawn from classes which are not substantially represented on these organisations and by themselves truly representative of the interconcerned. In doing so, the aim should be to courage separatist tendencies and accord represention only to such interests as cannot be affilitated all-India organisations.

The Standing Committee should maintain its present composition, but it should derive its powers from the Labour Conference. It should deal with specific general questions referred to it by the Conference for detailed examination and report, as also matters on which Government may desire similar examination before fuller discussion at the Conference. The latter will partake somewhat of the double-discussion procedure in vogue at the International Labour Organisation. The recommendations and reports of the Committee should be made to the Conference except when the Conference itself directs the Committee to address them to Government or in cases of considerable urgency when to avoid delay, Government may require early advice of the tripartite organisation, but it will be open to the committee to advise that no action should be taken in the latter class or case except after a full discussion at the Conference. The Committee also Considered "that it would be difficult to set up a Labour Welfare Committee to deal with labour subjects on an all-India basis and preferred that a start should be made with *ad hoc* committees on a tripartite basis either for different industries or on a regional or on all-India basis, according to requirements of each case." When the report of the Committee was discussed, workers' representatives desired the establishment of industrial committees on the lines of the I.L.O. The matter was left there, and a final decision was deferred for the time being.

7. Government have now decided to set up Industrial Committees for all principal industries. A Committee has been set up for Plantation Labour. Committee have been organised for coal mining and cotton textile industries. It is also proposed to set up Committee for other important industries. These Committees will discuss various specific problems special to the industries covered by them and submit their reports to the Conference, which will co-ordinate their activities. In urgent cases, Government may take action on the basis of conclusions reached by the Committees, but even then a report will be made to the main Conference of the action taken by Government.

8. The constitution of these Industrial Committees raises the question whether some change is not required in the Constitution and functions of the Labour Conference and the Standing Labour Committee. If both these bodies are to serve as deliberative bodies, there is clearly no need for three meetings in a year or even two. Unless its Constitution is revised, the Standing Labour Committee cannot serve as an executive body of the Labour Conference either. It is too big a body to serve as an efficient Executive Committee. It has been set up more as a deliberative body than as an executive organisation. It is, therefore, suggested that the Standing Labour Committee should be abolished and should be replaced by a Standing Committee consisting of 12 replaced by a Standing Committee consisting of 12 members, 6 from the Government group, 3 from employers and 3 from workers. Even 12 is a somewhat unwieldy

number for an executive body and a committee of eight members might be just the right one. The Standing Committee which will be an executive body might be entrusted with the duty of giving full consideration to the agenda of the Conference, to submit a report of the conclusions on each item for the consideration of the Conference. This would provide for a preliminary examination at a fairly expert level of the various items comings up for the agenda. Discussions at the Conference would be more purposeful and to the point, if this preliminary examination could be arranged for. In addition, the Standing Committee may also consider the programme of the Conference and its future agenda. This would provide the necessary link between Conference and Government in regard to the agenda. In other words, while Government will continue to finally determine what the agenda should be they would have an opportunity of knowing the views of employers' and workers' representatives on the subjects that may be suggested for discussion at the Conference. The Standing Committee will meet before the Conference, but in addition, meeting of the Committee could be arranged as and when found necessary.

9. Another question for consideration is whether the Labour Conference should consist of 44 representatives, and if so whether representation should be assigned to the various bodies. For example, in regard to workers' representatives the question has been raised that equal representation should not be given to all organisation, irrespective of their size and standing in the country. The points for consideration are :

(i) should the representation assigned to the different organisations represented at the Conference be modified, and if so, how ;

(ii) should any other organisation be asked to nominate representatives, and if so, which; and

(iii) should Government continue to have a right to nominate some of the employers' and workers' representatives as at present and if so, what arrangements should be made to provide for proper representation of unorganised employers and workers?

10. So long as the main Conference was dealing both with general questions and specific problems, there was probably justification for the presence of advisers. For, the newly set-up Industrial Committee will discuss all specific problems relating to individual industries. If

the suggestion in paragraph 8 is accepted, the Conference will have the benefit of a preliminary examination of the items on by agenda by the Standing Committee, so that the plenary session will deal with only general principles. This being the case, there would be no necessity for advisers. If this is accepted the right of delegates to bring advisers might now be withdrawn.

APPENDIX X

RESOLUTION ON INDUSTRIAL TRUCE

In December 1947 the Industrial Conference consisting of representatives of Government (Central, Provincial and Indian States), employers and workers unanimously adopted the following resolution on industrial truce :

RESOLUTION

This Conference considers that the increase in industrial production which is so vital to the economy of the country cannot be achieved without the fullest cooperation between labour and management and stable and friendly relations between them. The employers must recognise the proper role of labour industry and the need to secure for labour fair wages and working conditions; labour for its part must give equal recognition to its duty in contributing to the increase of the national income without which a permanent rise in the general standard of living cannot be achieved. Mutual discussion of all problems common to both and a determination to settle all disputes without recourse to interruption in or slowing down of production should be the common aim of employers and labour. The system of remuneration to capital as well as labour must be so devised that while in the interests of the consumers and the primary producers excessive profits should be prevented by suitable measures of taxation and otherwise, both will share the product of their common effort after making provision for payment of fair wages to labour a fair return on capital employed in the industry and reasonable reserves for the maintenance and expansion of the undertaking. For attaining these objectives, this Conference recommends :

(i) That the fullest use should be made of statutory and other machinery for the resolution of industrial disputes in a just and peaceful manner; where it does not exist, it should be created without delay. Such machinery should as far as possible be uniform throughout India.

(ii) The establishment of machinery, Central, regional and functional, for the study and determination of fair wages and conditions of labour, and fair remuneration for capital; and methods for the association of labour in all matters concerning industrial production, such as the formation of Central, Regional and Unit Production Committees.

(iii) The constitution in each industrial undertaking of Works Committees representing management and duly elected representatives of labour for the settlement of any dispute which may arise from day to day.

(iv) That, as a first step towards improving the standard of living of workers immediate attention should be devoted to the problems of housing of industrial labour; the cost of such housing should be shared in suitable proportions between the Government, employers and labour, the share labour being given in the shape of a reasonable rent.

The principals enunciated above having been accepted, this Conference calls upon labour and management to agree to maintain industrial peace and to avert lockouts, strikes or slowing down of production during the next three years.

This Conference invites labour and management to assist Government to secure, promote and guarantee such agreements between the parties as will usher in a period of contented and orderly advancement towards a co-operative Commonwealth.

APPENDIX XI

INDUSTRIAL TRUCE RESOLUTION, 1962

(Adopted at the joint Meeting of Central Organisations of Employers and Workers held in New Delhi on 3 November 1962)

Realizing that a grave emergency has overtaken the nation on account of the Chinese aggression and the need has arisen for taking urgent steps, in every direction, to prepare adequately for the defence of the country and repelling the invasion of its territory the Joint Meeting of all Central Employers and Workers' Organisations, held today, November 3, 1962, resolves that no effort shall be spared to achieve maximum production, and managements and workmen will strive in collaboration in all possible ways, to promote the defence effort of the country and reaffirms their pledge of unstinted loyalty and devotion to the country. Towards these ends, the following steps shall be taken :

I. *Climate*

It is important that a suitable climate should be created and preserved for ensuring sustained effort and resolute action in pursuance of the aforesaid aim. Both sides should exercise restraint and forbearance, so that nothing is allowed to come in the way of their single-minded and concerted endeavour, in support of the defence of the country. Positive step should be taken to promote constructive co-operation between management and workers, in all possible ways.

II. *Industrial Peace*

(i) Under no circumstances shall there be any interruption in or slowing down of production of goods and services.

(ii) In respect of their economic interests both workers and employers will exercise voluntary restraint and accept the utmost sacrifice, in an equitable manner, in the interest of the nation and its defence efforts.

(iii) There should be maximum recourse to voluntary arbitration and adequate arrangements should be made for the purpose.

If necessity for a reference to adjudication arises, the processes connected with it should be completed with the utmost promptness.

(iv) The industries mentioned in the First Schedule to the Industrial Disputes Act, 1947 and such other industries as may be considered necessary, e.g., petroleum and its products, chemicals, etc., may be declared as public utility services under sub-clause (vi) of clause (n) of Section 2 of the Act.

(v) All complaints pertaining to dismissal, discharge, victimisation and retrenchment of individual workmen, not settled mutually should be settled through arbitration. For this purpose, the officers of the Conciliation Machinery may, if the parties agree, serve as arbitrators. Dismissals and discharges of workmen should, however, be avoided as possible.

(vi) The Labour administration at the Centre and States should be streamlined so that grievances and disputes are settled promptly and cordial industrial relations are maintained.

III. *Production*

(i) All impediments in the way of better and fuller utilisation of men, machinery and materials should be removed. There should be no idle plant capacity or waste. Managements should exercise the maximum economy in their operations.

(ii) To maximize production, Establishments should work, wherever possible, extra shifts, extra hours or on Sundays and holidays by mutual agreement. Full co-operation should be extended by all in this respect. All advantages accruing to industry out of the extra effort of the workers should go to the consumer and/or be made available for defence efforts.

(iii) Absenteeism and turn-over should be discouraged and reduced to the minimum. Negligence of duty, careless operation, damage to property and interference with or disturbance to normal work should be denounced by the unions. Similarly any lapse on the part of the management that contravenes the spirit of the defence effort should be condemned and put right forthwith.

(iv) Technical and skilled personnel in short supply should be switched over to emergent work having a bearing on defend. Simultaneously, steps should be taken to increase the supply of technical and skilled personel through apprenticeship and other training programmes.

(v) In the production drive the well-being and health of the working class should not be ignored.

IV. *Price Stability*

(i) Every effort should be made to ensure that prices of industrial goods and essential commodities are not allowed to increase.

(ii) To ensure supply of essential commodities at fair prices to the working class, steps should be taken, whenever necessary, to organise consumers' Co-operatives in each unit and in industrial areas.

V. *Savings*

(i) The imperative necessity of increasing savings in the larger interest of the country should be brought home to workers and managements and arrangements to facilitate greater savings should be provided forthwith.

(ii) Workers may be persuaded to contribute to National Defence Fund and/or invest in Defence Bonds every month an amount equivalent to at least one day's earnings. Managements also agree to contribute liberally towards National Defence Fund and/or invest in defence Bonds: the basis of their contribution will be settled in consultation with Government.

APPENDIX XII

MODEL GRIEVANCE PROCEDURE

1. *Grievance Machinery*

A. Grievance Machinery will be required to be set up in each undertaking to administer the Grievance Procedure. The minimum requirements of such a machinery would be as follows, except where an established procedure is already working to the mutual satisfaction of either party. Even in the latter case, every effort shall be made to bring the procedure in conformity with the Guiding Principles.

For the purpose of constituting a fresh Grievance Machinery, workers in each department (and where a department is too small, in a group of departments) and each shift, shall elect, from amongst themselves and for a period of not less than one year at a time, departmental representatives and forward the list of persons so elected to the management. Where the union(s) in the undertaking are in a position to submit an agreed list of names, recourse to election may not be necessary. Similar is the case where Works Committees are functioning satisfactorily, since the Workers Committees member of a particular constituency shall act as the departmental representative. Correspondingly, the management shall designate the persons for each department who shall be approached at the first stage and the departmental heads for handling grievances at the second stage. Two or three of the departmental representatives of workers and two or three departmental heads nominated by the management shall constitute the Grievance Committee, the composition of which is indicated in Annexure. In the case of appeals against discharges or dismissals, the management shall designate the authority to whom appeals could be made.

B. *Grievance Procedure*

While adaptations have to be made to meet special circumstances such as those obtaining in the Defence Undertakings, Railways, Plantations and also small undertaking employing few workmen the procedure normally envisaged in the handling of grievances should be as follows :

(1) An aggrieved employee shall first present his grievance verbally in person to the officer designated by management for his purpose. An answer shall be given within 48 hours of the presentation of complaint.

(2) If the worker is not satisfied with the decision of this officer or fails to receive an answer within the stipulated period, he shall, either in person or accompanied by his departmental representative present his grievances, to the Head of the Department designated by the Management for the purpose of handling grievances. (For this purpose, a fixed time shall be specified during which on any working day, an aggrieved worker could meet the Departmental Head for presentation of grievances). The Departmental Head shall give his answer within 3 days of the presentation of grievance, if action cannot be taken presentation of grievance. If action cannot be taken within that period, the reason for delay should be recorded.

(3) If the decision of the departmental head is unsatisfactory, the aggrieved worker may request the forwarding of his grievance to the 'Grievance Committee' which shall make its recommendations to the Manager within 7 days of the worker's request. If the recommendations cannot be made within this time-limit, the reason for such delay should be recorded. Unanimous recommendations of the Grievance Committee shall be implemented by the management. In the event of a difference of opinion among the members of the Grievance Committee, the views of the members along with the relevant papers shall be placed before the Manager for final decision. In either case, the final decision of the management shall be communicated to the workman concerned by the Personnel Officer within 3 days from the receipt of the Grievance Committee recommendations.

(4) Where the workman is not satisfied with the final decision of management, he shall have the right to appeal to management for a revision. In making this appeal the worker, if he so desires, shall have the right to take a union official along with him to facilitate discussions with management. Management shall communicate their decision within a week of the workman's revision petition.

If so agreement is still possible the union and the management shall refer the grievance to voluntary arbitration.

(5) Where a worker has taken up a grievance for redressal under this procedure, the formal Conciliation Machinery shall not intervene till all steps in the procedure are exhausted. A grievance shall be presumed to assume the form of a dispute only when the final

decision of the top management in respect of the grievance is turned down by the worker.

(6) If a grievance, arises out of an order given by management, the said order shall be complied with before the workman concerned invokes the procedure laid down for redressal of grievance. If however, there is a time lag between the issue of order and its compliance, the grievance procedure may immediately be invoked but the order nevertheless must be complied within the due date, even if all the steps in the grievance procedure have not been exhausted. It may, however, be advisable for the management to await the findings of the grievance procedure machinery.

(7) Workers' representatives on the Grievance Committee shall have the right of access to any document connected with the inquiry maintained in the department and which may be necessary to understand the merit or otherwise of the workers' grievances. The management's representatives shall have the right, however to refuse to show any document or give any information which they consider to be of a confidential nature. Such confidential document(s) shall not be used against the workman in the course of the grievance proceedings.

(8) There shall be a time-limit within which an appeal shall be taken from one step to the other. For this purpose, the aggrieved worker shall, within 72 hours of the receipt of the decision at one stage (for if no decision is received, on the expiry of the stipulated period) file his appeal with the authority at the next higher stage, should he feel inclined to appeal.

(9) In calculating the various time intervals under the above clauses, holidays shall not be reckoned.

(10) Management shall provide the necessary clerical and other assistance for the smooth functioning of the grievance machinery.

(11) If it is necessary for any worker to leave the department during working hours on call from the Labour/Personnel Officer or any other officer of the established grievance machinery, previous permission of his superior shall necessarily be obtained. Subject to this condition, the worker shall not suffer any loss in wages for the work—time lost in this manner.

(12) If, however, there be any, complaint against any individual member of the staff, who is nominated by the management to handle grievance at the lowest level, the workman may take up his grievances at the next higher stage, i.e., at the level of Departmental Head.

(13) In the case of any grievance arising out of discharge or dismissal of a workman, the above mentioned procedure shall not apply. Instead, a discharged or dismissed workman shall have the right to appeal either to the dismissing authority or to a senior authority who shall be specified by the management, within a week from the date of dismissal or discharge. At the time the appeal is heard, the workman may, if he so desires, be accompanied by either an official of the recognised union or a fellow worker, as the case may be.

ANNEXURE I

GUIDING PRINCIPLES FOR A GRIEVANCE PROCEDURE

Existing labour legislation does not provide for a well defined and adequate procedure for redressal of day-to-day grievances in industrial units. Clause 15 of the Model Standing orders in Schedule I of the Industrial Employment (Standing Orders) Central Rules, 1946 specifies that 'All complaints arising out of employment including those relating to unfair treatment or wrongful exaction on the part of the employer or his agent, shall be submitted to the manager or the other person specified in this behalf with the right to appeal to the employers.'

In some industrial units, however, detailed grievance procedure has been worked out by mutual agreement. In the absence of a satisfactory grievance procedure, day-to-day grievances are allowed to pile up with the result that the accumulated discontent culminates sometime or the other in cases of indiscipline, strikes, etc. In what follows, therefore, an attempt has been made to draw up Guiding Principles for a Grievance Procedure. It is realised that it may not be possible to apply all these principles in respect of each and every industrial unit. However, all units should endeavour to conform, as much as possible, to these principles.

Complaints affecting one or more individual workers in respect of their wage payments, over-time, leave, transfer, promotion, seniority, work assignment, working condition and interpretation of service agreement, dismissals and discharges would constitute[1] grievances. Where the points at dispute are of general applicability or of considerable magnitude, they will fall outside the scope of this procedure.

A Grievance Procedure should take note of the following principles :

1. *Conformity with existing legislation*

A Grievance Procedure forms part of the integrated scheme intended to promote satisfactory relations between employers and workers.

---

1. In the case of Defence undertakings, however, a special provision may have to made.

This procedure should be designed to supplement the existing statutory provisions and it may, where practicable make use of such machinery as is already provided by legislation. The Grievance Machinery can be availed of on the receipt by the worker of the order causing a grievance. The operation of the order, however, need not be held up till the grievance machinery is completely exhausted. Whatever possible, attempts should be made to complete the grievance procedure the time the order is passed and when it is acted upon.

2. *Need to make the machinery simple and expeditious*

(a) As far as possible grievances should be settled at the lowest level.
(b) No matter should ordinarily be taken up at more than two levels, i.e., normally there should be only on appeal.
(c) Different types of grievances may be referred to appropriate authorities.
(d) A grievance must be redressed as expeditiously as possible and towards this end, the employer, in consultation with workers should decide upon the time limit required of settling a grievance.

3. *Designation of authorities*

The workmen must know the authorities to be approached and it should, therefore, be incumbent on the management to designate the authorities to be contacted at various levels.

It may be useful to classify grievances as those arising from personal relationship and others arising out of conditions of employment. In the former case, a grievance should be taken up, in the first instance, with the authority in the line management immediately above the officer against whom the complaint is made. Thereafter, the matter may go to the Grievance Committee—comprising representatives of management and workers. The composition of the committee shall be decided at the unit level (see Annexure).

Other grievances should be taken up, in the first instance, with the authority designated by the management. Thereafter, a reference may be made to the Grievance Committee.

Where the matter goes to the Grievance Committee in the first instance, an appeal shall lie with the top management.

ANNEXURE II

CONSTITUTION OF GRIEVANCE COMMITTEE

1. *In the case where, the Union is recognised*

Two representatives of management plus a Union representative and the Union departmental representative of the Department in which the workmen concerned work.

2. *In the case where the Union is not recognised or there is no Union but there is works committee*

Two representatives of management plus the representatives of the Department of the workmen concerned on the Works Committee plus either the Secretary or Vice-President of the Works Committee this is in case the Secretary of the works Committee is also the workmen's departmental representative.

It is suggested that in the case of the management, their representatives should be the Departmental Head plus the official who dealt with the matter at the first stage, or personnel officer should act as an adviser.

The size of the 'Grievance Committee' should be limited to a maximum of four to six otherwise it becomes unwieldy.

APPENDIX XIII

INTER-UNION CODE OF CONDUCT

We the representatives of four Central Labour Organisations, namely, INTUC, AITUC, HMS and UTUC, agree to observe the following basic principles for maintaining harmonious inter-union relations :

1. Every employee in an industry or unit shall have the freedom and right to join a union of his choice. No coercion shall be exercised in this matter.
2. There shall be no dual membership of unions. (In the case of Representative Unions, this principle needs further examination).
3. There shall be unreserved acceptance of, and respect for, democratic functioning of trade unions.
4. There shall be regular and democratic elections of executive-bodies and office-bearers of trade unions.
5. Ignorance and/or backwardness of workers shall not be exploited by any organisation. No organisation shall make excessive or extravagant demands.
6. Casteism, communalism and provincialism shall be eschewed by all unions.
7. There shall be no violence, coercion, intimidation or personal vilification in inter-union dealings.
8. All Central Labour Organisations shall combat formation or continuance of Company Unions.

It was generally felt that machinery consisting of representatives of the four Central Labour Organisations, with an independent Chairman, might be set up for implementing the code of conduct. For the time being, Shri Nanda, the Union Labour Minister, might invite the parties, from time to time, for further developing and amplifying the Code.

APPENDIX XIV

MODEL PRINCIPLES FOR REFERENCE OF DISPUTES TO VOLUNTARY ARBITRATION UNDER THE CODE OF DISCIPLINE

The right to refer a dispute to voluntary arbitration rests with the parties concerned. Ordinarily, therefore, there should be no difficulty when both the parties to a dispute agree to refer the same to voluntary arbitration.

Arbitration may normally be sought when efforts little a dispute through mutual negotiations/conciliation have failed.

Disputes may not, however, be referred to voluntary arbitration :

(a) If there is an illegal strike or lockout or a strike or lockout resorted to without seeking settlement by means provided by law and without proper notice or in breach of the Code of Discipline as determined by the machinery set up for the purpose unless such a strike, or direct action, or lockout, as the case may be is called off.

(b) If the issues involved are such as have been the subject matter of recent judicial decisions or in respect of which unduly long time has elapsed since the origin of the cause of action.

1. Individual Disputes

Disputes covered by item II(v) of the Industrial nice Resolution i.e., those pertaining to dismissal, discharge, victimisation and retrenchment of individual workmen not settled mutually should normally be referred to arbitration and in particular :

(i) if there is case of alleged victimisation or unfair labour practice;

(ii) if the Standing Orders in force or the principles of natural justice do not appear to have been done to the workers.

(iii) if it appears prima facie the injustice has been done to the workers.

Cases of discharge and dismissal wherein breach of the Code of Discipline has been established by the settlementation Machinery concerned and also the workers where settlements have been reached with a recognised union may not be referred to voluntary arbitration.

Cases in which breach of the Code of Discipline have been alleged but not established may not be referred to voluntary arbitration unless the concerned officer of the Industrial Relations Machinery, dealing with the case, after investigation, *prima facie* comes to the conclusion that there is no breach of Code of Discipline involved or there is a room for doubt in reaching a conclusion as regards the breach of Code of Discipline.

7. In respect of dispute, which either of the parties alleges to be frivolous or vexatious, the dealing officers of the Industrial Relations Machinery may not normally suggest to the other party for reference to arbitration unless he, after preliminary investigation, feels that the dispute merits such a reference.

8. Disputes regarding grievances which have gone through the grievance procedure and the management and the union have not come to an agreement may be referred to arbitration.

II. Collective and General Disputes

9. Disputes which do not fall in the category of individual disputes i.e., which concern an industry as a whole or a large number of workers may also be referred to arbitration if the parties agree, provided the arbitrator is a person of status i.e., a senior officer of the Industrial Relations Machinery concerned or a judicial authority including a retired judge.

10. Such disputes, however, may not normally be referred to arbitration if :

(a) a substantial question of law if involved or
(b) new rights are sought to be created which are likely to have wide repercussion or
(c) large financial stakes are involved.

11. the following types of disputes may also be considered proper for arbitration :

(a) Disputes arising out of application or interpretation of law, collective bargaining agreements or settlements, and the awards of tribunals.
(b) Disputes on mere calculation or computation or benefits or sums where the rights are not disputed.
(c) Disputes between workmen and workmen or unions and unions, etc., if they affect the smooth working of the industry.

APPENDIX XV

CRITERIA FOR RECOGNITION OF UNIONS

1. Where there is more than one union a union claiming recognition should have been functioning at least one year after registration. Where there only one union, this condition would not apply.

2. The membership of the union should cover least 15 per cent of the workers in the establishment concerned. Membership would be counted only those who had paid their subscriptions for at last three months during the period of six months, immediately preceding the reckoning.

3. A union may claim to be recognised as a representative union for an industry in a local area if it has a membership of at least 25 per cent of the workers of that industry in that area.

4. When a union has been recognised, there should he no change in its position for a period of two years.

5. Where there are several unions in an industry establishment, the one with the largest membership should be recognised.

6. A representative union for an industry in an area should have the right to represent the workers of all the establishments in the industry, but if a union of workers in a particular establishment has a membership of 50 per cent or more of the workers of that establishment it should have the right to deal with matters of purely local interest, such as for instance, the handling of grievances pertaining to its own members. All other workers who are not members of that union might either operate through the representative union for the industry or seek redress directly.

7. In the case of trade union federations which are not affiliated to any of the four central organisations of labour, the question of recognition would have to be dealt with separately.

8. Only unions which observed the Code of Discipline would be entitled to recognition.

APPENDIX XVI

PROCEDURE FOR VERIFICATION OF MEMBERSHIP OF TRADE UNIONS, EVOLVED ON THE BASIS OF DECISIONS OF THE 16TH SESSION OF THE INDIAN LABOUR CONFERENCE (NAINITAL, MAY 1958)

The existing procedure of requesting the four all-India organisations (viz., INTUC, AITUC, UTUC and HMS) to furnish particulars of their claimed membership on or before 15 August every year will remain unchanged. The unions affiliated to these organisations are required to furnish the annual return to the Registrars on or before 31st July every year. The all-India organisations may, therefore, furnish the claimed lists (10 copies) by 15 August to the Chief Labour Commissioner.

2. A copy of the claims of membership submitted to the Chief Labour Commissioner by each of the all-India organisations will be made available to the other organisations in the third week of August. These four organisations will be given a fortnight's time to raise objections, if any in writing with regard to the claims furnished by other organisations. Any objections received in this connection after the prescribed time-limit, i.e., 15 days will not be taken into consideration. The Chief Labour Commissioner will get these objections examined through the field officers of his machinery during the course of verification and they will be asked to make specific enquiries in respect of these objections.

3. In the meanwhile scrutiny will be made by the Chief Labour Commissioner of the claims furnished by the organisations to ensure that, the claimed, lists are furnished in the prescribed form, giving details, in respect of registration and affiliation number. The total membership and the grouping of the trade unions in the various sub-heads will also be examined. The claimed lists along with the objections, as referred to above, will be sent to the various Regional Labour Commissioners for verification by the third week of September. The Regional Labour Commissioners will complete the verification works within a period of eight weeks.

4. The verified lists will reach the Chief Labour Commissioner's office by the third week of November. The copies of the verified lists will then be furnished to the four all-India organisations in the first

week of December. They will be again given a fortnight's time to raise objection in writing (6 copies), if any, in respect of verification results of the unions affiliated to their own organisation, as well as to the other organisations. Any objections received after the prescribed date will not be taken into consideration.

5. The objections received will be placed before a committee composed of one representative each of the four central trade union organisation. This committee will meet in the first week of January and, will be presided over by the Chief Labour Commissioner or his representative. All the objections raised will be taken into consideration by the committee and efforts will be made to resolve the disputes. In case any further investigation is considered necessary by this committee, Regional Labour Commissioners or their representatives will be asked to conduct spot inquiries in the presence of the representatives of the four all-India organisations who would form a panel in various localities for this purpose. Such panels will be set up in each State. Ordinarily a month's time should suffice for the Regional Labour Commissioners to submit their reports in consultation with the panels. These reports would, therefore, be expected to reach the office of the Chief Labour Commissioner in the second week of January.

6. After consolidation the reports referred to above the committee composed of the representatives of the four all-India organisations will again meet by the end of February to examine the reports received and to resolve the disputes with the help of the information received. Such of the disputes as this committee fails to resolve will be reported along with the necessary particulars to the Ministry of Labour and Employment in the first week of March. If considered necessary steps to refer these disputes to an independent agency will be taken by the Ministry of Labour Employment.

7. The C.L.C.'s office will compile and consolidate the verified figures leaving those under dispute as referred to in para 6 above and the verified information industry-wise/State-wise/organisation-wise would be furnished to the Ministry of Labour and Employment by the end of April.

II

A meeting with the representatives of all-India trade union organisations was held at 3 P.M. on 21 March 1959 to discuss certain issues arising out of the verification of trade union membership for the year ending 31 March 1958.

A number of issues were taken up for discussion and it was unanimously decided as under :

1. As the present verification was being done on the basis of test check and random sampling, the results obtained through this general verification process, should be utilised only for purposes of giving representation to the central trade union organisations on the international and national councils, conferences, committees.

2. As regards counting of membership of those who had paid at least 3 months subscription during the period of six months ending 31 March 1958, it decided that since this method of counting membership has so far been followed, the same should be continued for purposes of general verification for the year ending with 31 March 1958. As the unions would require some time to adjust to this system of counting membership and to amend their constitutions accordingly, their membership for purposes of verification for the year ending with 31 March 1959 should be counted on the basis of the unions' constitutions as was the practice in respect of verification prior to 1958, i.e., the rule regarding payment of at least 3 months' subscription during the last 6 months should not be insisted upon unless the same way incorporated in the unions' constitution.

3. Where a dispute arises about strength of membership for recognition of individual unions verification on an *ad hoc* basis will have to be carried out. The procedure of verification in such cases will be the same as that of general verification except that it will naturally be a detailed check. The machinery to be utilised for this purpose in the case of unions falling in the Central sphere will be the same i.e., the Central Industrial Relations Machinery. In the case of unions falling in the State sphere. The same procedure may have to be followed and the State Government machinery will be responsible for verification.

4. If in any State statutory provisions for ding recognition to the trade unions exist, the same will continue to apply for purposes of recognition.

5. As the result of general verification were to be utilised only for purposes of giving representation to be all-India organisations on international and national councils, conferences and committees, the elaborate procedure outlined in the revised verification procedure forwarded with this Ministry's letter No. LC-37(2)/8, dated 31 July 1958 will not be necessary. Objections received after circulating the

verified lists amongst the four all-India organisations will be placed before a committee composed of one representative each of the four all-India organisations. This committee will try to resolve the disputes and if there are any unresolved matters, these will be referred by the Chief Labour Commissioner to the Ministry of Labour and Employment. Paragraphs 5 and 6 the revised procedure referred to above will be deemed to be modified as follows :

> "Objections received will be placed before a committee composed of one representative each of the four central trade union organisations. This committee will meet under the chairmanship of the Chief Labour Commissioner or his representative. All the objections raised will be taken into consideration by the committee and efforts will be made to resolve the disputes. Such of the disputes as this committee fails to resolve will be reported along with the necessary particulars to the Ministry of Labour and Employment."[1]

1. It was subsequently clarified that this provision would not preclude the reference of such unresolved disputes to independent agency referred to in paragraph 6 of the procedure for verification and that it was the intention that disputes which the committee failed to resolve would be referred to an independent agency.

APPENDIX XVII

PROCEDURE FOR VERIFICATION OF MEMBERSHIP OF UNIONS FOR THE PURPOSE OF RECOGNITION UNDER THE CODE OF DISCIPLINE[1]

1. On receipt of a representation from a union for recognition under the Code of Discipline, the Central/State Implementation Machinery will first ascertain :

(a) the names of unions functioning in the establishment together with their number and date of registration by reference to the Registrar of Trade Unions concerned;

(b) whether any of the unions functioning in the establishment was responsible for an established breach of the Code during the past one year. (By an established breach of the Code' is meant a breach reported to and on enquiry established by the Implementation Machinery of the State or the Centre);

(c) whether the existing recognised union, if any, has completed a period of two years of recognition.

2. After ascertaining the above facts the Implementation Machinery at the Centre will request the Chief Labour Commissioner to arrange verification of membership of unions entitled to recognition under the Code. In the States, either the Implementation Officer will carry out this verification or get it done through the State Labour Commissioner, depending on the practice obtaining in each State.

3. The verification officer will ask the unions by registered post/A.D. to produce before him within 10 days, at the stipulated place and time, a list of their members who have paid subscription for at least 3 months during the period of six months immediately preceding the date of reckoning along with (i) membership-cum-subscription register, (ii) receipt counterfoils, (iii) cash and account books, (iv) bank books, and (v) a copy of the constitution of the union. If the number of members of a union is more than 10,000 a longer time on the basis of one additional day for

---

1. This procedure will not be applicable in the States where recognition of unions is regulated by a Statute.

every 2,000 members over 10,000, should be given for submission of its list of members and records.

If any of the unions fails to produce the list of its members, and records, a second and final notice will be given by registered post/A.D. as mentioned above, if membership of the union exceeds 10,000 at the stipulated place and time. If the union fails to produce the list and records on the second occasion also no further attempts will be made to verify its membership. However in respect of the union which has submitted its list and records, the verification officer will examine them and report its membership without inviting objections from the rival union, i.e., the defaulting union, and without doing any personal verification as mentioned in para (7) below. If more than one union produces its lists and records, the verification officer will check their membership in the manner described below ignoring the union which fails to produce its records.

4. The date of reckoning, mentioned in para (3) above will be taken as the first of the month in which verification begins, i.e., when the verification officer ask the unions to submit their lists and books for scrutiny.

5. The verification officer will then check the list of members with the membership register and receipt counterfoils and exclude those who have not paid 3 months' subscription during the period of six months preceding the date of reckoning. This examination will be 100 per cent and will be done in the presence of the office bearers of the union concerned but not in the presence of the office bearers or representatives of the rival union. If the union objects, to the elimination of any member from its membership register, it will have to give full and valid reasons for such an objection. The verification officer will then re-check the records (i.e., membership register, receipt books, etc.) to ascertain the correct position. The verification officer will scrutinise carefully the cash and accounts books as well as the bank book maintained by a union to ascertain that the amount of subscription shown to have been received has been properly accounted for and that the amounts received as subscription are not incompatible with the total number of persons shown in the register and the list furnished by the union. The verification will also ensure that only those workers are included in the lists of the unions who were on the Muster Roll of the management on the date of reckoning.

6. The verification officer will thereafter intimate in writing to the unions concerned that the verified lists of their respective members are ready for inspection by the union representatives at an appointed

time and place. The union will also at the same time be informed that after inspection of the verified list of members of the rival union(s). they should send, in writing. Their specific objections, if any, to the entries in these lists, within 10 days [or a longer period if the number of objections is likely to exceed 10,000 on the basis of one additional day for every 2,000 objections over and above 10,000] on the date of inspection. It should be made clear to the unions that general and vague objections like inflated membership etc., will not be considered : the objection should give names of persons whose membership of a union is objected to and the reasons therefor.

[The union representatives will be allowed to make notes from the verified lists shown to them in the presence of the verification officer : they will, however, not be allowed to take any of they will, however not be allowed to take any of the lists, nor a copy of the lists will be given to them.]

7. The objections received from the unions will then be verified by personal interrogation by the verification officer, of the members on the basis of the following systematic[1] sampling system :

(i) if the objection list finished by a union consist of 500 or less names of members, the number of persons to be personally interrogated should be 20 per cent subject to a minimum of 100 ;

(ii) if the objection list furnished by a union consists of more than 500 but not more than 1,000 names, the number of persons to be personally interrogated should be 15 per cent subject to a minimum of 100;

(iii) if the objection list furnished by a union consists of more than 1,000 but not more than 2,000 names, the number of persons to be personally interrogated should be 10 per cent subject to a minimum of 150;

---

1. A systematic sample means sampling from a list by taking individuals at equally spaced intervals called sampling intervals. The Sampling interval should be :
total number of persons in the objecion list

number of persons in the sample

Thus, for example, if there are 400 workers in the objection list and a sample of 100 workers is to be selected the verification officer should select every (400/100th) or 4th worker in the list. It is, however, not necessary that in all cases the third or the fourth. Thus, for example, if the first name is selected as the first sample then subsequent samples will be 5th, 9th, 13th etc., names : if, howerer, the second name is taken as the first sample, the subsequent samples would be 6th, 10th, 14th, etc., names in the list.

(iv) if the objection list furnished by a union consists of more than 2,000 but not more than 5,000 names, the number of persons to be personally interrogated should be 5 per cent subject to a minimum of 200; and

(v) if the objection list furnished by a union consists of more than 5,000 names, the number of persons to be personally interrogated should be 2 per cent, subject to a minimum of 250.

The persons selected for personal interrogation should among other things be asked whether they are members of a particular union and whether they had paid subscriptions for three months within a period of six months from the date of reckoning and if so, the amount of subscription paid, the months for which it was paid, etc. The verification officer will maintain a list of members personally interrogated, giving their ticket numbers, names of section where working, the result of personal interrogation, etc.

8. Where the sample check reveals that certain members interrogated deny membership of a union, its lists of members will be modified proportionately. For example, if on checking records, it is found that a union has 2,000 valid members and the rival union objects, to say, 800 of these members, a 15 per cent sample of the latter has to be drawn, i.e. 120 persons have to be interrupted personally. If on personal interrogation it is found that 30 of the 120 persons (i.e. 25 per cent) deny membership of the union, the strength of the union will be reduced by 25 per cent or 800 persons whose membership was objected to, i.e., by 200. In other words, the final strength of the union will, in this case, be 1,800;

[2,000–(25 per cent of 800) = 1,800]

If the persons who, on interrogation, deny their membership of the union claiming them as their members, inform the verification officer that they are members of a rival union, the verification officer will check their membership with the list of members and records of that union and adjust its list accordingly, i.e., their names will be added to the list of the rival union if they are not already included in it, and excluded, in the manner mentioned above, from the list of the claimant union.

9. While conducting personal verification as mentioned in para (7) above, the verification officer will not allow the representatives of any union or management to be present.

10. The verification officer will report his findings to the Central/State Implementation Machinery which in turn will communicate its decision to the management as well as to the unions. In his report the Verification Officer will also indicate the total number of workers in the establishment and the percentage of the verified membership to it.

APPENDIX XVIII

The GREGORY COMMITTEE'S REPORT ON THE GENERAL PRINCIPLES OF FIXING DEARNESS ALLOWANCE TO EMPLOYEES IN INDUSTRIAL CONCERNS, 1944

EXTRACTS

13. The question of rationalising dearness allowances was discussed by the Plenary Labour Conference held at New Delhi on the 6-7 September 1943, in terms of a questionnaire which covered the main points at issue. We think it desirable that we should adhere to the same questionnaire, in what follows, then we give our answers to the separate issues posed.

14. The first question was : Is it necessary to have general uniform principles, for fixing dearness allowance, or bonus?

To this our answer is a two-fold one : "First, it is in our opinion indispensable that the issue of dearness allowance should be kept rigidly apart from any question of bonus. A dearness allowance should be granted, for the purpose of compensating changes in the cost of living or changes in the purchasing power of money. Whether a particular industry is so prosperous that, after, paying dearness allowance on the scale considered desirable, it is still in a position to make further grants to its workers, is another matter altogether. There has in fact, been a considerable degree of confusion of thought as to the conditions which justify, respectively, a wage-change, the grant of a dearness allowance and the grant of a bonus. Second, we regard it as absolutely necessary that there should be general principles for fixing dearness allowance. The present state of affairs is completely chaotic, e.g., some employers have paid dearness allowances in place of higher wages, others have paid higher wages in place of dearness allowance. This state of affairs should not be allowed to continue.

15. The second issue was formulated in the questionnaire as follows : "If the reply to (1) is in the affirmative.

(a) what should be the general principles? Should the general principles allow for different rates for different industries, or for different regions? If so what should be the governing factors and the demarcation of regions?

(b) Should it be laid down that the degree of assistance given towards the increased cost of living should diminish as wages increase above subsistence level? If so, how?''

16. Sub-head (a) obviously concerns three separate matters of which the first is clearly the most important. At the risk of repetition at later points in our report, we wish at this stage to set out in some detail what in our opinion the general principles'' guiding the grant of dearness allowance should be.

17. It will be obvious that at a time of universal shortage, it is impossible to compensate everyone, throughout the whole range of industrial incomes, without the compensatory action, becoming self-stultifying. At some point in the income-scale, a line must be drawn, beyond which it must be assumed that the *de facto* income, though no longer buying as much as it did before the war, yet buys such a sufficiency of real things as not to require any special consideration. We put this dividing line at the amount fixed by the Payment of Wages Act, viz. 200 rupees. But this is the least difficult of the issues that we have to face. Within this income limit, if dearness allowances are to be paid, they can be paid on two alternative hypotheses, viz., on the assumption that each individual should be treated in exactly the same way as every other individual, or on the assumption that even with a ceiling income above which no compensation is necessary, there are differential standards of life, so that, taking incomes of 75, 100 and 150 rupees for instance the amount of dearness allowances should rise in absolute amount with the income itself. In other words, if the limit of income is 200 rupees, and if the income within that limit is to receive full or partial compensation, should every one receive that amount of compensation, stated in so many rupees, or in such and such a percentage of actual income? And if an absolute amount of compensation (i.e., so many rupees) is to be paid, to what income in terms of rupees, is it to be related?

18. We have reached the conclusion that it is desirable that the amount of dearness allowance should be an absolute amount i.e., that it should be a fixed amount in terms of rupees (subject to a portion at the whole of it being paid in kind and subject also, in the opinion of some of us to a limit governed by reference to the actual wage received on the lines of the second proviso enunciated below). That is to say we reject the idea that dearness allowance should be laid down *ab initio* as a percentage of percentage of actual income. But this still

leaves us with considerable difficulties. It is clear that there are some incomes so low that they required full compensation and that, if the amount of compensation required can be stated in terms of rupees, that amount of rupees when applied to larger incomes will result in a diminishing percentage of compensation. We have, however, been to agree among ourselves as to the precise detection of the incomes which should be compensation full, and we, therefore, present below the alternatives which have found favour with the members of our Committee. We premise what with the following condition; that earnings in formulae are understood to refer to a full normal of employment for adult male workers. Separate calculations should be made for workers other than male workers. Where an individual has, in an period of time, worked less than the normal his dearness allowance shall be calculated not assumption that he has worked the full period, but on the earnings for the actual nine days that he has been at work. In such case of earnings, receipts on account of overtime should be excluded. Subject to the aforesaid fundamental alternatives are as follows :

(1) The absolute amount of dearness allowance should be equated to full compensation for the weighted average of the earnings of all wage groups below the ceiling wage of 200.

OR

(2) The absolute amount of dearness should be equated to full compensation weighted average earnings of all you below the weighted average as can the first of these formulae.

Some of our colleagues are of the opinion the first of these formulae is adopted, the full compensation shall be adjusted to 75. per cent of the actual average : that is to say (in formula No. 1), if the weighted average is say 40 rupees, compensation shall be on the assumption that the weighted average is 30 rupees. Other members are of the opinion that, whether the first or the second of these formulae is accepted, in the case of a person whose actual earnings are below the weighted average, his dearness allowance shall be calculated on the actual earnings.

The establishment of what actually constitutes the weighted average of earnings under either of the formulae mentioned above would have to be determined by Government.

19. The adoption of either of the two main formulae proposed will, of course, mean that the lower and lowest income-groups, will

receive compensation in excess of what they would receive if the compensatory payments were based on their actual earnings : on the other hand, the higher wage-groups would inevitable receive less. Some members of the committee believe that this general result is in accordance with social need. But, as the qualifications set out in paragraph 18 above will indicate, other members also think that it is necessary to go further in the provision of additional safeguards, either to avoid the danger of accentuating the inflationary spiral or to avoid the danger of an undue disturbance of the established wage-structure.

We wish to make it clear that where a worker at present drawing dearness allowance would be entitled to a higher dearness allowance if either of the main formulae (subject, of course, to the limitations of either of the provisos, if accepted) were adopted, the amount of such allowance must be determined in the light of the indices actually employed in the industry or region in which he is working. The suggestion in para 12 that unsatisfactory cost-of-living indices should be replaced by retail price-indices should be applied *pro future* only, to govern variations in the amount of dearness allowance after the initial adjustments have been made. Apprehensions have been expressed lest the fall in the cost of living should reduce earnings to below the level ruling at the outbreak of the War. This apprehension arises on the assumption that the rise in living costs has not been reflected in dearness allowances and that whereas less than 100 per cent of the rise has been given the full 100 per cent will be taken off in the fall. It is clear, however, that dearness allowance can only be reduced to nil and that wages as such will not be reduced thereafter merely because of the fall in the cost of living. Where dearness allowances have been given in the shape of a rise in actual wage levels, it is presumed that wages will not be allowed below the 1939 levels merely because of the fall in the cost of living.

20. To turn now to the second question of part (a) of the question as set out in paragraph 15. We think the ideal procedure would be that in each region there should be a single dearness allowance to which the workers in the region should be entitled : but we are aware that, in fact, a considerable measure of differentiation exists among different industries within the same region. Though we do not regard bonus as substitute for dearness allowance, it may be considered whether it is not desirable for industries paying dearness allowance above the standard to reduce it to the standard level and for the time being to compensate their workers by a deferred bonus to the extent

of the excess. In the interests of uniformity, we recommend that excess profits rules be adjusted correspondingly.

21. There are obvious variations in the cost of living in different parts of India at the present time. It is never easy to draw dividing lines, though the fact that food prices are governed by provincial policy and stand at markedly different levels even in neighbouring provinces, suggests that for the moment at any rate, the provincial area, rather than an suggested regional area, should generally be adopted. Our attention has, however, been drawn to the circumstance that portions of a province may economically be more closely linked with a neighbouring province than with the life of the province of which it forms an administrative part : in such cases, in the grant of dearness allowance notice should be taken of the circumstances.

As regards sub-item (b) i.e., "Should it be laid down that the degree of assistance given towards the increased cost of living should diminish as wages increase above subsistence level" we would point out that the adoption of either of the formulae set out in paragraph 18 above would automatically result in a diminution of the proportion which dearness allowance bears to wages as the wage rises above subsistence level.

22. The third main issue in the questionnaire was stated thus : if and when such principles are laid down, should they be so worked that not only are tendencies to give higher allowances checked but that such allowances as fall below the prescribed standard are raised?

We answer this question in the affirmative, and are of the opinion that the adoption of either of the alternatives mentioned in paragraph 18 above would in fact raise the allowances below the prescribed standard and lead to a check in granting higher allowances.

23. The next question raised is this : Should the allowance be automatically related to increases or decreases in the cost-of-living index? And should the scale of neutralisation diminish as prices rise above a certain level?

It is obviously not possible to change the allowance with every change in the guiding index, which, as we have indicated, should in the future, until comparable cost of living indices are available, be the local, regional or provincial retail price-index, (subject to such exceptional areas as are referred to in para 12[1]). In that sense, we

1. In para 12 the Committee accepted Shri Deshpande's suggestion. . . that the retail price index numbers compiled under the Central Scheme may be made use of in all centres with the possible exception perhaps of Bombay, Cawnpore and Madras and also of Ahmedabad, Sholapur and Nagpur if weightages for the last three centres are

reject the idea of an automatic increase with every small change in the index. On the other hand, we take the view that rising or falling retail prices (or, *mutatis mutandis,* a rising or falling cost-of-living index) should justify additional or diminishing allowances related to the rise or fall. We have stressed throughout our Report that our concern is primarily with the low income-groups and these obviously suffer most as prices rise. It appears to us to be a negation of the idea of a dearness allowance to reduce the scale as prices rise, since this would afford a smaller degree of relief precisely when circumstances demand the opposite course of action.

24. The fifth issue is : Should the allowances be fixed on a percentage of wages or incomes or at flat rates in slabs varying according to wage levels? The sixth issue is so closely associated with the fifth that we prefer to deal with both of them together. The sixth issue is as follows : If the allowances are at flat rates should there be only one flat rate or two flat rates or more? It follows logically from the scheme already set out in a previous paragraph, that we are in favour of one flat rate of dearness allowance for all workers, consequently we desire to see one slab only.

25. The seventh question which the questionnaire posed was this : Should there be a limitation that no allowances or/and bonuses should place the person in a better position than he enjoyed in 1939 before the Wars?

For reasons which we have already pointed out it is impossible at a time of general shortage to improve the position of the community all round and any attempt to do so will merely result in an inflationary spiral. For this reason we take the view that, in general, dearness allowance should obviously not place the individual in a better position than he enjoyed before the War.

To this general rule some Members of the Committee are consciously prepared to make one exception under either of the two formulae set out in paragraph 18 above, the lower and lowest ranks of wage earners are entitled to be better off than they were before the War, since the dearness allowance will be adjusted to an average higher than the actual wage they have been drawing. On balance these Members believe that the result is socially justified, but they are not prepared to generalise this concession.[1] We wish to emphasise

---

revised on the receipt of more recent enquiries.

1. If the proviso that where a worker is in receipt of earnings below the appropriate weighted average the dearness allowance should be calculated on his actual earnings were accepted, this result would be automatically achieved.

that these remarks apply only to dearness allowances. Particular industries may find themselves in a position to pay bonuses to their workers. With such grants we are not concerned, since we have not been asked to lay down any general principles by which the grant of bonus should be governed.

26. The eighth question is as follows : In view of the need to fight inflationary tendencies, should the cash element of allowances be fixed at a minimum and the bulk of the allowance be made available in kind, through supplies of essential articles at concessional rates?

We strongly favour this suggestion not necessarily because it has any very decided influence on the inflationary problem, except to the extent that competitive buying is eliminated but on the ground that the individual worker actually obtains the constituents of his standard of living, instead of having to struggle with others, perhaps at rising prices, in order to obtain them, possible finding himself unsuccessful in the end.

27. The ninth question series contained in the questionnaire is as follows : "How should the general principles be implemented? Should there be legal compulsion or can voluntary experiment achieve the desired results? Should authorities be set up in different regions or for different industries to decide finally on all questions relating to dearness allowance and bonus, apart, from the adjudication procedure already provided for?"

A majority of members oppose and a minority support implementation of general principles by legal compulsion apart from the adjudication procedure already provided.

28. Whilst we have been concerned in this Report purely with industrial labour, we desire to make it clear in our opinion that clerical and lower-paid supervisory classes have also suffered severely from the rise in the cost of living, and the limitation of our recommendations to the industrial classes as such should not be interpreted as excluding the consideration of the position of the clerical and lower-paid supervisory classes.

APPENDIX XIX

REPORT OF THE INDUSTRIAL HOUSING SUB-COMMITTEE OF THE STANDING LABOUR COMMITTEE (EXTRACTS)

I. Terms of Reference

This Sub-committee was appointed at the seventh meeting of the Standing Labour Committee held on 28 August 1945 to consider the following matters relating to the housing of workers :

"(i) whether there should be a building fund for the housing of workers and the manner in which it can best be raised, and in particular the manner in which they raised, and in particular the manner in which the cases of those employers who have already provided housing can be dealt with;

(ii) the basis on which the workers can be required to pay rent;

(iii) the minimum standards required for workers' houses;

(iv) the most suitable manner of administering any funds which may become available (whether from Government, Employer or Worker) for the housing of workers; and

(v) the facilities that are required to be granted by the Central and Provincial Governments and local authorities to facilitate the housing schemes of workers."

2. The appalling conditions under which the industrial worker is forced to live is common knowledge trial worker is forced to live is common knowledge and since the problem has already been examined by different commissions and inquiry committees it seemed to us unnecessary to devote any more time to the collection of data. After consideration of our terms of reference we decided that the whole question could be most conveniently examined under three separate heads :

1. The minimum housing standards necessary—covering item (iii).
2. The basis on which to charge rent—covering item (ii).
3. The need for a fund, and the ways and means for implementing, financing and administering housing schemes

resulting from our recommendations—covering items (i), (iv) and (v).

II. Summary of Recommendations

.......We make the following recommendations in answer to the specific questions referred to us by the Standing Labour Committee :

(a) (i) There should be a Building Fund provided to finance the housing of workers who are unable to pay an economic rent for the minimum standard of housing laid down.

(ii) The Fund could best be raised as follows :
Government (Central and/or Provincial) should make available long-term interest free loans for housing built to approved standards, and such loans should be redeemed by the building authority by means of a sinking fund spread over a period of not less than 30 years.

(iii) No question arises in the case of those employers who have already provided housing for their labour until accommodation to the extent of 100 per cent of the demand is provided for industrial workers in any areas. Provided that if any special form of direct taxation on industry is introduced by Government, such taxation should include provision for rebates to employers in respect of any existing housing which though not complying with the prescribed standards may be approved by the building authority under such conditions as they may prescribe.

(b) The Committee were unable to arrive at any agreed decision as to the basis on which workers can be required to pay rent.

(c) The minimum standards we recommend for workers' houses are set out in the Annexure.

(d) The Housing Found, and in the first instance, the housing Subsidy we have recommended, should be administered by a National Industrial Housing Board, including representatives of the Provinces, the Centre, the States, employers, labour and other interested parties. This Board should have a whole-time Chairman who, while responsible to the Central Government, should having the maximum liberty of action possible. In addition to National Industrial Housing Board, Regional Industrial Housing Boards, representing Provincial Governments, the States, local authorities, employers, labour and other interested parties, should be set up to co-ordinate regional schemes before they are submitted to the National Industrial Housing Board.

(e) (i) To enable a start to be made with a nation-wide housing of our poor worker we recommended that Provincial and Central Governments between them provide the necessary finance by making available long-term interest free loans for approved schemes complying with the minimum standards we have recommended. In addition to the provision by Government of interest-free loans, we recommend that employers be asked to pay a sum of Rs. 2 per month per house for every house allotted to them. Any deficit that may remain over and above that covered by employers contribution and the interest-free loan should be met by a further subsidy raised by some form of general taxation.

(ii) To ensure that houses are constructed as cheaply and as efficiently as possible it is essential for the Central and Provincial Governments to co-ordinate their building programmes through the National Industrial Housing Board, and to ensure that the requirements of raw materials for the various Provincial housing schemes all over the country are co-ordinated by the Board and bulk orders at controlled rate placed by the Board for these materials Government should also take every step possible to encourage and develop mass production methods.

(iii) Provincial and Local Authorities should be responsible for making available properly developed sites for approved housing schemes. Local Authorities and where a large new township is being set up the township itself should be responsible for the provision of all the amenities we have recommended and for the conservance services.

G. PEACE
Chairman

ANNEXURE

1. A house to accommodate an industrial worker and his family should comprise at least :

> two rooms, a kitchen with storage space for food and fuel, an independent bath room, a lavatory, verandahs, preferably both in front and at the back, and a courtyard in the case of single storey houses

and be provided with an adequate supply of water and where possible with water borne sanitation.

2. *Standard of accommodation*

(a) The total floor area of the two main rooms exclusive of verandahs, should not be less than 240 sq. ft.

(b) The height of the two main rooms should not be less than 10 ft. measured from the floor to the lowest part of the ceiling, and neither of the two main rooms should have a cubic capacity of less than 1,000 c.ft.

(c) At least on verandah, and preferable youth, should be not less than 7 feet wide.

(d) Shelves should be provided in the kitchen for keeping utensils and built-in shelves or almirahs provided in the main rooms.

3. *Standard of ventilation*

(a) An efficient form of top ventilation should be provided.

(b) The main rooms should be provided with doors and windows providing adequate light and through ventilation.

(c) It is most desirable that houses be so designed that the two main rooms are not one behind the other. Where this is not possible, ample ventilation to the outside air should be provided in both rooms.

(d) The kitchen should be provided with a chimney or a flue and a well designed *chulah* economical in fuel.

4. *Standard of lighting*

(a) The window opening in each of the main rooms and in the kitchen, exclusive of doors and opening to the outside air, should not be less than 10 per cent of the floor area of the room.

(b) Electric light should be provided wherever possible.

(c) Every house should be white-washed at least once a year.

5. *Sanitation and drainage*

(a) A family lavatory, not a common lavatory, is to be preferred on all grounds, social and hygienic....

(b) All drains other than sullage drains, which must be installed underground, should be "pucca" and, unless there are exceptional circumstances justifying some other course, covered and underground.

6. (a) Houses should not be built back-to-back and it is most desirable that blocks of houses be limited in size, and wherever possible laid out on the lines of a garden city.

(b) Houses should be allocated on the basis of one family to one house. Any family houses remaining surplus after meeting fully the requirements of married workers may be allotted to single workers on the basis of four workers to a house.

(c) Provision against subletting and taking in boarders should be made by formulating suitable tenancy conditions and providing adequate machinery for their enforcement.

7. *Dormitories*

The Committee recognise that dormitories may be necessary and even desirable in some cases. Where provided they should conform to the general principles of planning we have recommended above, and the sleeping space for each person should not be less than 50 sq. ft., this space being in addition to the provision of common dining rooms, baths, lavatories, etc. Dormitory accommodation should not be let to families or to persons of different sexes.

8. *"Neighbourhood unit"*

In open development where a large number of houses are proposed to be constructed it is most desirable that the housing estate should be planned as a self-contained community or a "neighbourhood." Each neighbourhood unit should be built round a civic centre providing adequate public amenities, such as playgrounds, schools, libraries, creches, a hospital and a shopping centre, depending upon its size. Community cattle sheds should also be provided where there is a demand for them.

9. *Undesirability of segregation of working classes*

It is socially and psychologically undesirable to build a large housing estate entirely for one class of the population, and it is essential for proper social progress and for a proper and full civic life that provisions be made for all types and classes........

10. *Population density*

In order to ensure the healthy development of a housing estate it is necessary to have proper safeguards against overcrowding, and we recommend that in the areas set aside for workers' dwellings the maximum number of houses to be built should be limited to 20 in any one acre. This number of housing density, should be calculated by including in the area the curtilages of the dwellings, access roads and minor open spaces and half the boundary roads up to a maximum of 15 ft. . . . We further recommend that the overall or gross density of the neighbourhood as a whole, including the areas to be developed for sale to private persons, should be limited to 10-12 houses per acre . . .

11. *Multi-storeyed buildings*

The Committee went into the question of vertical construction in great detail and, while there were no two opinions as regards the desirability of single storey buildings, the more general view was that it might be necessary to provide multi-storeyed buildings in certain areas for the following reasons :

(a) insufficient land available within reasonable transport range;
(b) excessive cost of land;
(c) cost of development and the limits to which an economic supply of sewerage and water could be given;
(d) The volume of housing in that particular locality. . . .

12. Notwithstanding the general recommendation made above, the Committee wish to record that some of its members hold very strong views on this question. They consider that the provision of multi-storeyed houses for the lower paid classes of industrial workers is most undesirable and where provided will only reproduce the slum they are designed to replace . . . .

13. *Transport*

Adequate and cheap transport facilities should be provided as a public utility for workers to and from their place of work as part of every housing scheme.

14. *Management and welfare*

We consider it of the first importance that adequate provision should be made by the local authorities concerned for well trained and paid welfare and management staff in connection with every new housing project and that compliance with this provision should be made a condition of the grant of a subsidy. . . .

15. *Costs*

In proposing a minimum standard of housing the Committee has not overlooked the fact that the greatest difficulty in implementing the scheme is the present high cost of construction. Figures of Rs 3,500 to Rs. 5,000 have been mentioned as the estimated cost of a house of the proposed standard. The country cannot afford this price for its working class housing. The rationalisation of the design and construction of the working class houses by the use of more modern methods and by the mass production of standardised parts and fittings to as large an extent as possible will probably result in an overall reduction in the cost of construction.[1]

1. One of the members (Shri Shri Ram) had reservations on paras 9, 10, 11 and 15. Another member (Shri Edward Souter) had reservations with regard to paras 10 and 11 and a third (Shri W.H. Prosser) with regard to para 12. Separate notes from the first two were appended to the Report.

APPENDIX XX

ORGANISATION OF CONSUMER COOPERATIVE IN THE INDUSTRIAL SECTOR

(Extracts from Memorandum placed before 20th Session of the ILC)

A scheme has now been drawn up in consultation with the Ministry of Community Development and Co-operation for setting up consumers' cooperatives of industrial workers. The scheme is for the consideration of this Conference. The basic idea is to set up viable units. It is thought that each consumer cooperative society should have a minimum membership of 250 and the value of each share should be at least Rs. 10. Thus the minimum share capital to be raised would be Rs. 2,500. In addition, each society will need an advance of Rs. 10,000 as working capital either from a sister cooperative credit society, if there is one with surplus funds in the same organisation, or from the State Bank of India or the Central Cooperative Bank or by way of deposit or loan from the employer or from members who are better off. For obtaining institutional finance, the problem of adequate security will prove a difficulty, here the employers can help. But the best method of financing would be for the employer to advance loans at a low rate of interest. The employer will no doubt associate himself closely with the activities of the society and will have opportunities for ensuring that sound business methods are followed and wrong investments are not made. At least during the first three years it would require some managerial subsidy. It is calculated that such subsidy (on a tapering basis) should be Rs. 900 for the first year, Rs. 600, for the second and Rs. 300 for the third year. As soon as such a society works up business worth one lakh annually with a margin of about 6¼ per cent. On average, it would become self-sufficient. In order that it could borrow its working capital. Its "owned assets" have to be strengthened. The borrowing limit of a cooperative society is always a multiple of its owned assets. The scheme for general consumers cooperatives provides for share capital participation by Government, on 50-50 basis. Thus if the minimum share capital collected by the members is Rs. 2,500, another 2,500 would be contributed by Government. So in the draft scheme for the consumers, cooperatives for industrial workers, it has been provided that the employer should contribute a share capital of Rs. 2,500 or make an outright contribution to the reserve fund of the society of an equivalent; amount (what has been described as 'foundation money' in the scheme). If there is share participation by employers, obviously the usual limit on the number of shares which can be held by a single member under cooperative law will have to be relaxed by the concerned Registrars of Cooperative Societies.

On the analogy of representation given to Government for contribution share capital on a matching basis, the employers representation on the Managing Committee of the Society could be upto one-third of the strength of the Committee. If however, the employer does not purchase shares but advances loan, it could be provided in the by-laws that at least one representative of the employer would be on the Managing Committee.

Briefly, the financial assistance expected from the employers (on the pattern of the assistance provided by Government for stores for general consumers) will be as follows :

		Rs.
1.	Share capital contribution or contribution to Reserve Fund	2,500
2.	Working Capital Loan	10,000
3.	Managerial subsidy[1]	
	First year	900
	Second year	600
	Third Year	300
4.	Accommodation for the store to be provided free or at nominal rent.	

It is true that the majority of the workers may not be able to purchase outright shares worth Rs. 10 each. Weekly or monthly contribution of small amounts towards share capital would be a long drawn out and complicated process. Now that the Employees' Provident Fund and the Coal Mines Provident Fund cover as many as 3⅓ million workers, it should be possible to make non-repayable advances from these two funds to those worker members who wish to join the co-operatives for the outright purchase of one or more shares. This would at once strengthen the share capital base of the consumers' cooperatives to be set up in a large number of establishments.

Since, a minimum membership of 250 per society is to be aimed

1. This amount, however, might vary and some societies with a good share capital base and adequate working capital advance from the employer may not need any subsidy. Other might need a little more than what is provided here.

at, we have to leave out for the present industries employing on the average less than 300 persons (workers and office staff). But there is nothing to prevent the smaller units from combining and setting up one viable consumer store for a number of contiguous establishments. It may also be provided that such smaller units in which the individual employers may not be able to provide the kind of financial assistance needed, should qualify for Government assistance under the Scheme for general consumers. Such units, if viable, could be included in the Third Plan Target of the State concerned.

The primary co-operatives of industrial workers and employees could seek affiliation to the district or central store, if any, or to the Apex wholesale store of the State.

This amount, however, might vary and some societies with a good share capital base and adequate working capital advance from the employer may not need any subsidy. Others might need a little more than what is provided here.

ANNEXURE

A SCHEME FOR A CONSUMERS' COOPERATIVE STORE AMONGST INDUSTRIAL WORKERS

I. Introduction

The scheme on Consumers' Stores indicated below has been drawn up in the light of the recommendations of the Committee on Consumers' Cooperatives as accepted by the Ministry of Community Development & Cooperation and endorsed by the last annual Conference of State Ministers of Cooperation.

2. *Objects*

The objects of the stores shall be :

(a) To arrange for the purchase and sale to its members and other consumers at reasonable rates all articles of consumption, domestic requirements and necessities of life bought by it or manufactured either by itself or in combination with other consumers' stores.

(b) To carry on for the benefit of its members wholesale and retail trade and subject to the sanction of Registrar, establish and conduct on co-operative principles such other lines of works, as for example, running of small processing and manufacturing units, as may from time be resolved by the general meeting.

(c) To provide for repairs and other services in respect of articles sold by the society to its members.

(d) To open a cafeteria or a canteen in the interest of the members.

(e) To do such other things as may be expedient for accomplishing the above objects or as may be incidental or conducive to the attainment of allow any of the above objects of the store.

3. *Membership*

Membership should be open to individual workers and members of the staff above the age of 18 years belonging to a particular commercial or industrial unit. It may be located in a residential colony or office premises. It is very necessary that adequate stress is laid on the economic size of the unit. According to the accepted recommendations of the Committee on consumers' Store, it is suggested that a store should not be stated unless it has about 250 members as the minimum to serve so that it can have a reasonable business turnover and pay its way. No member should be permitted to withdraw any of the shares held by him in the store or to resign his membership of the store within one year from the date on which he was admitted as a member.

4. *Share Capital*

The share capital of the store may be divided into 5,000 shares or so of small denomination. The value of a share may be fixed at Rs. 10 payable in instalment within 2 or 3 months according to the capacity of the members.

5. *Liability of the Members*

The liability of the members of the store for meeting the debts of the society in the event of its being wound up shall be limited to the face value of the shares subscribed. A share transfer fund should be created to enable the society to repay the share money to the outgoing members till suitable arrangements can be made for transfer of the share to the incoming members.

6. *Business Operation*

A consumers' store amongst workers should generally start by dealing in a few selected commodities of daily necessity like foodgrains and provisions which have quick turnover so that its capital does not remain locked up for a long period. Later on as it establishes itself it should expand the field of coverage also. The variety and range of commendations and needs of consumers. It may affiliate itself with the apex wholesale society of the state or district marketing societies supplying such consumer goods on wholesale basis to the consumers store. Sales should be on cash basis unless suitable arrangements can be made to ensure weekly or fortnightly or monthly recoveries from members by deductions from their salary bills. Sales should be made on market rates to avoid competition with the private traders. Members should be given purchase dividend at the close of the year according to the purchases made out of net profits accruing to the society from business turnover.

7. *Financial Implications*

A consumers' store should run on fairly efficient lines so as to enable it to compete effectively with the private trade. It is, therefore, necessary for a store to maintain a minimum paid staff as roughly indicated below :

		Rs.
(i)	one manager-cum-accountant at Rs. 125 x 12	1,500
(ii)	One salesman at Rs. 75 x 12	900
(iii)	One weighman at Rs. 50 x 12	600
(iv)	One delivery man at Rs. 60 x 12	720
		3,720
(v)	Other establishment cost etc. excluding shop and godown rent	2,280
		6,000

This amount of establishment cost can only be earned if the society can have sales turnover of rupees one lakh per year with earning at Rs. 6¼ per cent. Then again to have a business of about rupees one lakh, it is necessary to have a revolving working capital of about Rs. 15,000 to 16,000. As against this requirement of working capital the society with 250 members can raise share capital of Rs. 2,500. This owned fund is too small as against its requirement. It will, therefore, be necessary for the employer unit to render financial assistance in the form of grant as foundation money or in the form of share capital contribution to its owned funds upto a minimum of Rs. 5,000 to enable it to borrow the balance of Rs. 10,000. In most of the states a Society cannot expect to get loans from financial agencies more than twice its owned fund. But it is also very doubtful how far the co-operative financing agencies would be able to cater to the needs of working capital of consumers' stores of industrial workers at this stage. It will have, therefore, to fall back upon the employee for a loan of about Rs. 10,000 at a low rate of interest for working capital.

Besides these requirements of working capital the society will be in need of purchasing shop equipment for about Rs. 2,500 or so. This fund may be provided as a grant by the employer ['foundation money'].

It may also be pointed out in this connection that it may not be possible for a consumers' store to reach a target of sales turnover of rupees one lakh during the initial stage and earn a margin of about 6¼ per cent, on average to maintain the staffs required. It will, therefore, be necessary for the employer unit to pay a subsidy towards managerial expenses on a tapering basis for about 3 years say Rs. 900 during the first year, Rs. 600 during the second year and Rs. 300 during the third year towards the pay of the manager. In addition to financial assistance the employer should make available suitable shopping accommodation to the consumers' store at a nominal rate of rent. Therefore, on this basis, the financial requirements of a consumers' store and assistance needed from the employer will be as indicated below :

	Financial requirements			*Financial assistance from the employers needed*	
		Rs.			Rs.
(1)	Share capital	5,000	(1)	Share capital contribution or foundation money	2,500
(2)	Working Capital	15,000	(2)	Loan	10,000
(3)	Managerial expenses	6,000	(3)	Managerial sub-sidy	
				First year	900
				Second year	600
				Third year	300
(4)	Accommodation			Free or at nominal rent	

APPENDIX XXI

CONCLUSIONS OF THE TRIPARTITE COMMITTEE ON WORKS COMMITTEES (NEW DELHI, 30 NOVEMBER 1959)

The Committee came to the following conclusions :

1. *Functions of Works Committees*

It was agreed that it was not practicable to draw up an exhaustive list of the functions of Works Committees. There should be some flexibility of approach for the system to work properly. Illustrative lists of items which the Works Committee should not normally deal with and those which it should not normally deal with were drawn up and approved (Annexure). It was agreed that the demarcation would not be rigid and the approved lists were flexible.

2. *Units in which the Works Committee should be Formed*

It was agreed that no change was called for in the existing statutory provisions in the Industrial Disputes Act limiting the number of workmen to 100 for the purpose of the formation of a Works Committee.

3. *Composition of the Works Committee*

It was agreed that no change in the existing provisions of the Industrial Disputes Act or Rules regarding the number of members of the Works Committee was necessary. As regards the number of representatives it was felt that at times the managements found it difficult to produce equal number of reprepresentatives as that of workers. But as, however, this was permissible even under the existing rules, no change therein was recommended.

4. Composition of the Workers' Side of the Works Committee

It was considered that the workers' representatives on the Works Committee should be elected by the workers without the constituencies being divided between workers who are members of a union and those who are not members of a union. The existing provisions regarding representation for different departments or sections should continue. As for election, the consensus of opinion was that ordinarily the employers should be responsible, therefore, but that where there is a dispute or an apprehended dispute or where either the employer or the workers make a specific request to the appropriate Government, a Conciliation Officer/Labour Officer deputed by that Government should supervise the election.

5. *Chairmanship of Works Committee*

It was agreed that the present provision in the Central Industrial Disputes Rules regarding the compulsory rotation of the office of the Chairman between employers and workers should be removed. At the same time it was felt that the workers representatives should not be barred from holding that office, if suitable persons were available from their side. It was agreed that for the next three years, the Chairman should be from the management side, who should, as far as possible, be the head of the organisation should be reviewed after three years.

6. *Periodicity of the Meetings*

It was agreed that the present provision, i.e., having a meeting at least once in a quarter needed no change. Meetings should be held more frequently if necessary.

7. *Facilities to Works Committee's Members*

It was agreed that the Secretary of the Works Committee should have the privilege of putting up notice regarding the work of the Works Committee on the notice board of the establishment.

8. *General*

The question was raised whether Works Committee should be established in commercial establishments also and not in factories only. It was pointed out that according to the existing provisions in the Act commercial establishments, might form the Work Committees whenever required.

ANNEXURE

I. *Illustrative list of items which Work's Committee will normally deal with*

1. Conditions of work such as ventilation, lighting, temperature and sanitation including latrines and urinals.
2. Amenities such as drinking water, canteens, dining rooms, creches, rest rooms, medical and health services.
3. Safety and accident prevention, occupations, diseases and protective equipment.
4. Adjustment of festival and national holiday.
5. Administration of welfare and fine funds.
6. Educational and recreational activities, such as libraries, reading rooms, cinema, shown, sports, games, picnic parties, community welfare and celebrations.
7. Promotion of thrift and savings.
8. Implementation and review of decisions arrived at meetings of Works Committee.

II. *List of items which the Works Committees will not normally deal with*

1. Wages and allowances.
2. Bonus and profit sharing schemes.
3. Rationalisation and matters connected with the fixation of workload.
4. Matters connected with the fixation of standard labour force.
5. Programmes of planning and development.
6. Matters connected with retrenchment and layoff.
7. Victimisation for trade union activities.
8. Provident fund, gratuity schemes and other retiring benefits.
9. Quantum of leave and national and festival holidays.
10. Incentive schemes.
11. Housing and transport services.

APPENDIX XXII

MODEL AGREEMENT REGARDING ESTABLISHMENT OF JOINT COUNCILS OF MANAGEMENT

Agreement between ....
(Name of employer) ....

and

....(Name/Names of Trade Union/Unions) ....

1. The company and the Union appreciate that an increasing measure of association of employees with the management of the works would be desirable and would help (a) in promoting increased productivity for the general benefit of the enterprise, the employees and the country, (b) in giving employees, a better understanding of their role and importance in the working of the industry and in the process of production, and (c) in satisfying the urge for self-expression.

2. It is, therefore, agreed that a Council/Councils of management consisting of representatives of the management and of the employees be set up.

3. The constitution of this Council/these Councils and the procedure to be followed by it/them would be as set out in the Annexure.

4. It would be the endeavour of the Council/councils (i) to improve the working and living conditions of the employees, productivity, (iii) to encourage suggestions from the employees, (iv) to assist in the administration of law and agreements, (v) to serve generally as an authentic channel of communication between the management and the employees, and (vi) to create in the employees a live sense of participation.

5. The Council/Councils would be consulted by the management on matters like :

(i) general administration of Standing Orders and their amendment, when needed.

(ii) introduction of new methods of production and manufacture involving re-deployment of men and machinery; and

(iii) closure, reduction in or cessation of operations.

6. The Council/Councils would also have the right to receive information, discuss and give suggestions on :

(i) General economic situation of the concern;

(ii) the state of the market, production and sales programmes;

(iii) organisation and general running of the undertaking;

(iv) circumstances affecting the economic position of the undertaking;

(v) methods of manufacture and work;

(vi) the annual balance sheet and profit and loss statement and connected documents, and explanation;

(vii) long-term plans for expansion, re-deployment, etc.; and

(viii) such other matters as may be agreed to.

7. The Council/Councils would be entrusted with responsibility in respect of :

(i) administration of welfare measures;

(ii) supervision of safety measures;

(iii) operation of vocational training and apprenticeship schemes;

(iv) preparation of schedules, of working hours and breaks and of holidays;

(v) payment of rewards for valuable suggestions received from the employees; and

(vi) any other matter as may be agreed to be the Joint Council.

8. All matters, e.g., wages, bonus, etc., which are subjects for collective bargaining are excluded from the scope of the Council/Councils. Individual grievances are also excluded from its/their scope. In short, creation of new rights as between employers and workers should be outside the jurisdiction of the Joint Council.

APPENDIX XXIII

CODE OF DISCIPLINE IN INDUSTRY

I. *To maintain discipline in Industry*

(both in public and private sectors)

There has to be (i) a just recognition by employers and workers of the rights and responsibilities of either party, as defined by the laws and agreements, (including bipartite and tripartite agreements arrived at all levels from time to time), and (ii) a proper and willing discharge by either party of its obligations consequent on such recognition.

The Central and State Governments, on their part, will arrange to examine and set right any shortcomings in the machinery they constitute for the administration of labour laws.

To ensure better discipline in industry

II. *Management and Union(s) Agree*

(i) that no unilateral action should be taken in connection with any industrial matter and that disputes should be settled at appropriate level;

(ii) that the existing machinery for settlement of disputes should be utilised with the utmost expedition;

(iii) that there should be no strike or lock-out without notice;

(iv) that affirming their faith in democratic principles, they bind themselves to settle all future differences, disputes and grievances by mutual negotiation, conciliation and voluntary arbitration;

(v) that neither party will have recourse to (a) coercion, (b) intimidation, (c) victimization, or (d) go-slow;

(vi) that they will avoide (a) litigation, (b) sit down and stay-in strikes, and (c) lock-outs;

(vii) that they will promote constructive co-operation between their representatives, at all levels and as between workers themselves and abide by the spirit of agreements mutually entered into;

(viii) that they will establish upon a mutually agreed basis, a grievance procedure which will ensure a speedy and full investigation leading to settlement;

(ix) that they will abide by various stages in the grievance procedure and take no arbitrary action which would by pass this procedure; and

(x) that they will educate the management personnel and workers regarding their obligations to each other.

III. *Management Agree*

(i) not to increase work-loads unless agreed upon or settled otherwise;

(ii) not to support or encourage any unfair labour practice such as, (a) interference with the right of employees to enroll or continue as union members, (b) discrimination, restraint or coercion against any employee because of recognised activity of trade unions, and (c) victimisation of any employee and abuse of authority in any form;

(iii) to take prompt action for (a) settlement of grievances, and (b) implementation of settlements, awards, decisions and orders;

(iv) to display in conspicuous places in the undertaking the provisions of this code in local languages;

(v) to distinguish between actions justifying immediate discharge and those where discharge must be preceded by a warning reprimand suspension or some other form of disciplinary action and to arrange that all such disciplinary action should be subject to an appeal through normal grievance procedure;

(vi) to take appropriate disciplinary action against its officers and members in cases where enquiries reveal that they were responsible for precipitate action by workers leading to indiscipline; and

(vii) to recognise the union in accordance with the criteria (Annexure I) evolved at the 16th session of the Indian Labour Conference held in May 1958.

IV. *Union(s) Agree*

(i) not to engage in any form of physical duress;

(ii) not to permit demonstrations which are not peaceful and not to permit rowdyism demonstration;

(iii) that their members will not engage or cause other employees to engage in any union activity during working hours, unless as provided in by law, agreement or practice;

(iv) to discourage unfair labour practices, such (a) negligence of duty, (b) careless operation, (c) damage to property, (d) interference with or disturbance to normal work, and insubordination;

(v) to take prompt action to implement award agreements, settlements and decisions;

(vi) to display in conspicuous places in the union offices, the provisions of this Code in the local language(s); and

(vii) to express disapproval and to take appropriate action against officer-bearers and members indulging in action against the spirit of code.

APPENDIX XXIV

SEMINAR ON THE WORKING OF THE CODE OF DISCIPLINE

CONCLUSIONS

The representatives of employers, workers and Government who participated in the Seminar generally felt that the Code of Discipline had worked well and introduced a positive approach in industrial relations and that there was need to take further steps to ensure more faithful observance of the Codes that its salutary effect could be sustained and enlarged. Most of the suggestions made towards this were constructive and helpful.

2. The representatives of two workers' organisations (HMS and AITUC) urged the adoption of ballot to determine the representative character of unions for the purpose of recognition. The representative of the INTUC was, however, opposed to ballot on the ground that it would equate a union member with a non-member in the matter of voting and the object of the Code to promote stable paid membership of unions would be defeated. He further suggested that the quality of a union and not merely its numerical membership should be the basis for grant of recognition. The representative of Hind Mazdoor Sabha stressed that free collective bargaining unhampered by compulsory adjudication would lead to the development of a healthy and strong trade union movement. In this connection the INTUC representative felt that a developing country like ours with a planned economy could not afford the luxury to abolish adjudication and let collective bargaining be the only means to settle industrial disputes.

3. It was also suggested that effective steps to revitalise the inter-union Code of Conduct be taken so as to eliminate inter-union rivalries which have often threatened industrial peace.

4. The main conclusions of the Seminar are as under :

(1) Implementation Machinery should take prompt action on complaints made to it under the Code of Discipline. As far as possible, enquiries into complaints should be completed within a period of three months, and the breaches, on being established, should be brought home to the erring party

which should be asked to set them right immediately or give an assurance that it would avoid such breaches in future. When serious and persistent breaches occur the Implementation Machinery should insist on sanctions being applied by the concerned Central Organisation. To make the Code effective the Central Organisations should not hesitate to apply sanctions against erring members.

(2) The Implementation Machinery should always inform the complainant party of the action taken on its complaint.

(3) The Central employers' organisation should ensure that their members establish a grievance procedure in their establishments on the line of the model grievance procedure. They should send to the Implementation Machinery concerned a list of their members who have so far set up a grievance procedure. Unions should co-operate with managements in the establishment of grievance procedure. Public sector companies and corporations should also ensure that this essential requirement the Code is fulfilled without further delay.

(4) Employers should not delay the grant of recognition to a union recommended by the Implementation Machinery on the result of verification conducted under the Code. If an employer does not recognise such a union with a period of three months, in spite of the request of this Central Organisation, the matter may be brought before the Implementation Committee concerned.

(5) Every effort should be made to avoid delay the verification of membership of unions for recognition. If there is undue delay in any particular case and if there is a demand for revising the date of reckoning the matter should be placed before the Implementation Committee and its decision taken before changing the date of reckoning.

(6) For the purpose of recognition the principle simple majority may be followed. The employers' representatives, however, felt that the dislodging a recognised union, a rival union should have a majority of at least 10 per cent membership over the recognised union.

(7) The existing practice of continuing recognition of a union for at least two years should continue.

(8) The existing provision for entitlement to recognition, namely, that a union should have functioned for at least one year in

the establishment concerned should continue.

(9) There was no agreement on the question amending the constitution of unions to provision for collection of subscription for membership on a monthly basis instead of annual basis. The representative or Hind Mazdoor Sabha reiterated that in case of annual subscription the membership of workers should be considered on a specified date such as December 31 or June 30 depending on whether the request for verification is made in the first half or the second half of the calendar year. It was, however, decided to refer this question to the Indian Labour Conference for decision.

(10) As there was no decision on the question of recognition of an industry-wise union under clause 3 of the Criteria for recognition of unions it was agreed that the matter should go before the Indian Labour Conference.

(11) In view divergence of views on the question of rights of unrecognised unions it was decided that the matter be placed before the Indian Labour Conference to review the decision already taken in this respect at its 22nd session in July, 1964.

(12) Both employers' and workers' organisations should take all steps to promote voluntary arbitration as a means to settle disputes particularly those relating to matters of local interest not involving wide repercussions or large financial stakes and a individual cases of retrenchment, dismissal, discharge and victimisation.

(13) The Central employers' and workers' organisations should take greater interest in the screening of labour disputes before these are taken to courts and in settling those out of court which are already pending in courts.

APPENDIX XXV

LIST OF CASE STUDIES/EVALUATION STUDIES CARRIED OUT BY THE IMPLEMENTATION AND EVALUATION DIVISION DURING 1958-1965

(Refer footnote at page 51)

1. A study of the 1958 strike in the Premier Automobiles Limited, Bombay from the point of view of Code of Discipline.
2. A study of the 1958 strike in the Calcutta Tramways Co. Ltd., Calcutta from the point of view of Code of Discipline.
3. Report of one member committee appointed to review the working of the Calcutta Dock Workers' (Regulation of Employment) Scheme, 1966.
4. Report of enquiry into breaches of the Code of Discipline in Modern Satgram Collieries, Raniganj, West Bengal.
5. Analysis of appeals regarding industrial disputes decided by the Supreme Court during 1957-58 with a view to ascertaining the legal principles or monetary stake involved in them.
6. Analysis of appeals to High Courts and Supreme Court against, industrial awards during the period 1947-58, with a view to determining their trend during the pre- and post-LAT period.
7. Study of the working of the Employees' Provident Funds Act in exempted establishments.
8. Study of the extent of establishment of Grievance Procedure in Coal Mines.
9. Study of the extent of establishment of Grievance Procedure in Iron Ore Mines.
10. Study of the extent of establishment of Grievance Procedure in Manganese Mines.
11. Implementation of industrial awards in the Central sphere during 1960-61.
12. Implementation of industrial awards in the Central sphere during 1962-63.
13. Attitude of employers and unions to voluntary

arbitration (January 1960 to June 30, 1961).

14. Attitude of employers and unions to voluntary arbitration (July 1, 1961 to June 30, 1963).
15. Reviews of the working of the Code of Discipline (June, 1958 to December, 1964).
16. A study of implementation of bi-partite agreement and the report of the court of enquiry on the abolition of contract system in coal mines.
17. Analysis of appeals relating to industrial disputes decided by the Supreme Court during 1960-1963.
18. Review of the working of the Industrial Truce Resolution (1962- 63).
19. Study of the industrial relations and implementation of labour enactments in :

A. Public Sector

1. Fertilizer Corporation of India Ltd., Nangal Unit.
2. Fertilizer Corporation of India Ltd., Sindri Unit.
3. Fertilizer and Chemicals Travancore Ltd., Alwaye.
4. Hindustan Housing Factory, Delhi.
5. Hindustan Insecticides Ltd., Delhi.
6. Hindustan Shipyard Ltd., Visakhapatnam.
7. Hindustan Steel Limited, Rourkela.
8. Hindustan Steel Limited, Durgapur.
9. Hindustan Machine Tools Ltd., Pinjore.
10. Hindustan Machine Tools Ltd., Bangalore.
11. Hindustan Cables Ltd., Rupnarainpur.
12. Heavy Machine Building Plant (HEC), Ranchi.
13. Foundry Gorge Plant (HEC), Ranchi.
14. Heavy Electricals Ltd., Bhopal.
15. Indian Telephone Industries Ltd., Bangalore.
16. Indian Oil Corporation Ltd., Barauni Refinery.
17. Bharat Electronics Ltd., Bangalore.
18. National Instruments Ltd., Bangalore.
19. National Newsprint and Paper Mills Ltd., Nepanagar.
20. Praga Tools Limited, Hyderabad.
21. Hindustan Aeronautics Ltd., Bangalore.
22. The Neyveli Lignite Corporation Ltd., Neyveli.
23. The Shipping Corporation of India Ltd., Bombay.
24. Hindustan Antibiotics, Pimpri, Poona.
25. Delhi Transport

Undertaking, Delhi (New Delhi Tpt, Corporation).
26. Indian Oil Corporation, Gujarat Refinery.
27. Fertilizer Corporation of India, Trombay Unit.
28. Hindustan Machine Tools, Hyderabad.
29. Surgical Instruments Ltd., Madras.
30. Hindustan Machine Tools, Kalamassery.
31. Cochin Refineries Ltd., Cochin.
32. Hindustan Cables Ltd., Rupnarainpur.
33. Hindustan Aeronautics Ltd., Kanpur Division, Kanpur.
34. Triveni Structurals Ltd., Naini Allahabad.
35. Hindustan Aeronautics Ltd., Hyderabad Division, Hyderabad.
36. Synthetic Drugs Plant, Hyderabad.
37. Hindustan Antibiotics Ltd., Rishikesh.
38. Bhilai Steel Plant, Bhilai.
39. Kolar Gold Mining Undertaking, Oorgauia (New Bharat Gold Mines Ltd.).
40. Zagar Mines of Hindustan Zinc Ltd., Udaipur.
41. Heavy Machine Building Plant (HEC), Ranchi.
42. Heavy Machine Tools Plant (HEC), Ranchi.
43. Foundry Forge Plant (HEC), Ranchi.
44. Gauhati Refinery, Gauhati.
45. Surgical Instruments Ltd., Madras.
46. National Instruments Ltd., Calcutta.
47. Bharat Opthalmic Glass Ltd., Durgapur.
48. Air India, Bombay.
49. Delhi Milk Scheme, Delhi.
50. Diamond Mining Project, Panna.
51. Three Captive Mines (Nandani, Hirri and Rayhara) of Bhilai Steel Plant, Bhilai.
52. Madras Port Trust, Madras.
53. Alloy Steels Plant, Durgapur.
54. Bharat Heavy Electricals Ltd., Hardwar.
55. Hindustan Steel Works Construction Ltd., Bokaro.
56. Indian Telephones Industries, Bangalore.
57. Hindustan Machine Tools (I & II) Ltd., Bangalore.
58. Hindustan Housing Factory, Delhi.
59. Central Inland Water Transport Corporation Ltd., Calcutta.
60. Neyveli Lignite Corporation Ltd., Neyveli.
61. Fertilizer Corporation of India Ltd., Gorakhpur.
62. ECIL, Hyderabad.
63. Cochin Shipyard Ltd., Cochin.
64. Hindustan Machine Tools (III) Ziankot, Srinagar.
65. Hindustan Photo Films Mfg. Co., Ltd., Ooty.
66. Hindustan Copper Ltd., Khetri.

B. Private Sector

1. National Beko Radio and Engineering Company Ltd., Bombay.
2. Standard Batteries Ltd., Bombay.
3. West Coast Paper Mills Ltd., Bandali.
4. Copper Engineering Ltd., Machine Tools Division, Poona.
5. Steel Plant (Private) Ltd., Bombay.
6. Indian Rayons Corporation Ltd., Veraval.
7. New Jamehari Khas Colliery, Burdwan Distt., West Bengal.
8. Hindustan Motors Ltd., Uttarpura, West Bengal.
9. Tata Iron and Steel Company Ltd., Jamshedpur.
10. Nararee and Jealgora Collieries, Dhanbad.
11. Premier Automobiles Ltd., Bombay.
12. Tata Engineering and Locomotive Company Ltd., Jamshedpur.
13. Kirloskar Oil Engines Ltd., Poona.
14. Kaymore Cement Works, Kaymore (M.P.).
15. Texmaco Ltd., Calcutta.
16. Ashok Leylands,, Madras.

APPENDIX XXVI

LIST OF THE CHAIRMAN OF VARIOUS SESSIONS OF THE INDIAN LABOUR CONFERENCE

SESSION		*DATE OF THE MEETING*			*VENUE*	*CHAIRMAN*
*1st	Session	22-23	January,	1940	New Delhi	Sh. Ramaswami Mudaliar
*2nd	Session	27-28	January,	1941	New Delhi	Sh. Ramaswami Mudaliar
*3rd	Session	30-31	January,	1942	New Delhi	Sh. Firoz Khan Noon
#4th	Session	07	August,	1942	New Delhi	Dr. B.R. Ambedkar
#5th	Session	06-07	Sept.,'	1943	New Delhi	Dr. B.R. Ambedkar
#6th	Session	27-29	October,	1944	New Delhi	Dr. B.R. Ambedkar
7th	Session	27-28	November,	1945	New Delhi	Dr. B.R. Ambedkar
8th	Session	21-22	April,	1947	New Delhi	Sh. Jagjivan Ram
9th	Session	19-21	April,	1948	New Delhi	Sh. Jagjivan Ram
10th	Session	20-22	March,	1950	New Delhi	Sh. Jagjivan Ram
11th	Session	11-12	August,	1951	New Delhi	Sh. Jagjivan Ram
12th	Session	08-11	October,	1952	Nainital	Sh. V.V. Giri
13th	Session	07-09	January,	1954	Mysore	Sh. V.V. Giri
14th	Session	14-16	May,	1955	Bombay	Sh. K.K. Desai
15th	Session	11-12	July,	1957	New Delhi	Sh. Gulzari Lal Nanda
16th	Session	18-20	May,	1958	Nainital	Sh. Gulzari Lal Nanda
17th	Session	27-29	July,	1959	Madras	Sh. Gulzari Lal Nanda
18th	Session	24-25	Sept.,	1960	New Delhi	Sh. Gulzari Lal Nanda
19th	Session	09-10	October,	1961	Bangalore	Sh. Gulzari Lal Nanda
20th	Session	07-09	August,	1962	New Delhi	Sh. Gulzari Lal Nanda
21st	Session	13	July,	1963	New Delhi	Sh. Gulzari Lal Nanda
22nd	Session	29-30	July,	1964	New Delhi	Sh. D. Sanjivayya
23rd	Session	30-31	October,	1965	New Delhi	Sh. D. Sanjivayya
24th	Session	29-30	July,	1966	New Delhi	Sh. Jagjivan Ram
25th	Session	20-21	April,	1968	New Delhi	Sh. Jaisukh Lal Hathi
26th	Session	12-13	November,	1969	New Delhi	Sh. Jaisukh Lal Hathi
27th	Session	22-23	October,	1971	New Delhi	Sh. R.K. Khadilkar
Tripartite N.L.C		17-18	Sept.,	1982	New Delhi	
28th	Session	25-26	November,	1985	New Delhi	Sh. P.A. Sangma
29th	Session	21-22	April,	1990	New Delhi	Sh. Ram Vilas Paswan
30th	Session	07-08	Sept.,	1992	New Delhi	Sh. P.A. Sangma
31st	Session	03-04	January,	1995	New Delhi	Shri P.A. Sangma
32nd	Session	23-24	November,	1995	New Delhi	Sh. G. Venkat Swamy
33rd	Session	24-25	October,	1996	New Delhi	Sh. M. Arunachalam

* held as Conference of Labour Ministers

\# held as Tripartite Labour Conference